The Survival of Culture

THE SURVIVAL OF CULTURE

PERMANENT VALUES IN A VIRTUAL AGE

Edited with an Introduction by

HILTON KRAMER
and
ROGER KIMBALL

IVAN R. DEE
Chicago 2002

For Donald Kahn

Library of Congress Cataloging-in-Publication Data:
The survival of culture : permanent values in a virtual age / edited
    with an introduction by Hilton Kramer and Roger Kimball.
        p.   cm.
    Includes index.
        ISBN 1-56663-466-0 (alk. paper) — ISBN 1-56663-465-2 (pbk. :
alk. paper)
        1. Civilization, Western. I. Kramer, Hilton. II. Kimball, Roger,
1953–

CB245 .S97 2002
909'.09821—dc21   2002028838

Contents

Acknowledgments

THE EDITORS would like to take this opportunity to acknowledge the dedicated help of their colleagues at *The New Criterion*, Sara E. Lussier, Susannah Luthi, Robert Messenger, James Panero, Robert Richman, and Maxwell Watman.

The editors would also like to acknowledge the many individuals and institutions that have, for two full decades, helped to support *The New Criterion*. We wish to thank in particular the Lynde and Harry Bradley Foundation, the John M. Olin Foundation, and the Sarah Scaife Foundation. Without their unwavering commitment, *The New Criterion* would not exist. We are especially grateful to the Bodman Foundation, whose special grant helped make possible *The New Criterion*'s series on The Survival of Culture and the publication of this book.

It gives us great pleasure to dedicate this book to our friend Donald Kahn. Mr. Kahn has for many years been a generous supporter of many cultural institutions, including *The New Criterion*. We are deeply grateful for his commitment to *The Survival of Culture*—and to the survival of culture.

Introduction:
The Survival of Culture

IN THE SPRING of 2001, when we began thinking about running a special series of essays in *The New Criterion* on the survival of culture, it was clear that we would not be telling an entirely cheerful tale. After all, when one looked around at the institutions that represented culture in contemporary society, one was likely to encounter a dismal spectacle. In our universities, museums, theaters, symphony orchestras, and other traditional bastions of high culture, one increasingly found not only a degradation of standards but also a corruption of will. Almost everywhere, it seemed, frivolity competed with outright nihilism in a race to the lowest common denominator.

Nor was this ominous spectacle confined to explicitly artistic or scholarly institutions. One saw an analogous devolution in the family, in the media, in politics, and—perhaps most ominously—in the law.

There were and are, of course, exceptions: little oases of sanity and resistance in the vast, encroaching desert of mindless conformity and rancorous political correctness. But those exceptions remain exceptions. The usual case was aptly described by the philosopher David Stove when he spoke, in an analogous context, of a "disaster-area, and not of the merely passive kind, like a bombed building, or an area that has been flooded. It is the active kind, like a badly-leaking nuclear reactor, or an outbreak of foot-and-mouth disease in cattle."

That, anyway, is how things seemed to us in the good old days, in the spring and summer of 2001, before the events of what has come to be called, in a universally recognized shorthand, 9/11. We are still too close to that day of infamy to comprehend its full implications. Indeed, it may be said that the sun has not yet set on the day that dawned September 11, 2001. A new era was born. The terrorist attacks not only killed thousands of innocent civilians, they also threw down a gauntlet. Those attacks were, as Binyamin Netanyahu put it, furious salvos in "a war to reverse the triumph of the West." How the West responds—and we are talking about something that will be measured in years, maybe decades, not months—will determine whether our culture in any recognizable shape maintains the capacity to survive.

MOST OF the contributions to *The Survival of Culture* were written in the aftermath of the terrorist attacks of September 11 and, inevitably, that event colors the tenor and argument of this book. The authors deal with a wide range of subjects, from the fate of research libraries in an age of digital information processing to the way partisan politics has undermined the independence of the judiciary, from the rise of new forms of anti-Western sentiment—not least in the West itself—to the attack of the very ideal of permanence as a cultural value. Within that diversity, however, there are recurrent themes. One prominent leitmotif concerns the struggle between civilization and barbarism—a battle that is proceeding on many fronts and in many different campaigns: in manners as much as in morals, in politics, public policy, and that shifting, unstable realm where private sentiment is educated into the light of common conviction.

When we inaugurated a series of essays on the survival of culture in September 2001, we quoted an admonitory passage that Evelyn Waugh had written in 1938, another moment when the storm clouds of barbarism gathered to threaten civilization. "Barbarism," Waugh wrote,

> is never finally defeated; given propitious circumstances, men and women who seem quite orderly will commit every conceivable atrocity. The danger does not come merely from habitual hooligans; we are all potential recruits for anarchy. Unremitting effort is needed to keep men living together at peace; there is only a margin of energy left over for experiment however beneficent. Once the prisons of the mind have been opened, the orgy is on. . . . The work of preserving society is sometimes onerous, sometimes almost effortless. The more elaborate the society, the more vulnerable it is to attack, and the more complete its collapse in case of defeat. At a time like the present it is notably precarious. If it falls we shall see not merely the dissolution of a few joint-stock corporations, but of the spiritual and material achievements of our history.

In their various ways, the essays that compose this volume all bear witness to the wisdom of Waugh's observations. Some are chiefly exercises in spiritual anatomy, others are primarily salvage operations. Together, they canvass some of the most significant institutions and trends defining cultural life today. If the tenor of several contributions is somber, their ultimate aim is deeply affirmative: to endorse permanent values in order that culture might not simply survive but flourish.

July 2002

The Survival of Culture

The New Epicureans
by Kenneth Minogue

I N A FAMOUS PASSAGE at the beginning of Book II of *De Rerum Natura*, Lucretius talks of the pleasure of watching other people endure dangerous situations. As Dryden rendered the passage:

> 'Tis pleasant, safely to behold from shore
> The rolling ship, and hear the tempest roar.

It isn't, Lucretius goes on to say, that we are pleased at the troubles of others, but that we take pleasure in realizing that these are troubles from which we're not suffering. Nature, Lucretius observes, in an early probe into the modern horrors of stress, wants only two things—the absence of pain, and the absence of worry.

This is part of the Epicurean art of living, and the way you achieve equanimity of mind is by a philosophical discipline requiring you to follow long chains of reasoning (about the nature of death, for example) and eschew the ephemeral pleasures of luxury and society. Lucretius's imagined philosopher finds it sweet

> To see vain fools ambitiously contend
> For wit and power.

Two roads to happiness confront us: that of action and that of contemplation. So far as the philosopher is concerned, there is no contest. Worldly commitments demand action, and action often leads to pain and failure. But the life of contemplation cannot fail, because we have withdrawn our hopes and fears from the world, and have understood ourselves as merely one object in a universal scheme. For most people in the past, the contemplative option was not available, or was available only in a religious form, which had its own dangers. The Epicurean contemplative was thus the fine fruit of a rich elite in the classical world, an elite that devoted itself to personal self-fulfillment. It is hardly surprising that the Roman general Fabricius, on learning about this philosophy, hoped that all Rome's enemies might adopt it.

As self-conscious beings, we are of course always in some degree the spectators as well as the participants in our own lives, but modern conditions have facilitated a remarkable shift in the balance between action and reflection. In reflection, we become spectators of the human comedy, and spectatorship as a mode of responding to the world has not only become possible but has even come to dominate the way we live our lives. In its most elementary form, this change results simply from the abundance of leisure we enjoy. Instead of the odd occasion imagined by Lucretius in which someone can watch a ship in trouble from the shore, we can through the media of film and television enjoy the interesting sensation of watching people in dire trouble from the comfort of our own homes. At this most elementary level, the contemporary Epicurean is the couch potato. We are sated on the pleasure of tranquillity as we watch terrible things (real or fictional) happening to others.

As we might expect in our modern complexity, spectatorship as a mode of responding to the world now comes in a variety of forms, though all of them involve detachment from particular commitments. This sort of "hanging loose" has become the axis on which our moral universe is revolving, and we may distinguish two distinct forms of it. The first consists in the deliberate avoidance of burdens, as when we prefer not to commit ourselves to marriage and children, or not to volunteer for military or other kinds of dangerous or burdensome service. A wife and children are, as Bacon put it, the hostages a man gives to fortune, and keeping tomorrow uncluttered by such things can be construed as the essence of freedom. Most philosophers in the past were detached from particular involvements of this kind, no doubt, but they were committed (as our modern Epicureans are not) to the philosophical pursuit of truth itself.

A second type of detachment is less conspicuous because it takes an intellectual or a political form. It consists in a self-understanding that is simultaneously highly particular *and* highly abstract. It contrasts sharply with the common self-understanding of earlier times, when most people defined themselves in terms of region, nation and state, or profession. In *Conditions of Liberty: Civil Society and Its Rivals*, Ernest Gellner wrote that the West was distinguished by "modularity" in which any person can fit into any social organization to perform (within limits) any task. Gellner contrasted this with the situation in traditional societies, in which status resulted from specialization. But specialization in a changing society can itself become a kind of hostage to fortune, and our contemporaries dislike its narrowness, and perhaps the contingent human costs that may go with it.

A society of spectators is as different from a society of participants as detachment is from commitment. For one thing, participants, by the very fact of cooperation, constitute a community, whereas all that spectators can do is *associate* with one another. The odd thing is that the spread of detachment as a way of life and the talk of perfecting community can both feature as powerful assumptions of our moral understanding.

I PROPOSE to explore both of these modes of detachment and to indicate some of the implications they have for the survival of culture. First, let us consider the most explicit form of this new Epicurean art of living: the straightforward avoidance of the burdensome. The decline of marriage is a conspicuous example. The increasing avoidance of marriage in contemporary Western society is often seen as resulting from nervousness about committing oneself. It might equally be presented as a triumph of Epicurean wisdom. In order to see what is at stake in the decline of marriage, we can begin by turning the question on its head and asking: why is it that lots of people still do actually want to get married and establish families? In earlier generations, the question would have made no sense, because everyone took it for granted that both duty and happiness guided us towards this pattern of life. To cross what Joseph Conrad called "the shadow line" from the insouciance of youth to the solidity of responsibilities was part of a complete life, involving marriage at least for women and jobs or careers for men. Today, however, less than a quarter of Americans apparently live in families with children. Much of this might be explained as a merely negative avoidance of the burden of responsibility, but the shape of a positive "ideology of singleness" is already emerging. In a long life, runs this doctrine, the commitment of two people to each other is a risky business, riddled with the illusions of romantic love. Children are an expensive luxury, and no longer necessary as an insurance against destitution in old age. The mother who works is likely to face hostility from fellow employees who resent the fact that they may have to stay late because she has had to attend to sickness or some school meeting. A bad sign is all the public sentimentality to the effect that "the interest of the children must come first." In fact, children are widely feared and regarded as tiresome, which indeed they sometimes can be. If you take happiness to be the avoidance of pain and worry, marriage and family life must feature as the quintessence of folly. And this mere *via negativa* sometimes becomes positive in an actual denigration of those who embrace this folly: the view that those who opt for parenthood are really a little sad—people who don't have enough to fill their lives. Children are not only a "lifestyle choice," but might even be thought a rather puzzling, even deplorable one.

In an article called "What Are Children For?" in the June 2001 issue of the British magazine *Prospect*, Laurie and Matthew Taylor found that most people with families today had difficulty saying why they had created children. Obviously in terms of cost accounting, children are an indulgence, and the economist Joseph Schumpeter long ago suggested that men and women would soon come to regard them as a bad bargain. Most parents when asked by Professor Laurie Taylor hesitated to say that they "wanted to have children because such children will be their *descendants*." In a future-oriented society, this is one aspect of the future that seems to be strangely occluded, perhaps out of fear of seeming to be concerned with such an individualist aspiration as wanting to perpetuate one's name and history. The idea is that one not only lives for the present, but also *ought* to live thus. And this attitude gives us some clue about the way society is moving. Remember that Burke back in 1790 thought he was merely reporting common opinion when he said that society was indeed a contract, but not any old commercial contract. Rather, it was a grand link uniting the living, the dead, and those yet to be born. Burke regarded human life as a linkage over time in which the individual gained his significance from where he came from and where his family was going. Indeed, the very fact of membership in a family imparted respectability. Slaves procreated, no doubt, but they did not have the status of families. The change in our attitude to families is thus related to our sense of ourselves in time and also to our sense of our relation to society. Slaves had a master, but otherwise they were marvelously detached.

If we apply the calculus of "rational choice," family life might well be seen as the solution to a problem whose time has gone. Sex and companionship are easily available without the trouble and expense of setting up one's own dedicated facilities. This release from practical necessity is another aspect of our liberation from biology as destiny. And along with that liberation has come a significant change in how we construe a human life. The traditional recognition that, organically speaking, we go through the stages of youth, maturity, and senescence, corresponding to innocent youthful dreaming, to purposive achievement, and ultimately to serene wisdom, has been lost. In the past, these were the inescapable modes of human experience.

Today human development is curiously flatter; modalities have disappeared. Children unwrap the gifts of life at a tender age and are already launched on a parody of adulthood by their early teens. Yet many remain who experience that curious restlessness that Conrad spoke of in *The Shadow Line*, "moments when the still young are inclined to commit rash actions such as getting married suddenly, or else throwing up a job for no reason." In Conrad's day, the essence of morality was still coherence. The marriage contracted on impulse might be hell, the job that had been abandoned turn out in retrospect to be the best possible, but one had made one's bed and one had to lie on it. In moral terms, the possibilities of the future were circumscribed by the commitments of the past, and the individual's life was a narrative of engagement and response.

Today, by contrast, people talk about "reinventing themselves." Very little is irrevocable. Marriages can be unmade, the job market is more flexible, and pleasant prospects always seem to be beckoning. This is a mode of life in which there is no essential difference between youth, maturity, and old age: all is a kind of youth, though less innocent, in which the same pleasures are pursued throughout life. Every recourse associated with any stage of life can reappear later, even crime. It has recently been reported that some old people, in need of a

bit of extra cash, have resourcefully turned to fraud, or holding up the local convenience store with a mask on. Do not
talk to me of the wisdom of old men, says the poet. The ideal
death envisaged by our contemporaries is heart failure at
about eighty in the arms of a lover.

Nor has theory been a laggard to practice. A good deal of
the stuff called "re-thinking" has been going into "relationships," a term that only acquired its current scope—covering
everything from a lover to a business contact—about the
middle of the twentieth century. "Close relationship theory,"
as it is called, explores the conditions of satisfaction possible
in intimate unions. The Canadian Bar Association is among
many legal organizations arguing that the current legal focus
on marriage should give way to a consideration of "the substance of relationships." The test of a relationship, according
to this reasoning, is whether it creates satisfaction; if it
doesn't, there is no reason not to change it. Love has no objective existence: it is "a shifting metric" by which each of us
defines whether or not a relationship ought to continue. Such
relationships are dyadic, and it will be clear that children are a
disruptive force. They feature in one book, alongside drug
addiction and alcohol, as potential threats to relationships.

This is perhaps the purest example of the Epicurean process
by which the conventions of particular involvement are dissolved in what one might call "soothing abstractions"—
soothing, that is, to anything that might frustrate an impulse.
Other ways in which this process operates are more oblique,
as we shall see.

Optimizing pleasure is, then, one way of treating life as a
spectacle. One stands aside and keeps calculating the hedonic
impact of the specific burdens that might result from participation. What does this growing doctrine of detachment
presuppose?

The idea behind it is a kind of individualism—the idea that

freedom is choosing—but it is an individualism quite different from that which launched the modern world. The earliest individualists were men (women generally came into it later) who had personal projects of their own to pursue and therefore found the expectations by which society stereotyped them restrictive. Their projects were often about making money, or spreading the true worship of God, or some political settlement. What distinguished these figures above all, however, was that they did not easily fit into a traditional society. This kind of individualism led over time to the emergence of the sovereign state, a remarkable institution that developed the authority to change laws without actually violating them. This power to repeal inherited laws and commitments was what made the modern European state so dynamic and flexible. Those who came to the fore in this new institutional world were deeply serious about their projects and were consumed by a passion for duty and a hatred of idleness. They had a rich inner life based on the imagery of the Bible and a morality requiring that they should keep their commitments in good repair. Kant argued that the moral essence of a human being was autonomy. This did not at all mean that the laws of God or nature were rejected, but it did mean that these individuals insisted on interpreting and deciding on actions for themselves.

In each generation, no doubt, individualism was something rather different, but in the first half of the nineteenth century a distinctly different view of individualism began to evolve. It signalled its appearance by a new vocabulary, and being an individualist became honorific. It was the time when the terms "individualist" and "individualism" came into currency. Before that, individualists resembled Molière's M. Jordan, who discovered to his delight that he had been speaking prose "for more than forty years without knowing it." They pursued their desires un-self-consciously within a law-governed world. When people sought to turn individuality into a mark of distinction, however, they narrowed it down to mere eccentricity. You were an individualist to the extent that you stood out from the crowd, like Gérard de Nerval taking his lobster for a walk along the streets of Paris on a leash. You demonstrated your individuality by not being conformist. Individualism became, paradoxically, a fashion, and the world filled up with simple people following the philosopher Sinatra by singing "I did it my way." This usually meant they had made a mess of it. Perhaps doctrines no less than revolutions can, as Marx put it, happen first as tragedy and then as farce. For clearly the individualism of Calvin and Kant, which could take people to the block for a principle, was a quite different thing from the light-mindedness of Sinatra.

How was it that the old severe individualism modulated into the new, light-minded one? The key idea orchestrating this transformation was the identification of individuality with choice. If individuality were merely the exercise of choice, then the freest man in the world would be someone wandering round a supermarket, or perhaps the sultan in his harem. This is the freedom of the bazaar. It is life as an endless traffic with options. The old individualist was a creature of desires, but in desires begin responsibilities. The new individualist was merely a creature of impulse. Desires entail responsibilities; impulses merely have consequences. But a change in conventions may remove the sting from consequence, as it has in the case of the unwanted pregnancies of single mothers. Or a benign government may step in to nullify the consequences of imprudence in health or work. The drift of the contemporary world thus seems to be the removal of necessity from life in order that we can everywhere indulge our "right to choose." A woman can be a soldier, a man can be a woman, sex can be a costless indulgence, the old can indulge the appetites of the young, and so on. Society comes increasingly to resemble a fantasy playground.

The problem with fantasy, however, is that it might nastily

collide with reality. Role-playing can be fun. But females are merely chocolate soldiers, men can have themselves surgically altered to resemble women but cannot bear children, and self-indulgent sex is to committed sex as tourism is to travel. No reality without cost.

The curious thing is that individualism is being destroyed in the name of individualism. Or maybe it isn't curious at all. For certainly the process by which this has come about replicates a standard rhetorical procedure for corrupting ideas. Corruption occurs when some abstract element of an idea, some part of it, is mistaken for the whole—in this case the whole morality of individualism as a form of freedom. To be an individualist in the old sense did indeed involve choice, but the morally serious individualist was someone who had evolved from understanding himself as a mere follower of rules to one who understood his life in terms of the coherence of his commitments. In most cases, such an individualist did not in fact make a great number of choices, for he was rooted in his own soil. If you remove this vast hinterland of responsibility from individualism, you are left with the superficial notion that being "free to choose" makes one an individualist. What is demanded is not just being free to choose—but to choose, and choose again, and again. It is hard to distinguish such shallowly revocable choices from mere drift.

One form of detachment, then, is the avoidance of burdensome responsibilities so as to be forever free to indulge a string of mere preferences. It can easily be mistaken for the hardier individualism on which our civilization was founded. I have sketched out an image of this new detachment in terms of family life, but might as easily have considered its effect on the way individuals discharge their responsibilities to country, church, and other civil associations. It is clear that what I am discussing abuts at several points recent studies of the declining potency of civil association in Western life, such as those of Robert Puttnam.

But there is another sort of detachment from particularity, one whose outward consequences do not always appear as dramatically as does the rejection of family life. This detachment consists in moving from a particular to an abstract way of understanding oneself, as when the member of a nation comes to think of himself primarily as a rights-bearing human being, or when a woman understands herself less in terms of specific family membership than under the abstract category "woman." Each of us grows up in a family, a neighborhood, a school, perhaps a trade, and this can constitute the whole world. In the past it often did. Today, of course, none of us can avoid at least some elementary map of the wider world. We get it from the media, the schools, and above all from higher education. Education is something only really possible to those few who have a reflective disposition, but in the modern world half the population is "intellectualized" by attendance at pedagogic institutions. They are supplied, that is, with a range of abstract ideas, a kind of sociology, which allows them to place themselves in some grand scheme of nations and the world. They may recognize themselves as members of a civilization, class, type of economy, religion, morality, and much else. Such self-recognition cannot help leading in some degree to detachment from the inherited loyalties. Schooling enhances the power of pupils at the cost of detaching them from their local roots. A little learning, as Alexander Pope observed, is a dangerous thing, and in the modern world it leaves most people bereft of their roots, yet at the same time little touched by the kind of sophisticated skepticism that could restore their sense of the tradition from which they came.

MUCH OF THE INTELLECTUALIZATION of modern life results from ideology. For over a wide range of curricula, schooling and the practicalities of ideology interpenetrate. An ideology is a form of thought which teaches people to identify themselves as members of an abstract class: proletarians, women, members of a nation or race, disabled, gay, etc. As such, an ideology supplies projects and scripts for these groups to live by. It has the effect of shifting political attention away from interests towards ideas. An interest is local and limited, and thus flexible; an idea is universal and unlimited. Interests can be negotiated, but ideas tend to be intransigent. The farmer, the entrepreneur, and the priest all have what can be recognized as interests. The intellectual and the bureaucrat are creatures of ideas: no matter what happens, they will always have suitable materials for their activity. Politics driven by an idea is an adventure for the young whose passion it is to enjoy change.

Twentieth-century politics abounded in dramatic examples of political adventuring which left interests far behind in order to gamble on ideal possibilities: something attractive only to people so detached from their interests as to have entirely lost their bearings. These adventures would have been impossible if their promoters had failed to find some actual class of people so detached from their society as to constitute a natural pool of followers. Marx thought that the people he had defined as a "proletariat" were alienated from the particular loyalties of their society, but it turned out that very many were not. Proletariats are definitionally constituted by a condition called "oppression" and many more have been created since Marx—to such an extent, indeed, that it is not difficult to present the whole of society as constituted of oppressed minorities.

We have thus arrived at the point where modern societies can be understood as essentially oppressive, even though no particular set of people is discovered to be the oppressors. The idea of oppression without an oppressor is, indeed, curious, but it makes sense if society itself is understood as a bad system. Just such an understanding has become the standard machinery for detaching individuals from particular allegiances. To understand myself as an oppressed member of the family, state, world, etc., to which I belong is the first step towards detachment. It is not, as we shall see, an end to participation in society, but it can be the prelude to a new type of participation.

How does the process of detachment work? Consider a feminist engaged in the proselytism called "consciousness raising." Its aim is to persuade women to detach themselves from the particularities of family life and to understand themselves under the abstract character of women. Feminist intellectuals rapidly equipped this new abstraction with its own history, sociology, and even a kind of politics. As an identification, it certainly had resonance, but it inevitably lacked the concrete immediacy of any specific commitment.

EDUCATION AND IDEOLOGY, although fundamentally different, currently function in the same way, detaching individuals from their particular loyalties. This is one reason that unfortunate peoples in non-Western societies fell into the trap of thinking ideology could be an instrument of modernization. Ideology is much easier than education; it is much easier to pick up the melodramatics of Communism, fascism, feminism, nationalism, and so on than it is to become educated. But with both, the increased range and power of thought that abstract ideas provide entail a certain loss of specificity. Willa Cather in one of her short stories observes about the immigrant communities of Nebraska that the older children who had to get jobs in order to support the younger children who were thus enabled to go off to college possessed a certain vitality of character missing in their more fortunate juniors. The sociologist David Riesman, writing about how Jews responded to the breaking down of the restriction of the ghetto after the French Revolution, remarks: "Many Jews in the main Western countries surrendered their inherited ethical system in return for a chance to participate in the wider world, thus losing their special sources of spiritual strength." Detachment from one's small platoon is an inescapable part of the package of modernity, and it has all the features of other kinds of "liberation," including cost. Of course, rootedness in any institution—family, ethnic heritage, religion—can be experienced as imprisoning. Children sometimes quarrel with their parents and run away to the city, where increasingly they find they will have status as abstract bearers of rights.

The rise of the abstract individual is most conspicuous in those extreme cases where individual impulse collides with institutional tradition. Consider the case of a pupil who decides she does not like the uniform of her school. In the actual case I am referring to, the school required girls to wear skirts. The girl in question, pleading that she was cold in winter, wanted to wear trousers like the boys. She took legal action against the school on the ground that her right to choose what she wore was being denied. Other options were of course possible, most obviously wearing warmer tights or changing schools, but she preferred to go to law so as to bend the institution to what she wanted.

Or consider the homosexual who wanted to be a Boy Scout leader, or the actress five months pregnant who complained about being dismissed from the production of a Gilbert & Sullivan operetta in which she was to play a virgin. We all have our favorite cases, but what links most of them is that the freedom of the "individual" is packaged as a right and used as a battering ram against the autonomy of institutions. Schools, theaters, and especially business firms are being forced to sacrifice some element of their distinctiveness in order to accommodate the demands of individuals. Little if anything is to be allowed to stand in the way of choice.

A schoolgirl, a pregnant actress, a homosexual—these are particular configurations whose characteristics, permanent or temporary, constitute the real diversity of society. In being what they are, and perhaps in suffering what they suffer, they would contribute willy-nilly to the real variety of society. But these people do not wish to develop or explore the inwardness of their particularity, given the sacrifices that that might involve. They all reject these particularities and deny that they can be legitimately judged by conventional social criteria. They wish to be understood abstractly as rights-bearing individual members of a society in which "anything goes." In the past, each of these characteristics would have been considered a destiny, even though the female pupil would grow up and the actress soon cease to be pregnant. Today, conventions and legal judgments allow any particularities that conflict with impulse to be jettisoned. Each person seeks to detach himself from his particular character and situation in order to find a preferred location at the level of universal humanity. Particularity—being a schoolgirl and subject to rules, being pregnant and subject to restrictions, being homosexual and subject to suspicion when engaged in certain tasks—are all seen as forms of imprisonment incompatible with an open society. And the warders of this prison are the institutions that constitute society.

EPICURUS AND LUCRETIUS thought that happiness resulted when the philosopher detached himself from the world and treated the human condition as a spectacle. This detachment could take two forms. One was withdrawing from burdensome involvement in the business of life, such as the family or the city. The other was an act of mind that allowed the philosopher to understand himself as a purely rational being standing above the passions of the herd. The modern world has greatly multiplied analogues of these modes of detachment. Even the humble couch potato is contingently detached from the violence around him, while the person who rejects familial or civic responsibilities could claim to exemplify the philosophic indifference of the Epicurean. Such indifference was not a heroic response to the world. As Gibbon was later to write, skeptical philosophers could not believe, and Epicureans could not act. The modern Epicurean, however, is by no means a mere drone; he or she is likely to be extremely busy, for modern circumstances are very different from those of the classical Mediterranean. Indeed, it is the activist character of modern detachment that makes it so pervasive.

This activism is certainly conspicuous in the case of perhaps the most subtle form of detachment that has emerged in modern societies. It is what detaches modern professionals from the traditions of their own practice. To be a modern professional was until recently not only to exercise a specific form of power, but often also to be marked out by different kinds of dress. The teacher wore a gown, the lawyer a wig, the soldier a variety of uniforms, and so on. These signs conferred status and marked off the professional from the man in the street. Today most of these insignia are being replaced by a determined informality ("casual Fridays," for example) whose explicitly egalitarian message is to say: "We are of the same clay as you, and our very competence would be in question if we could not show that we have shared most of the experiences of life with you."[1]

In any case, the professional was also distinguished by other signs of his profession beyond the sartorial. The soldier could be recognized by his bearing, the lawyer by his dryness, the teacher by his pedantry, and so on. Each had what the French call a *déformation professionelle*. To enter a profession, as indeed to do anything else serious in life, was to embrace a limitation that excluded the practitioner from other possibilities. Yet precisely this distinctiveness has come to be understood as a kind of prison unwelcome to intelligent people

---

[1] Even politicians are affected by this tendency. After the Conservative Party in Britain was disastrously defeated in the election of June 2001, a political journalist was asked what they must do to return to favor. "They must give up their ties," he replied, and he meant neckties.

eager to "play a full part in society." Some professionals—lawyers and clergymen, for example—suffer the additional indignity of being caricatured in intellectual circles as mere props of a status quo widely thought to be unjust.

The stress induced by this reputation has been remarkable, but it had a simple cure—liberation, which turned out to be so easy. It involved becoming critical of society and taking on a new and interesting responsibility, not to clients but to society as a whole. The point was to improve it. Those liberated professionals experienced the pleasing realization that they had in their hands powers they had not previously used: the teacher dealt with the minds of the rising generation, the lawyer felt dissatisfied with the dry technicalities of tribunals and was tempted to implement his judgment about what justice required, the doctor began to take an interest in the social and political implications of epidemiology, and so on. In other words, the liberation of the professional resulted from embracing democratic responsibilities that might well clash with the narrow demands of a profession. The lawyer was no longer satisfied with saying: "This, alas, is the law, and if you want a different result, you had better get the politicians to change it. But you should not forget that hard cases make bad law."

The case of the entertainment industry, now reputedly the largest industry in the United States, has its own special features. Film and television are the purveyors of fantasy to the nation. Like the investigative journalist, the actor and director want to improve the world by revealing concealed truths. Exposing evils gave artists a function, affirming ideals gave them a respectable identity. Actors have always been on the margins of society and have as a consequence generally been at war with its conventions. Like artists of all kinds, indeed, rather like children, they actually need conventions and boundaries in order to subvert them. In the modern world, in which every activity has become material for the journalist and the actor, we cannot escape the derisive laugh of the irresponsible exploiter of absurdity. It is not by seeing things in context that the writer and the film producer produce the *frisson* they seek, but precisely by detaching them from context. And such detachment is a form of abstraction: the world as mere horror, mere comedy, mere tragedy, etc.

Detachment from the small platoon of everyday commitments is increasingly the character of the world we live in, and it can be understood in terms of both its causes and its deeper significance. So far as its causes are concerned, I shall simply list them, partly because they are widely discussed and partly because they raise issues that go far beyond my concerns. Clearly the first cause lies in the social and geographical mobility of Europeans. Having spread throughout the world, Europeans created a technology that makes it easy for people to follow opportunity wherever they think it may be found. Travel is the most elementary form of detachment.

The second cause lies in the prosperity of the modern economy, or what those who dislike commerce call "capitalism." Commerce means that relationships can be evaluated in terms of whatever benefits they produce, and loyalty to family, firm, or even religion may well be judged irrational. Modern economies have produced such wealth that most people now have the resources that will allow them to change their situation pretty radically if they should choose. And modern technology has allowed us to find alternatives to situations that previously we had to endure.

The third cause lies in democratic government which, taking its bearings from the poor, imposes a kind of dependence on everyone. But this is a dependence that has the outward show of independence: governments provide us with medicine, education, pensions, and welfare. In a socialist society everything is free. That's not quite the case with us today, but many things have been socialized in this way.

These are forces in modern life so powerful that it is

remarkable that anything can stand against them. Yet in a modern society, loyalties of all kinds, remarkably, do survive. But they live in shallow soil.

THE COMMONEST WAY of understanding the detachment I have been analyzing is in terms of the dream of liberation. Particular loyalties are thrown over because they are seen as prisons, and the life of an abstract bearer of rights is embraced because it seems to correspond with freedom. The roots of this idea are immensely complicated and like much else they emerge from theological controversy. But their character can be illustrated by that famous passage in which Marx (in *The German Ideology*) speaks of the life of man under socialism. The passage attacks the division of labor as an alienation from true communal life imposed by a class-divided society. According to Marx's fantasy of life under Communism, however, no one has an exclusive sphere of activity. Anyone can become anything, which means that one could "hunt in the morning, fish in the afternoon, rear cattle in the evening, criticize after dinner, just as I have a mind, without ever becoming hunter, fisherman, shepherd or critic."

Here is a remarkable dream of a society that is not a society. Everybody floats. The examples chosen are no doubt a little odd and would hardly be so plausible if I were to substitute being a brain surgeon in the morning and an airline pilot in the afternoon, but they do call to mind one of the features of modern life: that a great deal of work consists of shuffling symbols in an office, and, that over a considerable range, one office worker can learn to do pretty much what another can do. All you need is a bit of "higher education." And this interchangeability is central to a world of abstract, multi-competent individuals.

The basic point, however, is that Marx construes as unfree, indeed as evil, the condition in which a person is limited to the character of a single profession. Any institutional involvement is a prison, a form of oppression that limits one's full participation in society itself. Families are no different. The Communist ideal is that children should be communally reared, and the supposedly furtive privacies of the household should give way to the communal restaurant and the dormitory. Community's the thing, and one is only free in being attached to that alone. In such a free community, there would be no privacy because there would be no need for it. An actual right to privacy is only valuable as an inadequate protection against the oppressive conventions of a class-divided society.

What is at stake in the ideal of detachment? It is, from one point of view, a version of Rousseau in which the citizen is free in being guided by the "general will" alone. From another point of view, it exhibits aspects of an infantile fantasy, a dream of life as a children's playground in which one might move, like a rich dilettante, from toy to toy according to the promptings of impulse. But it is hard not to think that there is more to it than this, and that it reveals to us a lot that is otherwise mysterious about the modern world.

The idea is clearly that the world is basically evil because it is restrictive, and hence that the business of life is to detach oneself from it. For we live in a world that suppresses our authenticity by forcing upon us all kinds of pretences, responsibilities, duties, etc. In the rhetoric of the modern revolutionary, this alienating world is referred to as "capitalism" and characterized root and branch as commercial, consumerist, oppressive, ruthless, profit driven, and unequal. And this is not just one political opinion among others, such as political parties disagree about. It is a conviction in our civilization so deep that it will surface again in some new form after every disaster. The burnt fool's bandaged finger, as Rudyard Kipling put it, wobbles ever closer to the fire.

Moths can never learn that it is not smart to fly into the flame. When human beings exhibit the same immunity to learning from experience, we had better recognize that we are dealing with something like a religion, which is to say a comprehensive understanding of the meaning of life. And in this case we can find an imperfectly concealed structure of civilizational self-hatred which exhibits its own morality, liturgy, demonology, and eschatology. It derives from many sources, ultimately from the gnostic beliefs that proliferated at the time that Christianity was developing.

Gnosticism was the belief that the world had been created by an evil power that competed with God for mastery of the world. Unlike orthodox Christianity, gnosticism was an esoteric form of knowledge, restricted to initiates, that was said to be necessary to achieve salvation. And in some versions, anything that served to sustain the continuance of this evil world, such as procreation, was forbidden. (Some gnostic sects had no problem with homosexuality as a preferred mode of sexual activity since it did not bring children into an evil world. The very etymology of the term "bugger" derives from a tenth-century gnostic sect in the Balkans called the "Bogomils.")

There is a remarkable modernity about Lucretius. He would have made a superb counselor. He attributed most of the unhappiness in the world to "superstition" (the word he used was *religio*, which referred to the convictions that bound Roman society together). He was a scientific materialist who did not believe in an afterlife, and he provided many reasons why it is irrational to fear death. The point of life was pleasure, by which he meant not luxury and excitement but the purring detachment of a somewhat self-satisfied philosopher. The roots of this doctrine are philosophical, though in Lucretius the philosophical patter largely serves one of those consolatory versions of the art of living that are hard to distinguish from do-it-yourself religions.

It certainly isn't because modern Europeans have been studying Epicurus that his doctrine exhibits such a remarkable affinity with the way our civilization is moving. It may rather be that we are in a civilizational situation similar to that of the Hellenistic Greeks, playing our games amid the fragments left by the achievements of greater ancestors. Or it may be that large segments of the population now find themselves released from necessity the way some Greco-Roman elites were. But there is no doubt that the modern educated consciousness is characterized by the kind of superior detachment from particular loyalties, and a disposition to enjoy life as a spectacle, which we find in the Epicureans.

THERE IS, however, a difference. The ancient Epicurean opted for a quiet, private life away from the hurly-burly of the world. He was, politically speaking, a rather feeble figure. Our abstract individualists, on the contrary, have detached their loyalties from state, church, and family only to attach them, in many cases, to a range of abstract causes expected through political action to achieve the perfection of human life.

The consequence is a transformation of our moral world. Morality has modulated into a kind of sociality. No doubt most people still understand goodness in terms of such virtues as honesty, integrity, kindness, and so on. But for many people, morality has become entangled with holding the "right" opinions, with support for so-called ethical causes such as environmentalism, aid to the Third World, and opposition to smoking, landmines, or torture.

Morality, in other words, becomes swallowed up in desirable public policy. Evil is identified as failure to support righteousness and, especially, with espousal of the wrong causes. The measure of this moral transformation is the way in which our moral vocabulary is nervous about using "right" and "wrong." It prefers to talk of the "acceptable" and the "unacceptable." And it is not the case that having these attitudes is now an additional criterion of goodness; it is an actual replacement, as the career of President Clinton in one way illustrates. To fail the test of opinionated high-mindedness is to reveal oneself not as a cad or a thief, but as racist, sexist, elitist, and so on. That is to say, morality, which used to be concerned with motive and with doing the right thing, has been politicized as orthodoxy of attitude. A great deal of the modish moral relativism of our time is merely a recognition that public policy has replaced morality, and that public policy is essentially circumstantial.

The Epicurean was also a moral revisionist, in that he focused everything around pleasure, but he was certainly not a civic activist. And as someone marginal to the traditional society of Greece and Rome, he did not seriously change the real character of those societies. They were in any case in decline; Gilbert Murray once characterized Hellenic philosophy as expressing a "failure of nerve." But the modern detachment that concerns me has transformed not only morality but also the social reality itself.

Here the key idea is diversity—an ideal so much admired that governments have taken it up as the figurehead of their legislative endeavors. The diversity they legislate concerns social and sexual categories, and demands the inclusion of so-called representatives of each defined category in all major social endeavors. The real diversity of the past, by contrast, covered a vast range of activities (not legal categories) and resulted from the spontaneous responses Europeans made to constantly changing circumstances. Europeans were involved in so many particularities that the society itself was impenetrably complex. It was in recognition of this fact that the wisest rulers—and the originators of liberalism—affirmed that government must be limited to essential functions. They opposed any attempt to turn a state into a right-thinking regime. The classical view of a human society pointed to its specialization. Menenius Agrippa in *Coriolanus* tells the rebellious citizens of Rome that they are the belly in mutiny against the head, and everybody knew that an artisan was a totally different thing from a senator. The diversity of society was expressed in the limitations of its individual members. In the modern world, a farmer is not essentially different from a president, a judge from a builder—all are self-conscious reflections of the social whole, which all are endeavoring to make more perfect, where perfection is understood in the Epicurean sense of avoiding pain and banishing worry.

The modern diversity exemplified by governments forcing various institutions to include women, ethnic groups, the disabled, those with different sexual preferences, etc., in their membership is, of course, a semantic swindle. It is simply homogeneity by government *diktat*. A Dickensian world of genuine diversity has been replaced by blandness. One cause of the blandness is to be found in the fact that individuals, by detaching themselves from rootedness in particular traditions, now exhibit many of the features and experiences that previously were scattered over many individuals. What we are dealing with is a new semi-individualized diversity that is glib, facile, and inevitably shallow. What I mean may be best illustrated by the difficulty the Roman Catholic church has in recruiting priests, who must be celibate. At a time when it is thought that everybody must experience everything, institutions must change to accommodate the new form of personality. Karl Mannheim once suggested that intellectuals could be characterized (in terms of their detachment from particular interests) as "free floating." Today, most people are in one degree or another "free floating." We are all intellectuals now—though one cannot help remembering that you can be an intellectual without being intelligent.

Finally, what are the political implications of this new social and moral order? What does it mean for the survival of culture and the vitality of the values upon which it thrives? On the face of it, what concerns the Epicureans is the perfecting of community. Yet these rather flighty creatures with their passion for choice and their tiny capacity for facing challenges without choosing the easier option seem hopeless material for any kind of community at all. Community entails limitation, and the communities of the past were not only restrictive, but also ordered by rules with which people complied. The new Epicureans are not very good at rules, but they are very sensitive to messages, role models, public education programs, advertising, fictional heroes, and everything else that imitation and fashion feed upon. The ideal perfection dreamed of in utopian literature depended upon a community in which everyone shared the same attitude to things. Such unanimity is a condition for a society without moral and political conflict. We live in a world busy constructing the pattern of right attitudes that will orchestrate such a terrifying harmony. The new Epicureans, abstractly considered, are those who have unwittingly volunteered to be the materials for whatever is the next stage in the West's search for a perfect society.

The Battle of the Book

by Eric Ormsby

I N SEVENTEENTH- AND EIGHTEENTH-CENTURY England
and France a boisterous debate, traditionally known as the
"Battle of the Books," raged for many decades. The issue at
stake was one of style: should we accept the "Antients" (to use
Jonathan Swift's spelling) as our models and exemplars in
matters literary, given their immemorial legacy of acutely expressive prose and verse, or should we rather forge a
"Modern" style and manner befitting our own age and its
peculiar requirements and contingencies? Charles Perrault in
France in the 1695 preface to his *Contes* sided resolutely with
the moderns, and this on moral grounds: the ancient fables
taught a destructive morality. Interestingly enough, he singled
out the pernicious effects of certain misogynistic classical tales
on young girls' moral nature and declared: "I maintain that
my fables deserve more to be related than most of the ancient
tales . . . if one considers them from the moral aspect."

Similar debates took place at other times and in other cultures. In ninth-century Baghdad, to name but one, poets
argued strenuously over whether it was better to ape the style
of those earlier desert-dwelling bards who had made the
original glory of literary Arabic or to forge an idiom and
manner reflective of the overly refined and courtly world in
which the poets actually lived. The scurrilous wag (and great
poet) Abû Nuwâs went so far as to lampoon the early poets

and to state that the only thing he himself sought in the ancient ruins was a good stiff drink.

Today, it seems, we are confronted with a new battle of the books. Ours, however, is not between two competing and irreconcilable types of book but between the book itself and its would-be surrogates, whether these latter take the form of CD-ROMS, video disks, digital encryptions, or indeed, formats and media not yet invented or even imagined. It is thus a battle of the book itself, rather than merely of one type of book against another. And in no institution has this battle been waged more confusingly or more protractedly over the last twenty-five years than in that supposed *asylum pacis*, or "haven of peace," the epithet that the great German scholar and library director Adolf von Harnack once gave the research library.

In a certain real sense, of course, this is a phony war. Books and computers work well together and have proved complementary, even symbiotic, on numerous ventures (Is publishing itself even conceivable now without automation?). But each format has come to stand for something in the minds of its adherents: if not a style, then a stance. For the book lover, it is the affection and reverence for tradition coupled with the conviction that the book as a medium is essentially unimprovable. (I should alert the reader that I share this conviction, even though I presided over the implementation of two large automated systems in libraries where I was the director.) For the advocate of automation, by contrast, tradition is itself the problem; there are bold and innovative electronic ways of building collections and of running libraries. The computer holds out the promise of resolving many of the old intractable problems: lack of space, deterioration of paper, the cumbersomeness of making bibliographic and intellectual connections using printed sources alone. The zealous computer fanatic sees the book lover as troglodytic; the staunch book lover regards the computer fanatic as barbaric. As you might suspect, both sides are right and both sides are wrong.

In developing his fable about the Library of Babel, Jorge Luis Borges noted that the library, which was a model of the universe, was infinite and unending. So, too, it often seems, are the problems underlying the history of research libraries over the past few decades. In what follows, therefore, I use a broad brush, all the while recognizing that the topics raised could each demand many pages for a full and nuanced treatment.

To understand this period of almost incessant change, two factors must be recognized. First, until quite recently, this has been an era of unprecedented budgetary crisis for libraries (and often for the universities that support them), with crunches and squeezes and freezes and clawbacks—the terminology alone is terrifying—of varying intensity affecting nearly every fiscal year since the affluent 1960s, and accompanied by staggering increases in the prices for both books and periodicals. And second, this has been the period in which, not by coincidence, automation began to be introduced swiftly—often, all too swiftly—into libraries, initially as a cost-saving strategem and then, increasingly, as an alternative to the long-accepted but expensive standard practices and services, such as original cataloging or collection-building by means of professional bibliographers, among other possible examples.

It is not easy to summarize this period dispassionately but all observers would agree, I think, that the effects of both of these factors have been far-reaching, occasionally destructive, and quite often traumatic. The trouble with budget cuts is not solely that they restrict growth but also that they open up opportunities for crisis managers, who for the most part have no stake in, or love for, the libraries they administer but grasp crises as opportune moments for self-promotion or the promotion of some not-so-hidden agenda. And the trouble with automation is not that it is itself unsuitable or deleterious to research libraries but that it has furnished an irresistible pretext for sweeping change, often for its own sake rather than for the sake of the libraries or those researchers who depend on them.

In *The Battle of the Books*, Jonathan Swift could speak, rather disingenuously, of "the publick Peace of Libraries." Whatever mood may reign in libraries, it is fair to say that over the past few decades, peace, public or private, has not been predominant. Rather, a stubborn engagement, with numerous skirmishes, several protracted sieges, and not a few premature cries of victory, has swirled around books and libraries even though the precise issues have often been unclear, even to— perhaps especially to—the participants. In all this, the book has not merely survived but has flourished even as myriad forms of automation, like upstart pretenders to the epistemological throne, have been touted and installed, sometimes with the quite blatant purpose of supplanting the book and all it represents. Millions upon millions of dollars have been expended, hundreds of careers have been embroiled (and not a few destroyed), and yet any final resolution remains in doubt. If we can indeed call this a "battle of the books," perhaps it is more of a brawl, a brawl carried out in slow motion and under cover of a rather ferocious gentility (only a seeming paradox in the world of librarianship). In fact, we have more books than ever (though whether libraries can keep up with the flow remains a troubling question), and we have ever more sophisticated, and ever costlier, automated systems, ostensibly to enable us to retrieve the "information" in those books.

In reality, alas, information has become its own *raison d'être* with the book considered, by surprisingly many members of the profession, as little more than a clumsy, outmoded, and luxurious obstacle to that quest. Small wonder that in my own thirteen years as a research library director, though I came to know many well-read and cultured directors, I never heard the book referred to at professional meetings, such as the biannual gatherings of the influential Association of Research Libraries, as anything but a kind of parasitic encumbrance, one that ate up space, generated noxious dust, deteriorated in various unseemly ways, and of which there yet never seemed to be enough to satisfy the ravening appetites of both students and faculty.

Formal public expressions of this are of course circumspect. In a statement of the priorities for the year 2000 of the 121 top-ranked American and Canadian libraries that are members of the Association of Research Libraries, we read of the need to "help research libraries and their constituencies move into a transformed and increasingly diverse environment through the development of human resources, programs, and services." Is this some sort of code or just terminal fuzziness? Judging from my own experience I would say that the key phrase is "a transformed and increasingly diverse environment." These weasel words mean almost nothing, to be sure, but to me at least the mélange of smarmy condescension and prissy buzz-words ("transformed," "increasingly diverse") suggests that these prestigious libraries are girding themselves for yet more disruptive change. Note too that the one thing the "constituencies" (those pesky faculty, students, and other researchers) will *not* be offered is larger or better book collections, but only "human resources, programs, and services." No doubt the "human resources" will take the form not of dowdy old librarians but of "cybrarians"—a new and ghastly coinage— which are not some race of alien mutants but librarians with the *libri* removed.

The next ARL priority pretty much gives the game away: "Ensure that research and learning will flourish through the development of advanced networking applications and Internet." This insurance, be it noted, is to be accorded not through the provision of books, journals, documents, microfilm, or even databases and other online resources, but rather through "advanced networking applications and Internet." This claptrap too is code; the sanctimonious phrase "research and learning" is intended to divert attention from the alternatives being recommended. Translated, this means that when your "constituencies" (librarians used to call them "users," so maybe this is an improvement) grumble that you're not purchasing the books and periodicals they need, offer them the smokescreen panacea of "networking." In other words, less misleadingly put: send them anywhere else but here.

READERS WHO WISH to have a preview of the not-so-brave world that awaits us at the hands of such hucksters need go no farther than Copenhagen. There the Royal Library has emptied the entire contents of its stacks and has replaced the books with computer terminals; the volumes themselves are warehoused in "remote storage" (another buzz-phrase, which really means: "Kiss your books goodbye"). When I visited the Royal Library scarcely ten years ago, its manuscript and print collections, thousands upon thousands of meticulously tended volumes, constituted its pride and joy; my enthusiastic hosts even insisted on taking me on a long and thorough trek through the many-tiered stacks. Now only a shell remains, traversed by the chattering of monitors with their ghostly "virtual resources." The Danish librarian who told me of this desecration of one of Europe's great collections had tears in his eyes as he spoke. I couldn't help thinking of the inadvertently prophetic words of Marcellus in *Hamlet*: "Something is rotten in the state of Denmark."

At the other extreme of this brawl of the book have been those bug-eyed and splenetic observers of the library scene, such as Nicholson Baker, whose recent onslaught (in his book *The Double Fold*) on conservation practices in research libraries has stirred so much acrimony. One reason, of course, why

Baker is viewed quite dimly by the library establishment is that he, or his type, has long been familiar: the aggrieved and expostulating professor who appears one day, frothing with rage, in the librarian's office waving some discarded tome and demanding to know how on earth so *indispensable* a title could have been discarded (or "de-accessioned," as librarians coyly put it). There is probably no book, pamphlet, leaflet, magazine, newspaper, comic book, or indeed, printed object of any sort, that does not have some research value, and in this, at least, the raving professor is right. I have known one librarian-collector of ephemera who dutifully amassed hoards of subway ticket stubs, empty shampoo bottles, and even designer sunglasses because all of these objects bore print on their surfaces. But libraries are institutions in which a principle of selection should reign, and this for very sound epistemological rather than pragmatic reasons. Selection, when carried out skillfully in a research library, is an art as well as a science, and it is this art, along with the collections it can shape, that we are in danger of losing in the current "battle," if indeed we have not already lost it. Much that Baker complains of is, of course, all too true, but the trouble is that he should have been proclaiming it twenty-five years ago, when it could have made a difference and when many librarians themselves might have welcomed such an ally. His fulminations are just too late.

One of the most troubling aspects of our battle of the books as it has been conducted, mostly behind the scenes, in our major university libraries is that there exists so little common ground between proponents of the traditional book with all its offshoots and the self-appointed apostles of a new approach. Swift could declare of his own conflict that "the present Quarrel is so enflamed by the warm Heads of either Faction, and the Pretensions *somewhere or other* so exorbitant, as not to admit the least Overtures of Accommodation." Worse still, few indeed have been those participants in our own battle who have had the courage or the foresight or the plain common sense to proclaim that the conflict is probably moot: indeed, we and our libraries—and by extension, that means our culture, and the survival of culture—require urgently *all* modes of knowledge, for in the end they are complementary, not antithetical. The invention of printing did not obviate the need for manuscripts or indeed for papyrus and palm-leaf scrolls and cuneiform tablets, all of which libraries still collect, or should be collecting.

One of my own frustrations as a library director lay in the difficulty, if not the patent impossibility, of persuading one side or the other that both books and computers were essential. On occasion, this took farcical turns. University administrators routinely cherish the plaintive hope that automation will somehow, in the near future, obviate the need for books, libraries, and traditional library buildings, the costs of which increase exponentially year after year (it is a rule of thumb that book prices rise by a year or more ahead of the Consumer Price Index). Researchers and students are, however, usually just as desperate to obtain print materials *in addition to* online resources; those who use the sources, especially in the sciences, often find both print and online formats necessary since they consult them at different times for different purposes: the online version in a lab in the heat of an experiment and the print version for writing up results. In the midst of such troubles, I found myself lunching with a university vice president who had been effectively blocking the construction of a new special library for over two years because, as he put it, "books will be extinct in five years, so why construct a new building to house them?" Suddenly, between the soup and the main course, he lost all patience and exclaimed, "Yes, yes, I know you book lovers all too well! The book is a sexual object for you. Think about it: those creamy white pages you love to spread wide, like a woman's thighs, the textures of the paper, even the smell of a fresh book. . . ! It is classically Freudian! Oh yes, I have you pegged!" The fact that my interlocutor was French-born and still possessed a Chevalieresque accent gave his words incredibly lurid emphasis.

Startled by this outburst, I yet had to admit upon later reflection that he had a point. A book is intensely physical, even sensuous. Reading is not a disincarnate, cerebral activity but a solidly physical process in which we deploy almost all our senses, and no doubt a Freudian pleasure-principle is at work while we read. After all, we are at least subliminally conscious of the weight of the book in our hands, the design and layout of the pages engage our eye, the typeface is pleasing or annoying or diverting, marginalia or underscorings may arrest our attention, we can smell the ink at times and graze the texture of the pages, the binding, the dust jacket with our fingertips. In her memoir *One Writer's Beginnings*, Eudora Welty put it this way: "I cannot remember a time when I was not in love with them [books]—with the books themselves, cover and binding and the paper they were printed on, with their smell and their weight and with their possession in my arms, captured and carried off to myself."

When we open an old book, or one we read in childhood, the scent of the past that rises up can bring back whole Proustian realms in its gust. By contrast, nothing could be less sensuous than a computer monitor with that cool filtering glow that emanates from it; even the touch of fingers on the keyboard is abstract compared to the feel of a cover or of pages. I do not write this as a nostalgic paean to the book as such (though I see nothing wrong in that), but I do wonder whether the knowledge gained from books may stick with us longer in part because it comes wreathed in these sensuous associations. In any case, the senses, if not the attention (try to distract a teenager from a computer screen!), seem more fully engaged by a book than by a monitor, however seductively the latter may twitter.

No doubt I am biased, but it strikes me that a covert complicity exists between book and reader that does not obtain between computer and user. Reading a book becomes an experience in one's life in a way that consulting a computer cannot be (or, at least, cannot be yet). The computer is unsurpassable for the transmission of facts, of raw information, as well as for its miraculous indexing properties, but it does not—again, perhaps, does not yet—engage our imaginations and intellects in quite the same way a book does. I believe that this has to do with the serial and sequential nature of a book, its succession of pages in linear alignment, as opposed to the scroll-like nature of the computer screen. There is a reason, after all, why the codex superseded the scroll; there is an affinity between the way in which information is presented in a book and the way in which we learn that has no analogue in the world of automation. As far as libraries are concerned, the most visible effect of this change, of this reversion to the scroll that computers represent, has been the relinquishment of the library card catalog. This too has been the subject of a much-discussed and rather silly essay by Nicholson Baker; however piquant Baker's complaints, he somehow missed the entire point of what the shift from card to online record betokened, for better or for worse.

The modern library, as it developed, especially in North America, over the past one hundred years or so, depended above all upon a precise and rather elaborate classification of human knowledge. The best-known of these systems of classification is probably the Dewey Decimal System, devised by Melvil Dewey around the end of the nineteenth century and which depended upon decimal increments to parcel knowledge by subjects. The system was much hated by school kids (myself among them) because it compelled you to use the card catalog, at least until you had a good enough grasp of the classifications to browse. Dewey's system rested upon an ancient conception: knowledge is not only classifiable but hierarchical. Some types of knowledge are more general (the domain of reference books such as encyclopaedias, gazetteers, atlases, etc.) and so occupy the first class. Thence we proceed from the general to the more and more particular along a scale of increasing precision and ever finer distinctions.

THE POINT OF ALL THIS is to say that in order to employ such a system as the Dewey with the utmost effectiveness, you have to have something of a general, if vague, understanding of a certain taxonomy of knowledge; there is an order between, and within, classifications and a strict logic obtains. Books (except fiction) are ordered by subject, not by author. If a given writer has composed a treatise on geology, it will be in a different classification from his or her slim pamphlet of lyrics. To be sure, this is but one principle of classification; books could be classified by author, as in the old Richardson system, or by other means. From the reader's viewpoint what obviously matters is being able to find the book. And yet, in using Dewey, one is necessarily reminded that a given book falls into one category and not another. Dewey and its analogues are, if you will, vertical principles of arrangement; they are arborescent systems from which sprigs and runners and branches are continually unfurling, at predetermined points along the trunk and nowhere else. The more elaborate certain sub-disciplines become, the more vertiginous the classifications and sub-classifications themselves become with call numbers spiralling into ever longer and unwieldier combinations. (Imagine the difficulty of classifying particle physics or quantum mechanics in a system developed in what was still a Newtonian world!)

Though Dewey, in its various revisions and permutations, is used worldwide and is probably the most successful and practical classification scheme yet devised, with that of the Library of Congress not far behind, nowadays all such systems have been rendered irrelevant and even otiose, at least for the average reader, by the advent of automation. The systems are still in use—books have to be analyzed and classified and shelved somehow and librarians are inveterate systematizers—but they have been effectively gutted of their epistemological structures. What librarians term "subject access" is no longer crucial in carrying out research in a library, and the old, massive, crimson-buckram-bound volumes of the Library of Congress index of subject headings, a concordance of Babel on an infinite Borgesian scale, is now more of a curiosity than anything else. Once it became feasible to conduct Boolean searches or simply to employ keywords, the entire edifice of subject classification and taxonomy began to totter. The old stuffy hierarchical categories have gone the way of the Great Auk, and anyone can now find *something* in the library as long as he has even the dimmest idea of what he is looking for. It would be intolerably elitist, I suppose, to lament this apparent dumbing down of the library. As opposed to the old vertical and hierarchical way of articulating knowledge, the new keyword approach is resolutely horizontal and "egalitarian"; not only can anyone use it, practically anything is connected to everything else. The notion of moving from the general or universal to the particular is made ridiculous. Who needs logic when you can enjoy random access?

It would be foolish to deny the usefulness of keyword searches and their analogues. At the same time, I have observed over the last two decades that research in libraries, among undergraduate and graduate students, is becoming shallower and shallower. If a title or an author is not instantaneously located in a database or an online catalog, the assumption is made (and is quite hard to shake) that the title or author does not exist. Gone are the days of tedious and often fruitless hours spent toiling through bibliographies and bibliographies of bibliographies for a single nugget of fact. Fair enough, and I will not lament their passing. Nor am I arguing that knowledge should be made difficult to obtain—

far from it. But, for better or worse, true knowledge is *by its very nature* hard to get; indeed, it is not just hard to get but tough, knotty, obdurate, resistant, and even harder to hold on to than to get, and we do no one a favor by pretending otherwise. In their tiresome stress on information over the last two decades, librarians have tended to place too great an importance on what should in fact be the beginning of a search for knowledge—the mere fact, the datum—and not an end in itself. A facility in surfing the internet is no substitute for the struggle to understand. If genuine learning were available at the stroke of a keyboard, by now we would all be Leonardos and Einsteins. The computer is good not because it makes learning simpler (it does not). It is good because it is fast and because it enables us to tackle tasks and challenges that are otherwise beyond our computational abilities. It is good because we can address the incredible complexity of problems that before we could not even have approached. And in libraries the computer is especially good because it permits almost instantaneous connections to be made between an infinitude of possible subjects. It articulates what would otherwise be Ovid's *rudis indigestaque moles*, a "rough disorderly lump" of chaotic data.

THIS SEEMINGLY SLIGHT SHIFT in the way we now seek for information in libraries—briskly and rapidly with apparently infinite "connectivity," as opposed to the old, laborious drudgery of toiling through card-files and reference shelves—has itself brought consequences, both good and bad, in its train and has affected not only the way in which research libraries function but also the very profession of librarian. "Information technicians" and re-tooled reference librarians may have thrived but at least two once-essential disciplines, that of cataloger and that of bibliographer, have been weakened, if not rendered obsolete. This has been one inconspicuous but destructive side effect of automation.

The bibliographer selects books; the cataloger puts them in logical and retrievable order. This sounds simple but is not. Incidentally, of all library specializations, these two are probably the most ancient, dating back to Ur of the Chaldees, if not beyond. Of course, catalogers are invariably (and often rightly) lampooned as fussbudgets and hairsplitters of the most exasperating sort, but then it is their nobly picayune craft to discern ever finer and more accurate footholds along the slippery ladder of classification. And cataloging, if not much honored today, can number among its distinguished practitioners many illustrious names, including the fourth-century B.C. poet and scholar Callimachus whose fabled *Pinakes* (literally "tablets") brought order to the immense holdings of the great library at Alexandria. In more recent times, Leibniz, Lessing, and Strindberg, as well as Philip Larkin (and Mao Zedong!), to name but these, served as librarians and devoted themselves to the creation of catalogs; and think of the prestige of lists and inventories in the works of Jorge Luis Borges, another librarian by profession. (To be sure, it is reported that Callimachus chafed at his post and was perhaps bitter because Ptolemy II never named him director; and Lessing quit the profession in disgust because he was sick and tired, he said, of acting both as the watchdog that guards the hay it cannot eat as well as the stable boy who must provide the cows with fodder on demand.)

As for the bibliographer, in bygone days most often a scholar-librarian with academic credentials the equal of any professor, he or she has been rechristened the "collection development" librarian or "subject specialist" and is expected to "network" and elaborate ever goofier and more unworkable schemes of "resource sharing." Most meretricious of these, in the turbulent quarter-century just past, was surely the ill-fated "Conspectus," aggressively promoted for years, over the objections of many bibliographers, by both the Research Libraries Group and the Association of Research Libraries.

The Conspectus was a cockamamie project by which libraries graded their own research collections, on a scale of one to five, for the purpose of facilitating a purely mythical "shared access"; since the Conspectus inevitably entailed highly subjective and not disinterested self-assessments, it finally collapsed under its own absurdity, but not before having frittered away millions of dollars that might have been spent on enlarging and improving the very collections libraries intended to share. (One flaw in the process was illustrated for me by an exchange with a colleague at the New York Public Library who after having read my ranking of Princeton's Persian holdings declared: "Since Princeton is so good in Persian, we can stop collecting it.")

Forgotten in all these grandiose (and hugely wasteful) sideshows is the fact that the truly wonderful and incomparable American collections, those, say, at Harvard's Widener Library or the New York Public Library or at Yale, Toronto, Indiana, Berkeley, Chicago, Princeton, and on and on, were in fact formed by rampant and often highly individualistic curators and bibliographers who were as much swashbuckling buccaneers in the book business as men and women of learning and scholarly shrewdness. (Their prototype, if not their patron saint, is J. P. Morgan, whose bibliographic acumen coupled with business ruthlessness created one of the glories of the world of libraries.) It goes without saying, of course, that few library administrators look with fondness on such potentially maverick staff members. Enter the computer. By holding out the rosy but specious possibility of "shared access," automation also offered a marvelous way of eliminating or "phasing out" such professionals under the snappy banner of "cost effectiveness."

Again it is not nostalgia that prompts me to lament the decline of the bibliographer and the original cataloger in research libraries. Both disciplines are as much needed now as ever before. Why? The original cataloger (that is, the cataloger who does not draw on the cataloging information provided by the Library of Congress or other libraries) works with rare, unusual, often esoteric material, e.g., Rabbinic commentaries on the Talmud with all their numerous super-commentaries, glosses and super-glosses, marginalia and excurses, etc. To catalog books of this sort may require hours or even days; all the authors, many of them obscure, must be traced and the authoritative versions of their names established, the relation of one commentary to a text or a gloss to a commentary must be teased out and elaborated, and so forth. But the result is a minute, almost microtomic dissection of a work and its intellectual and physical history that is of incalculable help to scholars. Naturally, such a specialty is both time-consuming and costly, and yet, is not this, and exactly this, what a research library should be providing? Who else will do this? True, the so-called "brief cataloging" that is now in favor does at least give researchers some grasp on complex collections, but it cannot be an adequate substitute for the full analysis and description intricate items demand.

As for the bibliographer, he not only scouts out and orders books; if he is any good, he also has a comprehensive grasp of the collection. He knows its lacunae; he has a long and detailed list of desiderata; he works to anticipate shifts in a scholarly field and to provide for them; above all, he strives to form a collection that is at once internally consistent and articulated: what may to the casual glance appear whimsical or superfluous will yet have its intrinsic place within the collection, and for good reason. Unlike the cataloger's work, however, that of the bibliographer is not easily quantified. Libraries must accept with a certain degree of trust that over time a good bibliographer will succeed in creating a rich and deep collection, much as universities trust that the professors to whom they grant tenure will eventually produce work of substance and significance. Such intangible covenants count for little in the library of today, and more's the pity.

Furthermore, not only have many of the most distinguished American bibliographers and curators literally been hounded out of their positions (yes, at the same Harvards, Princetons, and Yales, whose collections they toiled to build), but the acquisition of books and journals has been widely relegated to automated "approval plans." Under such plans, believe it or not, it is the bookdealers themselves who select and often catalog the very books that they sell to libraries. Multinational bookdealers now routinely create "collection profiles" for research libraries and then proceed to ship books as they, the bookdealers, see fit. Libraries have the right to return unwanted books but rarely do; it is simply too much bother. Despite the obvious risk of conflict of interest, these plans are not all bad since certain imprints, such as titles from university presses, are almost invariably acquired by libraries; why waste the time of a highly paid bibliographer on such routine purchases? And yet, the titles that fall through the cracks of the plans can only be retrieved by those very specialists who are now more and more being replaced by rank-and-file librarians. If this is bad enough in the realm of English-language publishing, imagine how it affects foreign and special collections for which subject expertise is indispensable. And the damage is usually irreparable; all the titles the library should have been acquiring when it was buying blindly quickly go out-of-print and become unobtainable; the special collection is diminished, usually forever.

Needless to say, this does not form any part of the rosy view of many university officials or library directors, most of whom yodel from their particular fence posts the latest eudaemonistic cock-cry of yet another false dawn. The administrators have been more to blame than rank-and-file librarians, most of whom are committed to an ideal of service, to provide whatever readers need. But library "managers" have almost universally seized upon, and pushed, automation as a magical cost-saving expedient.

IN ONE SENSE, this is understandable. Over the past twenty-five years, book and journal prices have soared to previously unimagined levels. I have my own benchmark for the surge in book prices: in 1971, almost overnight, the price of E. G. Browne's *Literary History of Persia*—published by Cambridge University Press and for over fifty years around $15 a volume—abruptly quadrupled and made havoc of my meager graduate student book budget. But even if we look at the very recent past, we can see the increases that have devastated acquisitions budgets. A law book that in 1984 cost $44, cost $82 in 1998; a book on literature cost an average of $24 in 1984, but $44 in 1998. (I should point out that there has been some abatement of book prices in the last two years but it is probably too soon to know whether this trend will continue.)

And journal prices, especially for scientific periodicals, have risen to truly obscene levels. A chemistry journal that in 1984 averaged $228.90 per year (a hefty enough price, one would have thought!) rose to $1,302.00 in the year 2000; a journal in mathematics that cost $107.00 annually in 1984 had quintupled to $517.00 in 2000. (In Europe the situation became even worse: the average German chemistry journal, for example, experienced a six-fold increase for the same period.) The history of scientific journal pricing and its horrendous rise over the last twenty years deserves discussion in its own right. Suffice it to say here that one of the chief pioneers of punitive price increases in academic journals—a particularly cruel and absurd cycle since publishers effectively sell back to university libraries at exorbitant prices the research that their own professors have produced—was none other than the late, unlamented Robert Maxwell, the self-styled "bouncing Czech." His progeny, particularly in England and Holland, continue to thrive at the expense of libraries.

BEGINNING IN THE 1970s, such constraints forced library directors and their bosses to cast about desperately for budgetary relief. The computer seemed the ideal answer. (It did not immediately become apparent that computers were, if anything, even costlier in the long term than books and journals.) But the largest irony of our own Battle of the Book is not that certain forceful advocates preferred computers to books for intrinsic reasons—in truth, they could care less— but that with the cynicism of panic, they latched on to that medium, whatever it might be, that looked cheapest, glitziest, and most "cost effective." If the book had been shown to be more cost-effective than the computer—with hindsight a not untenable position!—such administrators would have been baying for more books and journals. As it was, opportunists soon abounded on all campuses, bringing in their wakes not only blatant hucksterism—of the sort we thought had gone out with the snake-oil salesmen of the previous century—but also all varieties of new, and not-so-new, "philosophies of scientific management" and strategic planning. With the advent of the computer, and its ability to provide minute statistical data on operations, came the hard-headed, clear-eyed, unsentimental, bottom-line purveyors of the MBA world-view, and universities—and their libraries—have not been the same since. Gentlemanly library directors (and they were all men), accustomed to submitting elegantly drafted and wryly understated annual reports, were now being asked to draw up "business plans" for their operations. Efficiency experts, systems analysts, and high-priced consultants were not far behind. In all this, perhaps the greatest harm occurred because the research library was simplistically likened to any other large and complex organization when in fact its distinctive operations, requirements, and, yes, institutional culture—in short, all those factors that had made our great libraries great—were utterly at variance with those of a factory or a corporation.

Many librarians accepted the changes with relief, others were dismayed. With the advantage of two decades of hindsight, one can say that the dismay was perhaps not exaggerated. Of course, libraries have been unusually resistant to change, and with justice: an institution and a profession whose sacred duty it has always been to safeguard and make available the records of our past should be conservative, indeed, should be exceedingly cautious, about change. Even so innocuous an innovation as microfiche or microfilm (*pace* Baker), as well as the unprecedented position of "microfilm librarian" ("fiche-wives," as my colleague Orest Pelech of the Duke University Library promptly dubbed them), originally seemed alarming to librarians who feared, without justification, as it turned out, that this new format would replace the book. My own first supervisor and mentor in a research library harbored such anxieties. An immensely learned scholar and bibliophile, he once led me on an excursion through the darkest and most remote regions of the stacks. As I followed in his wake, I noticed that he was mumbling something indistinct but fervent. As I came closer, I saw that he was stroking the spines of the shelved books, and I heard him muttering, "I will never let them turn you into microfilm, my darlings!"

Of course, there is no question of a "return to the book" or any other such quasi-Luddite approach. Not only would that be ill-conceived, it would also be superfluous, for the book is thriving as perhaps never before. (According to *The Bowker Annual*, that bible of the library profession, some 100,405 titles were published in 1999 in the United States alone. And on the authority of Dr. Knud Dorn, of the firm of Otto Harrassowitz Buchhandlung in Wiesbaden, I am told that book publishing *in English* has increased enormously in recent years in Europe, probably because of the EU.) This is not parallel to, or in spite of, advances in automation but because of it, for printing technology has been revolutionized like everything else and the robust state of publishing, at least in terms of production, owes much to automation.

At best the computer and the book are symbiotic. What the

computer does well—sorting, indexing, linking, retrieving, etc.—no book can equal but what the book can do—proffer knowledge as a vital experience—computers mimic only very imperfectly. Among many possible examples, let me give two that represent for me the opportunities computers offer to research libraries; one is drawn from my own field of research, the other from my experience as a library consultant.

IN ISLAMIC INTELLECTUAL HISTORY, my particular discipline, manuscripts form a core around which entire subsidiary literatures have developed; usually these consist (as in the Rabbinic examples I noted earlier) of school texts with their ancillary commentaries and glosses, but they may also contain counter-commentaries or even wholly original treatises inspired by a work. In short, a given text may have spawned dozens or even hundreds of subsidiary texts which themselves often span centuries; an author who wrote in the twelfth century may find a glossator today in the madrasahs of Qum or Fez. To amass and compile all of these texts in printed or handwritten or microfilmed form is a daunting job and to collate them is even harder. But through such devices as hypertext, it should be possible not only to convert such writings to electronic form but to index them, so that at the touch of a finger, all the relevant explications on a given theme or problem, from any century whatever, could be summoned to the computer screen. This is in fact happening; the Qur'ân is available on CD-ROM together with two of its standard commentaries. Rather than rummaging through several densely printed volumes, one now can call up a definition or an explanation instantaneously. What is possible for Islamic texts is possible for those in other fields: the creation of a stratified palimpsest of related writings which are mutually transparent. Imagine such a simultaneous array of the different manuscripts of *Ulysses* or *King Lear.*

For the second example, when I worked as a consultant in

Morocco, I found that the quickest and best way of building new library collections from scratch was to acquire materials in an online format. Automation has in effect made it possible for Third World institutions to replicate the laboriously assembled collections of great Western libraries, and by this I mean not only their catalogs but much of their holdings as well. Newspaper files, government documents, scientific databases, huge electronically indexed collections of poetry, fiction, and history in several languages are available and more or less affordable. Here the approval plans of various book-dealers, used as a cost-cutting expedient in the West, proved indispensable for the acquisition of printed books and journals. Such "instant" libraries are springing up in the wealthier countries of the Arab world. Of course, they lack the depth of the rich old collections but at least they have a viable foundation on which to build. Moreover, many such collections are available gratis. More and more libraries are offering the full texts of rare and unusual resources. At McGill University Library, for example, it is now child's play to access and download special collections as disparate as those on the Northwest fur trade or the history of the treatment of tuberculosis.

RESEARCH LIBRARIES in their inherent conservatism have always striven for balance and it seems to me that in these, and other ventures, a new equipoise is taking shape. Both the Ancients and the Moderns represent extremes and extremes are antithetical both to libraries and to librarians, who have a fine-grained instinct for equilibrium. It behooves librarians, who are the guardians of collective memory, to look back into their own history for exemplars.

As one example, almost a century ago, in 1904, a figure emerged in the world of librarianship who is now forgotten but whose practice and thinking, in my own opinion, provide pointers for the future. Adolf von Harnack was the keeper of the Royal Library in Berlin from 1904 to 1921 and a renowned historian of early Christianity. Like our own two most recent Librarians of Congress, von Harnack came to his director's post not from the ranks of librarians but from the professoriate (and was heartily resented, at least at first, by the profession, as were both Daniel Boorstin and James Billington). This is worth mentioning because von Harnack administered the Royal Library with a scholar's eye; from long training and practice, he knew exactly what a great research collection and its services should be, and he set out to create them. To this end, he not only expanded and improved the holdings of the library but refined and enhanced the positions of the librarians who were responsible for its continuance. As it happens, von Harnack wrote frequently and well on his new position and its entailments. During his fifteen years in the directorship his view of scholarly collections evolved and became quite subtle, particularly so when juxtaposed to our present "approval plan" approach. Here is how von Harnack enunciated his guiding principle of selection in his 1911 work *Aus Wissenschaft und Leben*:

> Only what is used or at least has a prospect of use should be conserved. The librarian's task in large libraries has become for this reason much more difficult, but also much more significant. The superfluous is always harmful. This is true for large libraries as well. On the other hand, however, it is true to say that even the least significant item is valuable as a mass phenomenon.

As a consequence of this principle and its inherent tension—there is no facile rule or formula—von Harnack argued that the librarian must resist simplistic solutions. When the Director of the University Library in Graz, one Ferdinand Eichler, argued that libraries should concentrate on acquiring only "the best" books, von Harnack argued, with considerable élan, that this was nonsense. The purpose of a research collection, he countered, was not to offer the best or the right ideas, whatever those might be, but all those writings, right or wrong, wise or stupid, that bear on a given subject. The formation of research collections will always therefore be something of an art, in which scholarship, experience, and sheer intuition play essential roles. Von Harnack's conception of the library is at once utopian and down to earth. In a 1923 article he wrote:

> From the time of Leibniz until the end of the 18th century, there existed in the domain of science, literary culture and social life a single educated type and a "private company" (*société anonyme*), to which the most varied spirits belonged. It encompassed Bossuet as well as d'Alembert, Leibniz as well as Kant, Newton as well as Voltaire—all those, indeed, who understood how to present their insights and points of view with wit and style; who knew how to listen to an opponent and to present him with a well-founded response from their own position. This "company" no longer exists, but it does survive in libraries and must continue to survive there. An eclecticism open to all sides must reign there, as it did in the period of the Enlightenment.

Quaint as such a vision may sound, I believe that it remains valid. A research library must be as capacious as is possible but it must become so by enlightened and balanced principles of selection. Today surely this implies the fullest deployment of all means at our disposal; in other words, not this format or medium as opposed to that, but *all* pertinent materials, whether they be found on the printed page or in digital form or on bamboo scrolls and cylinder seals. In a fascination with the means, librarians have lately tended to ignore and neglect the ends. But the purpose of a library is not to cut costs or to showcase new gadgetry or to serve as a mausoleum for books fallen into desuetude; rather, it is to make possible that instant of insight when all the facts come together in the shape of new knowledge. It has always struck me as paradoxical that so many tons of concrete, so many miles of shelves and wires and circuitry as even a modest library contains, are required to prompt that most evanescent of human experiences which a new understanding entails. The poet Paul Claudel wrote that for the flight of a single butterfly, "the entire sky is necessary," and so it is as well, I think, in the empyrean of knowledge.

As THE MOTTO for the Royal Library, von Harnack took the Latin tag *Biblioteca docet*, "the library teaches." By this he meant not that the library staff offer evening classes but that the library itself make a genuine experience of knowledge continually possible; as a historian he knew that past, present, and future are not merely sequentially linked but interlaced by myriad crisscrossing strands.

What strand in all this belongs properly to the librarian? For von Harnack—and I think that he was right, however archaic his vision may appear—it is still the book itself:

> the literary document as such, as the bearer of literature and science, the book with its general and yet highly particular natural history from inception to binding, the book with its provenance and distribution, the book as an object to be collected, because one book is no book (*ein Buch ist kein Buch*).

Librarianship, when it is "vivified by love of books, is the sum total of knowledge about the library and the book in themselves (*an sich*)." All of von Harnack's musings on libraries are tinged with his own religious sentiment. For this reason he can go so far as to term the librarian a "minister of written and printed words" (*minister verbi scripti et impressi*). And if it is indeed the word—whether it appear on a printed page or a computer screen—that is important, this definition still holds good.

In *The Battle of the Books*, Jonathan Swift indulged the fancy that each book somehow preserved the fighting spirit of its author and that libraries were really cemeteries haunted by the spirits of authors who continued to do battle and oust each other:

> So, we may say, a restless Spirit haunts every Book, till Dust or Worms have seized upon it; which to some, may happen in a few Days, but to others, later; And therefore, Books of Controversy, being of all others, haunted by the most disorderly Spirits, have always been confined in a separate Lodge from the rest; and for fear of mutual violence against each other, it was thought Prudent by our Ancestors to bind them to the Peace with strong Iron Chains.

Perhaps, undetected by our grosser senses, some such bellicose and divisive spirits hover over our computer terminals and urge the susceptible to engage in new "battles of the books," from which either the printed page or the monitor will finally emerge triumphant. I hope not. If the past twenty-five years have proved anything, it is that, for the survival of culture, we need all the help we can get, whether in words baked on ancient tablets, set in cold type, or amid the pixels of the scanner and the computer screen.

The Felicific Calculus of
Modern Medicine

by Anthony Daniels

I N MAY OF 2001, one of Britain's most wanted criminals, a
man called Ronald Biggs, returned to Britain after thirty
years of exile in Brazil. Now aged seventy-one, he was arrested
on arrival and taken straight to prison. Biggs was one of the
men behind the "Great Train Robbery" of 1963, whose daring
astonished the country and netted the robbers about $60 mil-
lion in today's money. Biggs was caught and imprisoned, but
he managed to escape to Brazil, a country with which Britain
does not have an extradition treaty. He decided to return after
so long a period of exile because he was ill and impoverished
(he had lived for years by granting interviews to British publi-
cations). He appeared to have calculated that the medical
treatment in a British prison would be superior to that given
to an indigent person of foreign extraction in Brazil.

ON THE DAY of his arrival back in Britain, a newspaper known
nationally for the robustness of its views asked me whether I
was prepared, as a doctor who works part-time in a prison, to
write an article to suggest that Biggs should be denied medical
treatment while he was a prisoner. After all, he was a professional thief who had evaded, defied, and humiliated the
British criminal justice system for many years; he had contributed no taxes to the exchequer, far from it, and now that
he had returned home his incarceration would cost the British

taxpayer a veritable mint of money. Plainly, he was not a deserving case.

I turned down the commission and promptly wrote an article in another newspaper of not dissimilar political bent to explain why Biggs should receive his treatment like any other patient. No doctor to whom he appealed for help could possibly say to him, "You are Ronald Biggs, you robbed a train and evaded justice for more than thirty years, and therefore I refuse to treat you." Indeed, it was the very unworthiness of the man that illustrated the strength of the medical profession's ethical commitment to treat individual patients irrespective of their moral qualities. A good man does not receive better treatment from his doctor than a bad one: at least, insofar as it is possible for the doctor, himself a human being when all is said and done, to divorce his actions from his feelings.

This restatement of an elementary principle of Hippocratic medical ethics called forth many vituperative letters from outraged readers. They said that if they were doctors, they would have no difficulty at all in letting Biggs die. On the contrary, they would do everything in their power to bring forward his well-merited demise. Hippocrates was a fool and a hypocrite: anyway, he had never existed. I suspect that if there had been a plebiscite at the time as to whether or not Biggs should be given medical treatment, a resounding majority would have voted for withholding it, if not for outright execution. This demonstrates that the Hippocratic ethic, like every other civilized cultural achievement, is not to be taken for granted; it has to be protected and defended, sometimes from majority opinion. Barbarism is a permanent temptation.

But there are threats to the Hippocratic ethical tradition that are far more serious and insidious than the gusts of anger that periodically sweep through the public like wind through a cornfield, leaving equally little trace because the memory of modern man is no longer than his attention span. Doctors have been expelled from the Hippocratic Garden of Eden (if they ever truly inhabited it) because they—and others—have eaten of the fruit of the Tree of Knowledge.

In the Hippocratic tradition, the doctor is the agent of the patient and of no one else. When a patient perceives he has an ailment, he visits the doctor. The benevolent doctor listens to the patient, examines him, and proposes a cure, if there is one to be had. The patient, grateful for the doctor's disinterested advice, pays him an appropriate fee for his trouble. The whole transaction is intensely simple and private: no one else need know anything about it. There are no ethical complications.

It requires very little knowledge of the conditions in which medicine is practiced nowadays to understand that medical ethics have become considerably more complex—that is to say, tense and controversial—than they were in the days of Hippocrates. To begin with, there are few Hippocratic patients any longer, those who are content to entrust or submit themselves to the wisdom and judgment of others: modern man finds that to do so in any circumstances whatever is an affront to his dignity, autonomy, individuality, and self-importance. Armed with a sheaf of raw information (and misinformation) downloaded from the internet, and unaware that right judgment is anything more than a matter of applying a simple algorithm to such information, the patient increasingly feels himself, rather than the doctor, to be the authority.

This is a minor problem, however, compared with that of third-party interference in the relationship between doctor and patient. The simple Hippocratic model assumes that the patient will reward the doctor directly from his own pocket, not from that of a vast and anonymous bureaucratic organization, which is driven by the need to make a profit or to contain costs, or both. But it has been a long time since so idyllically simple a relationship has existed between doctor and patient—at least, in the vast majority of cases.

Medicine long ago passed the stage at which the doctor performed an examination that cost nothing except the value he attached to his time, and then prescribed a regimen or a few simple unguents or chemical remedies well within the financial capacity of his patient to buy. Medical investigations, procedures, and treatments have become so technologically sophisticated and expensive that for the great majority of mankind they are available only by means of insurance. Only the very rich and the very poor (who, in rich countries, are able to rely on public charity) can afford not to insure themselves against future medical expenses.

It is hardly surprising under the circumstances that the Hippocratic ethical injunctions—for example, that the doctor should never knowingly kill his patient—have been superseded in practical importance by the more pressing ethical principle that he who pays the piper calls the tune. And this is so regardless of whether the third party that pays the piper is an insurance company (as in America) or the state (as in Britain). The complaints of British and American doctors about the erosion of their independence by outside interference are remarkably similar despite the very different systems of medical insurance under which they practice. This fact should lay to rest the widespread notion that the American medical profession has brought its troubles on itself by overcharging and greed: for precisely the same dissatisfactions are voiced by the British medical profession, whose ability to express its greed in practical action has been severely limited by the virtual nationalization of medical practice in 1948, which turned most doctors into salaried workers.

FOR A TIME, the third-party insurers who paid for the medical treatment of patients were content to leave the medical profession to its own devices. They did not exercise their implicit power, leaving doctors to inhabit something of a fool's paradise. But as the escalating costs of technologically advanced medicine combined with ever greater levels of public scrutiny of all aspects of human existence, outsiders to the profession came to feel they had not only the right but also the duty to come between the doctor and his patient.

Since costs were so high, it was obvious to those who administered the funds that paid for medical treatment (which ultimately derived, of course, from the patients and potential patients themselves, a fact that administrators everywhere were apt conveniently to forget) that value for money should be sought. If demand was infinite but supply was limited, some pretty elaborate calculations would have to be done to ensure that money was not wasted and that the maximum good was procured per dollar expended. A brand of utilitarianism descended over medical practice: not the greatest good for the individual patient, which had been the doctor's traditional aim, but the greatest good for the greatest number. Unfortunately, doctors (with the exception of the very few among them who were epidemiologists) were by temperament, training, and tradition limited to the individual patients who consulted them; therefore they were ill-placed to decide how to bring about the utilitarian heaven in which every cent counted and not a one was wasted. Others than they would have to stand *in loco parentis* for the patients and their insurance premiums.

There have been a few practical problems with this medical felicific calculus, but these have not been regarded as at least theoretically insuperable by those who would constrain the independence of the medical profession. How, for example, do you compare the benefit produced by a liver transplant or a hip replacement with that of treating adolescent acne? (Let us leave aside for the moment the vulgar, pragmatic question of whether you can instantaneously turn a dermatologist into an orthopedic or transplant surgeon, or vice versa, were such a change of medical priorities found to be desirable.) For any such calculus to work, it is clear that commensurable units of medical benefit be found, a kind of euro of medicine, and, since whatever is necessary must be possible (for how could anything that was impossible be necessary?), it follows that such a unit is awaiting discovery. Indeed, some have claimed to have found it already, in such measures as the QALY, the Quality Adjusted Life Year; though, as with the euro, skeptics remain. But what is clear is that, in the search for the universal measure of health benefit, such disciplines as physiology, molecular biology, and pathology can no longer claim to be the queens of the medical sciences: the throne has been well and truly usurped by health economics.

The effects of this usurpation are likely to prove unfortunate. I give as a small example an instance from the experience of my wife, also a doctor, who practices entirely among the elderly. She sees a lot of patients with Alzheimer's disease, and recently drugs have been discovered that, at least for some patients, produce slight improvement in cognitive function or delay somewhat the progression of the disease.

These drugs are, however, relatively expensive: a year's supply costs in the region of $1,500–$1,800. The Director of Public Health for her area has advised that doctors refrain from prescribing these drugs on the grounds that, in times of financial stringency such as ours (and, personally, I have never lived in times other than those of financial stringency), the money could be better spent elsewhere: that is to say, could produce more benefit per dollar expended. From the Director of Public Health's point of view, the question is all the more urgent because the population is aging, and therefore there will be ever more patients with Alzheimer's disease for whom these expensive drugs might be prescribed. He has accordingly asked that the doctors in his area who persist in prescribing the new drugs be reported to him by dispensing pharmacists. Although as yet he and his type have no legal powers to enforce their recommendations, an atmosphere of intimidation, coercion, and threat has been successfully created as a first step in depriving doctors of choice on behalf of their patients, and there is no intrinsic reason why the recommendations of medical bureaucrats should not eventually be granted the force of law. Regulation of this kind is admittedly easier to implement in state-dominated systems of health care such as Britain's, but less formal, monolithic, and draconian controls can nevertheless be implemented without much difficulty by third parties such as insurance companies. The underlying logic is the same.

My wife, however, has not accepted the medical bureaucrat's fiat. She still believes that, state employee or not, her duty is to her individual patient and not to the general good as interpreted by a civil servant. Indeed, she could not possibly have justified failing to prescribe to a patient drugs that she believed to be potentially beneficial by claiming that she was only obeying orders: that excuse has been unacceptable for a number of years, thanks to certain well-known events. On the contrary, she threatened to report the Director of Public Health to the medical licensing authorities, for his gross professional misconduct in recommending that doctors do other than their best for their individual patients: a violation of a fundamental principle of medical ethics to which, even in this weak piping time of cost-benefit analysis, we still pay lip service.

The situation was rendered all the more fraught by the publicity the new drugs had received, so that many of her patients (or rather, their relatives) had heard of them, and by the fact that, in all the areas surrounding hers, the Directors of Public Health, armed with precisely the same data about the drugs as the Director of Public Health from her area, had come to the opposite, but equally rational (or irrational), conclusion—namely that in their areas, the drugs should be prescribed for people with Alzheimer's disease.

A patient and his relatives are, naturally enough, concerned for the welfare of only one person at a time: namely that of the patient himself. The general good is of no interest to them, and they are unlikely to wish to forgo beneficial treatment of the patient merely because a medical bureaucrat, on the basis of some very dubious calculations indeed, has concluded that more people would benefit if the money were spent otherwise. No one loves humanity so much that he will voluntarily suffer a treatable condition.

Thus "rational" cost-benefit analysis promotes bitterness and social conflict. Not only are its calculations highly contentious—it is not uncommon, for example, to see the figure attached to the economic burden of a given disease vary by one or even two orders of magnitude—but, unless they result in the same policy being implemented worldwide, they will also fuel resentment. Man is a comparing animal, never more so than in an information age, and the inhabitants of country X who suffer from an illness will soon enough learn that their counterparts in country Y receive better treatment than they. There are no longer any carpets under which disagreeable information can be swept.

Needless to say, it is possible to reduce any argument whatsoever, including that against cost-benefit analysis, to absurdity. If, for example, there were a treatment that cost $1 million per patient to extend life by one minute, the gain would clearly not be worth the expenditure, but this conclusion, though it relies upon the reasoning of cost-benefit analysis, is obviously arrived at *grosso modo*: no elaborate (and therefore untrustworthy) calculations are necessary to reach it.

There are pressures upon the doctor, however, other than the merely financial, to treat his patient less as an individual in need of succor than was ever envisaged by the Hippocratic ideal: pressures that come from within medical science itself. Explicit statistical calculation has now entered medical practice so thoroughly that it cannot be removed—nor ought it be. A very large proportion of the work of a modern doctor inevitably concerns the treatment of not a person but a statistic. I can illustrate the difference between Hippocratic medicine and modern medicine by considering the treatment of two conditions: hypothyroidism and hypertension. The first can be treated according to the Hippocratic tradition, the second not.

A patient with hypothyroidism visits his doctor with symptoms that the doctor attributes to an insufficiency of thyroid hormone, which he then prescribes. If he gets the dose right (and it is easy enough to do so), he can be confident that his patient will return completely to good health. The doctor has treated his patient as an individual.

High blood pressure, by contrast, is a symptomless disease (except in its last stages). It is likely to be diagnosed as a chance finding during a visit to the doctor for other reasons. The decision to treat the symptomless disease is based upon the knowledge that people with high blood pressure are at increased risk of a premature heart attack or stroke. The risk is reduced if the blood pressure is lowered by the use of drugs. For an elderly patient with, shall we say, moderately raised blood pressure, it is more likely than not that he will fail to suffer the premature heart attack or stroke whose prevention is the object of treatment. Moreover, it is more likely than not that, if treated, the reduction in his blood pressure will fail to effect the desired end result, that is to say, the non-occurrence of either of these serious medical conditions. The doctor would have to treat about one hundred patients with moderately raised blood pressure for five years in order to prevent one stroke or heart attack.

Nor is this all: the drugs that the doctor prescribes to reduce his patients' blood pressure have unwanted side effects, in some if not all cases. A symptomless disease is transformed by the doctor's attention and by his resort to statistical reasoning into one with symptoms, albeit those caused by his treatment rather than by the disease per se. Where now is the most famous of all Hippocratic injunctions, first to do no harm?

In his defence, the doctor can say that one stroke avoided is worth more than the relatively mild side effects experienced by, say, fifty other patients. But the difficulty of the situation is compounded by the impossibility of knowing which patient it is whose life will be, or perhaps has already been, preserved from a stroke or heart attack. The person who benefits might or might not be one of those who suffer from the side effects. No one can possibly know. What is clear is that the doctor can justify his treatment of high blood pressure only if he resorts to a utilitarian argument: that the sum of the good he does outweighs the harm, and not to any given individual, but to a class of individuals, namely those with high blood pressure.

Leaving aside the question of whether it is in principle knowable how many side effects suffered are equal in the felicific calculus to one stroke avoided, it is clear that the doctor is departing from his commitment to individuals when he treats a patient with hypertension: for in any individual case, he has a much greater chance of doing harm (even if of a relatively trivial kind) than of doing good (even if of a significant and life-saving kind). In fact, much of what the modern doctor does, including routine screening for cancer and other serious diseases, is inevitably based upon the same utilitarian logic. And whatever objections might be raised against utilitarianism as an abstract moral theory (and there are many such), it would be a strange modern doctor who never, under any circumstances, used utilitarian thought to guide his conduct.

The treatment of hypertension is a good lens through which to view the sacred cow of modern medical ethics: patient autonomy. I asked a friend of mine, a clinical pharmacologist of distinction, for his estimate of the number of patients treated for high blood pressure who were aware of the logic upon which such treatment was based:

"Two," he answered with characteristic decisiveness.

"You mean 2 percent, or two in a thousand?," I asked.

"No," he replied. "I mean two in the whole of Great Britain."

In other words, he thought there were scores and possibly hundreds of thousands of people who took tablets each day for their blood pressure who had only the haziest understanding of why they were doing so. By coincidence, I was consulted shortly afterwards by a man of about average intelligence who had high blood pressure, who had stopped taking his pills for lack of a repeat prescription, and who asked whether I would renew it. I asked him why he had taken the pills in the first place. "Because," he replied, "my doctor told me to." I then asked him why he thought his doctor had told him to. "Because he thought they would do me good." I explained, as clearly as I could, the logic of antihypertensive treatment. His eyes glazed over as if what I said had nothing to do with him, as if I were the village pedant. At the end of my explanation, I asked him whether he had understood what I told him, and he replied that he had.

"So what do you want?," I asked.
"I'll do whatever you think is best, doctor."

He was an old-fashioned patient, who didn't want autonomy; he wanted to be told what to do, as I have wanted to be told what to do on the few occasions in my life when, though a doctor, I have been seriously ill. The last thing I wanted when I was near death's door was to make a consumer choice, informed or otherwise. I do not think that he and I are the only people in the world who have sometimes wanted others to decide things for us.

To be sure, my patient's abrogation of his autonomy was itself a decision taken autonomously, just as the man who sells himself into slavery acts freely. To have demanded, therefore, that he choose for himself whether or not to take the pills would have constituted a denial of his autonomy. It remained for me to act in his best interests, but how was I to decide what were his best interests in a situation like this, independent of the wishes he either could not or would not express? It is easy enough to decide when a patient arrives unconscious at a hospital in diabetic ketoacidosis; it is vastly more difficult when the chances of doing slight harm are very much greater than those of doing considerable good.

In the event, I decided—as most doctors would—to obey that most glorious of all modern medical ethical imperatives, the need to avoid litigation, and prescribed the medication for him. (It sometimes seems that patients consult doctors not so much in the hope of a cure, but in the hope of a cause, or pretext, for litigation: for even settlements out of court, without admission of liability, produce sums of money for the litigant that he is unlikely to accumulate in any other way.) The courts, in assessing negligence, are apt to take as their standard what most doctors would do in the circumstances, and what most doctors would do in the circumstances is usually determined by what the most gung-ho and activist of expert witnesses would do. There is thus an inherent bias against what, in the days of therapeutic nihilism, used to be called "masterly inactivity." In these circumstances, the doctor is not treating his patient; he is treating his own anxiety.

But there is another direction from which traditional medical ethics is under attack. Willing as many patients still are to surrender their autonomy to doctors, many others—an increasing proportion—demand complete sovereignty over their own body. The doctor thus becomes a mere technician whose job is to satisfy the whims of his client (a patient no longer).

Recently in Britain, a surgeon caused a stir by amputating the perfectly healthy leg of a patient who claimed that, ever since adulthood, he was convinced that nature had made a dreadful mistake in supplying him with two lower limbs and that he could not be happy unless the appendage surplus to his requirements were removed. The surgeon justified the operation by saying that, in satisfying his patient's desire, he was improving the quality of his life. He was also reducing the risk of a dangerous, botched auto-amputation. And since the operation was performed under Britain's National Health Service, the surgeon was also able truly to claim that he had no pecuniary interest in the operation, and, living as we do in a highly materialistic age, a lack of pecuniary interest in an action almost automatically justifies it from the moral point of view in the eyes of a population rendered cynical by universal greed.

The surgeon's approach, to satisfy the autonomous desire of his patient whatever his desire might be, leaves doctors permanently open to blackmail. A person has only to say to a doctor that his life is miserable without drug or operation X and threaten either to procure it for himself by illicit or dangerous means or to commit suicide for the doctor to feel obliged to comply with the demand. Oddly enough, an emphasis on personal autonomy goes *pari passu* with the demand that doctors should bring about harm reduction: individuals being autonomous only as far as the satisfaction of their desires is concerned, not for the ill consequences of the satisfaction of their desires, the responsibility for the diminishment of which they are only too happy to delegate to doctors and other authorities.

It would not have surprised Edmund Burke to learn that the surgeon who amputated his client's leg was soon inundated by people requesting the same operation. There is nothing quite like the prospect of satisfaction to provoke bizarre desire; and, as if patriotically to preserve her nation's reputation for rococo excess, an American woman flew to Britain in the hope of having both her legs amputated—by a trained and competent surgeon, of course. The public revelation that there exists a sexual underworld, complete with its own websites, of people who are erotically excited only by amputees, put a temporary stop to the amputations, but surely only a temporary one, until a court somewhere in the world rules that it is man's inalienable right to have bits lopped off him if he so wishes.

It is the combination of technical advance, the concept of man the sovereign consumer (whose life consists, or should consist, of nothing but the endless extension of choice), and the doctrine of universal equity and human rights that produces so many of the ethical dilemmas that have given rise to a new profession: the medical ethicist. The idea that extension of choice is invariably a good (indeed, is the whole and sole purpose of life) is now deeply entrenched the world over. The triumph of the American Declaration of Independence has been complete: if every man has the right to pursue his happiness, and his happiness entails the amputation of his leg, it follows (does it not?) that he has a right to pursue and eventually to have such an amputation. No possibilities should therefore be ruled out a priori, certainly not on the grounds that they are unseemly, disgusting, or sacrilegious; for to do so is to impose standards that are not provable or universal, and therefore constitutes an abridgement of freedom.

CONSUMER CHOICE HAS become itself the beginning and end of wisdom. In a recent autobiographical book, one of the scientists principally responsible for the development of the contraceptive pill, Carl Djerassi, had this to say: since sexual behavior and attitudes are such personal matters, and at the same time so much a part of each culture's identity, differences should be accommodated rather than fought. Only a contraceptive supermarket—a multiplicity of choices to fit the peculiar software aspects of a given society—will provide such accommodation. In other words, the only way to preserve diversity is to turn the whole world into an existential Wal-Mart.

The unwillingness of modern man to place limitations upon his own appetites—the natural consequence of a pagan worship of the right to choice in everything—is seen around us every day. Shortly before I wrote this, *The Guardian* newspaper reported that a British judge had ordered DNA tests on the five men with whom a woman had slept in four days, with a view to finding out (for purely financial reasons) who was the father of her child. Apparently, she had been so desperate to have a child that she had slept with as many men as she could find during her fertile period, in the hope that at least one of them was himself fertile.

The egotistical shallowness of such behavior beggars description, let alone comment, but it is now undoubtedly a mass phenomenon. The woman had taken her right to a child—that is to say, the absence of any legal authority with the right or duty to prevent her from having a child—to mean that she had a positive right to one, regardless of circumstances. Her right soon transmuted itself into a desire, as such imagined rights so often do, until it became the existential itch that she had to scratch. All other considerations, such as the welfare of her future child, or a regard for the decent opinion of mankind, counted for nothing: she was but an atom in a social vacuum, the Brownian motion of her whims being for her the measure of all things.

We live, moreover, in an age of equity and equality (the two are usually equated). If one person in the world is entitled to something, then it follows that everyone else in the world must be entitled to it also. Thus, if a woman in her sixties in Italy is helped by in vitro fertilization and hormonal manipulation to have a baby, it follows that every other woman in the world who so desires it must have a right to similar treatment: for otherwise an injustice will have been done. This is the way that desires previously unheard or undreamt of enter the mind and there fester.

There is, as the Marxists used to say, a dialectical relationship between technical possibility and the whimsicality of man. It so happened that unprecedented progress in molecular biology, which now opens up Promethean possibilities previously unsuspected, occurred just after the rise of mass self-importance as a cultural phenomenon. The prospect of increasing control over some of the most elemental aspects of human existence has made us less tolerant than ever before of its inherent limitations. There are many things fundamental to our lives that we would once have accepted as being beyond our control that we no longer accept as such, and appear to us to have become a matter of choice.

To be sure, Prometheanism has a long and distinguished history, and has done much good. Let me take a single example, by no means the most important: osteoarthritis. It used to be accepted (because it had to be) that old people's joints became stiff to the point of immobility. A British surgeon with a background in engineering, John Charnley, had the idea of implanting artificial ball-and-socket joints in the hips of people crippled by osteoarthritis, since which time joint surgery has progressed almost exponentially. It is difficult to see in this anything but unadulterated good: much suffering has been relieved and many lives enriched by it. But such advances are not of deep or philosophical significance. They do not affect the human personality in any fundamental way. And they are wholly to be welcomed. Suffering might be good for the human soul (and in any case is unavoidable), but so is the search for the relief of suffering.

Increasingly, however, medical procedures are not so much directed at relieving suffering as at fulfilling desire. Of course, the distinction is not entirely watertight, for the thwarting of desire can itself (especially when it is believed that relief is possible) lead to suffering. That is why a dictum enunciated by an old acquaintance of mine, Dr. Colin Brewer, contains more than a grain of truth: misery increases to meet the means available for its alleviation. The plastic surgeon who carries out a rhinoplasty might be relieving the most terrible social phobia that renders life intolerable, or pandering to the mere vanity of his patient, or anything on the continuum between the two. Modern plastic surgery started as an attempt to repair the terribly disfigured faces of airmen during the war who were burned when their aircraft crashed, work that was both infinitely painstaking and noble, but it soon took up the search for eternal youth to which some of the rich believed their money entitled them.

Though the distinction is not clear-cut, there is a difference between what is done to relieve suffering and what is done to satisfy desire. A hip replacement is different from a sex change, a bowel resection from a facelift. The startling advances in molecular biology (as yet little translated into clinical practice) are set to bring about both the relief of suffering and the satisfaction of desire. Not only might the advances lead to a form of negative eugenics—the "culling" of undesirable embryos before they are born—but also to a form of positive genetics. Children might one day be born to specification, as cars are ordered with or without their various extras. We will no longer accept that life is, to some extent, a lottery: we will demand control over everything. The fact that the satisfaction of such a demand will always be illusory, will always shimmer like a mirage beyond the next technical advance, will be likely to make us bitter rather than happy. Certainly, it will inflate our sense of our own importance.

A recent case exemplifies the coarsening effect upon human sensibility (of patient and doctor alike) that technical possibility can exert, when it accompanies the radical individualism of which the libertarian right and the subversive left both approve. A British woman agreed, via the internet, to act (for a fee of $19,000) as the surrogate mother for a California couple. The California woman was infertile, and so a donor's ovum was fertilized in vitro by her consort's sperm.

The resultant embryo was implanted into the British woman's uterus.

The agreement between the couple and the surrogate mother was that if the pregnancy should turn out to be multiple, as is commonly the case with in vitro fertilization, it should be "reduced" by selective abortion. (The use of the euphemistic term "reduce" in these circumstances surely points to a guilty conscience, an implicit acknowledgment that an abortion is not an operation like any other.) The selective abortion was to take place, however, only if it were demanded before the twelfth week of gestation.

In the event, it was a twin pregnancy, but the California couple did not request a "reduction" until the thirteenth week. At this point, the surrogate mother turned tender towards the contents of her womb, for after twelve weeks, there was a risk that an attempt at selective abortion would result in a total, that is to say, a double, abortion. While she regarded it as perfectly ethical to kill one fetus, she jibbed at killing both: to do so would have been beyond the moral pale.

The California couple, however, had ordered one child, not two. As consumers, why should they now be forced to accept what they had not wanted, indeed what they had specifically stated that they did not want? They therefore abrogated the agreement unilaterally, claiming that the surrogate mother had not kept her side of the bargain, leaving her holding the babies, as it were, that she had never wanted for herself either (she was already, it goes without saying, a single mother).

What could any decent surrogate mother do in such circumstances but sue for breach of contract and punitive damages? There was in any case a rumor to the effect that the California couple had grown less keen on the whole surrogate-motherhood arrangement since discovering that the donor of the ovum suffered from an eating disorder— either anorexia or bulimia—and, fearing that the condition was wholly or partially genetic, and not wishing ever to be faced with the prospect of a fasting or vomiting teenager, they found a pretext for escaping from the contract. A legal battle ensued: for it is an ill wind that blows no lawyer any good.

The moral (or perhaps one should call it the immoral) of the story hardly needs pointing out. What is clear, however, is that the medical profession not only made the squalid situation possible, but also actively cooperated in its production. At no point did any doctor have the courage to resist the egotistical wishes of the three people involved. They prostituted themselves to the whims of this trio.

WHAT, THEN, is the future of the traditional practice of medicine: that is to say, of the relief of individual suffering brought about by discernable pathology? The value of that tradition has been brought into question by the barbarians within the gates—by the kind of academics and intellectuals who believe that the whole purpose of the human intellect is to mock and devalue what all previous intellect has wrought. Thus the history of medicine is now taught not as that of the arduous, difficult, painful, and contorted path of man from ignorance to knowledge, from suffering to the relief of suffering; it is taught as that of the search for power and prestige by a group of grasping, elitist, exploitative, and comically ignorant men. The fact that countless thousands of them struggled in vain, as best they could, to unlock nature's secrets, or that the efforts of such giants as Vesalius or Harvey did not bear practical fruit for hundreds of years, is not taken as a sign of the nobility and faith of the enterprise, but of its misguidedness, foolishness, or unimportance. From the security of our modern comfort, in the knowledge that many of our illnesses can be cured and most can be alleviated, the efforts of the past are denigrated or ridiculed, reduced in scale, denied their worth, and so forth, using all the instruments of an exaggerated station whose object is not to find truth but to destroy traditions, customs, institutions, and confidence in the worth of civilization itself.

One of the products of our civilization is, of course, the vast intellectual edifice upon which medicine has been built. The plain fact is that the Western medical tradition is incomparably greater in achievement than that of the rest of mankind put together and quintupled. This is a thought too horrible for our academics and intellectuals to contemplate, especially as their own contributions to the welfare of mankind are usually exiguous, to put it generously. Destruction is the best they can manage, and so, with the full force of their insincerity, they turn their rhetorico-critical faculties on the achievements that have made their lives of ease possible.

It is important, however, not to be apocalyptic when no apocalypse is at hand (though the opposite error is even more dangerous). As my polymath friend Raymond Tallis repeatedly points out, one of the errors bedeviling the reporting of medicine in the press is the use of numerators without denominators: one wouldn't want to ruin a good story by putting it in some kind of perspective. For example, a surgeon in Britain recently removed the wrong kidney from a patient, and there was something of an outcry against the incompetence of surgeons. Such gross errors should, in the abstract, never happen, but, as Hippocrates said, art is long, life is short, and the occasion fleeting. Man is not a failsafe mechanism. In all the ensuing outcry, not a single newspaper thought it necessary to investigate how many kidneys had been correctly removed by surgeons for each one removed incorrectly: about 25,000. Personally, I doubt whether only one in 25,000 statements made by journalists is in error.

So it is necessary to put the threats to the traditional medical relationship (in its ideal form) into some kind of perspective. Again, Professor Tallis might be of help here. He analyzed the one thousand complaints received in a year from patients at a large teaching hospital. One thousand sounds like a horribly large figure, but only one hundred complaints related to the clinical care the complainants had received, the rest being concerned about incidentals, such as bad food or the rudeness of porters, etc. Professor Tallis estimated, conservatively, that there had been 5.89 million interactions between clinical staff and patients in the same period—which means that there had been one complaint for every fifty thousand clinical interactions. This is prima facie evidence of a high general level of satisfaction.

Satisfaction and satisfactoriness are not quite the same thing, of course. People can complain too much or they can complain too little. But the fact is that, despite the threats from financial pressure, epidemiological modes of thought, and technical advances that dissolve the distinctions between the permissible and the impermissible, the traditional medical relationship between doctor and patient lives on.

A Malign Legacy

by David Pryce-Jones

Wherever on this planet ideals of personal freedom and dignity apply,
there you will find the cultural inheritance of England.
—Karel Čapek

M OST OF THE WORLD for most of the time has lived under tyranny. Choice does not come into the matter. Years, centuries, have to pass in order for people to be able to build the culture and supporting institutions of a democratic society—that is, one in which individuals have to be responsible for themselves and their choices. A highly complicated balance operates in a democracy between the myriad choices of individuals and the procedures of accountability they set up to adjudicate the moral, social, and political outcomes of their choices. There is no history, in Emerson's shorthand for the hard-won primacy of the individual over tyranny, only biography.

To be autobiographical, then: among my earliest memories is the exodus from Paris in June 1940 to escape the incoming German army. An image of the blurred faces of refugees along the road has stayed with me. Together with relatives, in due course I was able to leave Vichy France and cross into Spain. Many people—the German literary critic Walter Benjamin for one—were not so fortunate on that same escape route.

Grown up, I began to come to grips with this experience.

Why would unknown Germans have hunted down my relatives and my four-year-old self? How had this complete collapse of democratic France come about? I read what I could
about Nazism. I spent a year in Israel, where I was able to attend the Eichmann trial, and to discover, to my surprise, that
the death penalty served to protect the innocent more than to
exact revenge. In Germany, I was to interview many Nazis,
some of them of the highest rank, intimates of Hitler. Albert
Speer was one. A day with him in his house in Heidelberg
brought me to a different conclusion from that of his biog-
rapher Gitta Sereny, who believed she detected regret, if not
repentance. Faced with a rerun of the past, it seemed to me,
Speer would have made exactly the same choices. Power cor-
rupts. Murder runs deep.

In the era of Brezhnev, I travelled in the Soviet Union and
its satellites. In *Memoir of Hungary, 1944–1948* (2001), a won-
derfully evoked work, Sandor Marai describes how his very
first sighting of Red Army soldiers in Hungary during March
1944 told him that these men were not going to bring him
freedom; they couldn't, because they hadn't any for themselves. So I found it. Social and cultural permafrost had set in.
In the presence of KGB minders, I sat in rooms with people
unable to risk the simplest human exchanges. These encounters were initiations in tyranny. I knew I was contributing
entries to their secret police dossiers and mine.

My relatives had had property in Hungary, deep in the
countryside. The house was now a tank garage. The surrounding poverty was startling. The villagers wept; they be-
seeched me not to forget them. One day, they said, the Soviet
occupation would be over. A former farm manager poured me
a drink in a glass with my family's monogram on it, and on
the wall behind him hung a portrait of a lady in the splashiest
fin-de-siècle style, evidently removed from my family's house.
I was glad that these token things had survived. Vladimir Na-
bokov made the point that he hadn't minded the Communists

taking away his fortune, but he did mind that they believed him to be the sort of person who would mind. I felt the same. As a boy, listening to stories of the past and looking at family photographs and my grandfather's annotated copy of the poems of Petöfi, I cherished romantic fantasies about Hungary, its beautiful country houses, and the Budapest cafes like Gerbeaud's, where the company would be the likes of Marai. More than material things, the Communists had stolen the freedom of the fully imagined life.

The Soviets had created a new type of man, it was widely held, whose identity was defined by class rather than nation. The Soviets and their satellites were also supposed to have built a socialist culture and an economy that, in the double negative of the persistent Stalinist apologist E. J. Hobsbawm, was in its own way "not unimpressive." Yet touts in the streets of Moscow would offer to buy my jeans off me. On a subway train to East Berlin, I was intrigued by the presence of a throng of young men speaking Arabic. I followed as they disappeared into the interior courtyard of a gloomy and run-down Wilhelmine block. There, in front of peddlers offering dollars, surrealistically the young men took off their trousers, and then the many sets of underpants that they had been wearing. The reality of the five-year plan was that smugglers alone provided basic garments.

Intellectuals come out of the twentieth century wretchedly. Those in favor of Nazism, to be sure, were few and too deranged to win much acceptance. On the other hand, the huge majority of those in a position to enjoy full freedom of expression regarded Communism as a peaceful and progressive utopia, when in fact it brought murder, tyranny, and poverty. Voluntarily, intellectuals were surrendering to others the responsibility of making choices for themselves, and accountability, too. The resulting climate of opinion, loosely wrapped up under the label of fellow-traveling, was altogether a denial of reality. All manner of people had been in the clutches of

Soviet Communism and escaped to bear witness. Among them were Stalin's secretary Bazhanov, Victor Serge, Anton Cilega, Franz Borkenau—truly impressive men. Systematically vilified, they were denied a hearing. Messianic delusions about Communism spread throughout the educated classes with a mass credulity and self-righteousness not seen since the Middle Ages.

Motives related to fashion and careerism—and no doubt stupidity and ignorance—drove this failure of intellect. Consciously or unconsciously, there was also primary fear. Each totalitarian power evidently had a huge apparatus for war and state violence. With few exceptions, democratic politicians throughout the thirties followed policies to appease these powers. Fellow-traveling was the cultural arm of political appeasement. Far from offering any resistance, the eminent commentators of the day—the Webbs, Bernard Shaw, H. G. Wells—accommodated themselves to the expected totalitarian future. Trotskyists, Fabians, socialists, Bloomsburyites, pacifists, Quakers rejoiced in finding more to blame in democratic societies than in totalitarianism. Everything was the fault of the British or of other empires, the white man's prejudices, his law, or his capitalism. It is perhaps natural for many people to shirk a test of character, but here surely was also a plea for the continuation of privileges hitherto so effortlessly and pleasantly enjoyed.

Again with rare exceptions, defenders of democratic freedom were too apologetic to be effective. When E. M. Forster asserted that he would rather betray his country than a friend, he was characteristically obscuring the idea of a just cause. At that point, morality begins to rot. Quite forgotten now but a well-known commentator in his day, Ramsay Muir was a decent liberal, absolutely representative in his worries, seeking to stiffen the weakening instinct for self-preservation in democratic countries. In 1934, in the aftermath of Hitler's takeover, he published a pamphlet with the title *Is Democracy*

A Failure? Yes, he thought, in large states it was "a thing of yesterday," and all of us were drifting apathetically, losing the heritage of freedom our fathers had won. To ward off dictatorship he proposed to reform parliamentary procedure and introduce proportional representation, measures not likely to frighten off Hitler and Stalin. J. M. Keynes—hardly a conservative—observed in October 1939 that the left had been calling loudly for resistance to Nazism before the war. The moment war was declared, though, the left rediscovered its pacifism, to leave the fighting to "Colonel Blimp and the Old School Tie," for which Keynes called for three cheers.

It is no exaggeration to say that without Churchill democracy might well have failed in the crucial test against Nazism. As the case of France proved, appeasement slid naturally into collaboration. In 1940 the French National Assembly voted in favor of its own abolition, an act of democratic surrender without precedent. Through will-power and personal example, Churchill in person refuted the Marxist theory of historical determinism, according to which the individual has no role to play in affecting the course of events.

Without President Truman, democracy might have failed in the crucial test against Communism. At the present moment in world history, as Truman put it in his famous declaration in 1947, "nearly every nation must choose between alternative ways of life." One way of life was based on the will of the majority, and the other was based on the imposition of the will of the minority on the majority. Communist parties in France, Italy, Spain, and Greece were prepared to take power through revolution. Stalin's preoccupation with digesting Red Army conquests in eastern and central Europe instead took priority. Without steadfast American input and inspiration, the Soviet challenge would have been left unanswered, and western Europe would have adopted the Pétainist solution of consummating appeasement in outright collaboration.

Throughout the Cold War, the degradation of intellectuals

became more and more widespread. Communists could act
with barbarity anywhere in the world and be sure to find
enthusiastic apologists in the West. However many millions
of victims fell to Communism in Hungary, Cuba, Korea,
Vietnam, Cambodia, and China, the Sartres and de Beauvoirs,
the Lillian Hellmans and Norman Mailers, the Noam Chom-
skys and E. J. Hobsbawms applauded—and then accused their
own democratic societies of every injustice and ill. "The white
race *is* the cancer of human history," exclaimed Susan Sontag.
Between Friends (1995) consists of the correspondence between
Hannah Arendt and Mary McCarthy. From her New York
apartment or her much prized house in Castine, Maine,
McCarthy imagined herself leading "Resistance" to the
Vietnam War as though she were living in Vichy France.
Anti-Communism seemed to her more dangerous than Communism. Law and order, she held, existed only behind the
Iron Curtain. Arendt did not think that fascism would prevail
in the United States but prepared nonetheless for exile in the
house she had bought in Switzerland. Comic though this
flight from reality might seem, many in the educated classes
shared it. Some future Edward Gibbon will have to do
justice to this abuse of privilege and dereliction of
intellect.

IN THE SIXTIES, a yet wider coalition assembled throughout
the democratic countries of groups that resented or hated
everything that had made them what they were. Most of these
protesters came from comfortable and privileged back-
grounds, taking for granted the freedoms they were so
blithely abusing, only a collect call away from parents apparently willing to indulge them endlessly. "Counterculture"
was a telling description of a nihilism that spread from pacifist
flower children and hippies, to the drug-crazed disciples of
Timothy Leary, to assorted terrorists, the Weathermen, the
Irish Republican Army, the Baader-Meinhof gang, the Red

Brigades. On the evidence, the democratic West was nurturing within itself those who would destroy it. For fear of the accusation of fascism, the governments under threat panicked, adding to their own destabilization. In fact, the terrorist groups almost without exception were armed and financed clandestinely by the Soviet Union, and were provided with safe houses and training behind the Iron Curtain. A few courageous journalists, Claire Sterling for one, gathered the evidence to that effect, only to be mocked for their "obsession" with the Cold War.

Violence—or "direct action" in the vocabulary of these groups—became counterproductive only at the last minute. The murder of a range of innocent people, from security guards to businessmen and the Italian prime minister Aldo Moro, outraged the public. Though attributed to the Bulgarian secret police rather than to the KGB, the attempted assassination of Pope John Paul II in 1981 seems to have been the last act in this widespread campaign of destabilization. By then, the Soviet Union was discontinuing a covert policy that so many Western intellectuals were consummating for them overtly.

The work of the Foucaults, Derridas, Lacans, and the shoals of their imitators extended political fellow-traveling throughout society and its culture. The French writer Jean Sévillia coined the apt phrase "intellectual terrorism" for the title of the book he wrote about the whole development. Contempt for democratic institutions was translated into contempt for the moral values that had underpinned those institutions. Henceforth, language was to be used against itself. If words are passing fancies without correlation to reality, then there can be no such thing as truth. Moral judgments are only so much hot air, nothing is what it seems, and everything can as easily be reversed into its opposite. Thus generosity is really a selfish indulgence; love is merely possessiveness; manliness is brutality, while femininity the submission to this brutality; art becomes whatever you want it to be; freedom itself is servitude.

George Orwell had the rare imagination to foresee such inhuman inversions, but he was long since dead. The thrust has been to break down and relativize every aspect of behavior in such a manner that nobody could confidently say what is right and what is wrong. Every act became its own justification; the more violent the act, the greater the justification. As the criminal becomes valued, the judge and the jail warden dwindle into servants of tyranny, the policeman into a "pig." The artist or writer who produces something particularly offensive is "controversial" or "disturbing," terms implying interest and acceptance on the part of right-minded people, leaving criticism—never mind forceful rejection—to the fools. Art and literature become auction-houses in which the most extreme transgressions fetch the highest prices, and there is not even the pretence of universal values. Such is the dead end of the humanist tradition that was Europe's contribution to civilization.

The events of 1968 and their aftermath constituted nothing less than a vote of no-confidence in democracy, and this led spontaneously to what looked like a terminal appeasement of and collaboration with the Soviet Union. I heard a famous French filmmaker say, as though preaching ex cathedra, "I don't read Solzhenitsyn, he's a right-wing writer." Two generations of intellectuals had taken a hard look at the balance of forces in the world, decided that the Soviet Union weighed in as the more powerful, and determined to have a career on the winning side. People thinking of their own skins prefer to be victimizers rather than victims.

"Because the trams run on time, they think it is a normal society," was the bitter crack of Osip Mandelstam on the Communism that was to murder him—one among the tens of millions. Mikhail Gorbachev and those who elected him certainly thought it was a normal society. The veteran Andrei

Gromyko characteristically announced that Gorbachev might have a nice smile but his teeth were iron. The railroad system functioned, the gulag was in good order. Gorbachev believed that Communism was perfectible through promulgation and exhortation and that his smile would prove more effective than his teeth for the purpose. Glasnost was a step in elementary truth-telling and perestroika an introduction of parliamentary representation, in however controlled a form. These reforms were enough to expose Gorbachev's notion of Communism as an illusion.

As THE SOVIET EMPIRE was falling, I was convinced that Gorbachev would reveal his true nature by imposing military rule, massacring thousands as an example to others, declaring a state of emergency, and instigating whatever else he might deem necessary to hold on to power, including threatening a nuclear exchange. Afterwards Gorbachev claimed that no such ideas had entered his or anyone's head. But after questioning a great many first secretaries and ideological secretaries throughout the empire, I realized that they too had expected some such major showdown. By the time the use of force became imperative for the survival of Communism, it was too late to resort to it. People had the chance to take responsibility for themselves and hold their oppressors to account. Freedom spread with the speed of a bush fire. At the fall of the Bastille, Charles James Fox exclaimed, "How much the greatest event it is that ever happened in the world! And how much the best!" The breaking of Communism in an almost carnival atmosphere was an event still greater. A true believer to the end, Gorbachev did the world a service by default. It still seems to shock him that his idealization of Communism bore no relation to its reality.

With a symbolism that leaves its stamp on history, eager crowds of anonymous people broke through the Berlin Wall one night, emerging into the open like the prisoners in the last act of *Fidelio*. They had the highest expectations of the West. On a continental scale, here was the mirror image of the moment in 1944 when Sandor Marai had looked to the arrival of Soviet soldiers for freedom. These hopefuls have been disappointed. The seventy or so years of Communism had emptied daily life in the Soviet bloc of moral content. Right and wrong had become void concepts to a population reduced to the simple purpose of survival. Now one alienated mass gazed at another. The West, it turns out, has had nothing very much to convey beyond an interest in material possessions: it demonstrated no great interest in the extraordinary fact that millions of people had suddenly been released from tyranny and were in urgent need of the institutions of democracy and the rule of law.

Russia has the resources to finance a society with democratic institutions. But the few with the will for such an end lack power to do much about it. Boris Yeltsin ruled the new Russia by decree, signing perhaps as many as 15,000 a year, far too many to read, and most of them put before him by unscrupulous courtiers. The Clinton administration took at face value the assertion of Yeltsin and his entourage that the content of these decrees was in the public interest. "Go, Boris, go!" was President Clinton's advice, as though he were in a sports stadium. Yeltsin held elections, and not even the subsequent shelling of his own parliament was enough to staunch the aid and subsidies. Who knew—or cared—into whose pockets the money went?

The Europeans were wrapped in their own exclusive concerns. Through the decades since the last war, Germany and France have been trying to come to terms with the historic enmity between them. A series of treaties have brought into existence what has eventually become the European Union. The collapse of Communism and the consequent unification of the two Germanys alarmed the French President Mitterand. He believed that the only brake he could devise on future German strength was to merge the French franc and other European Union currencies with the deutsche mark. The German Chancellor Helmut Kohl agreed on the ostensible grounds that otherwise a too powerful Germany might not be responsible for its actions in the future, tempted—as two of Kohl's close aides put it—to settle relationships with their neighbors "in the traditional manner." The effort to integrate East Germany has already cost a sum in the order of a hundred billion dollars, a figure likely to double. Far from feeling grateful, half the former East Germans still hanker after Communism. Once the consequences of glasnost and perestroika were spelling the end of the Party's monopoly on power, the nomenklatura looked to its future. Claim as they might to be the vanguard of the proletariat, these people were in reality privileged thieves, living off the fat of the land, exclusive managers of state enterprises, with access to the best houses, cars, and aircraft, as well as foreign currency and travel. The one thing missing was title to the wealth they enjoyed. Privatization, they were quick to grasp, would provide them with title. They had only to devise the paperwork for conveying to themselves the public property in their hands. The era of Boris Yeltsin completed a national asset-stripping launched in the era of Gorbachev.

This gigantic redistribution of wealth has been a civilian version of wartime plundering. On the one hand, it was a bribe huge enough to buy off the nomenklatura from resorting to a widespread massacre in defence of privilege and monopoly. On the other hand, it was a continuation by other means of that same privilege and monopoly. Blatantly corrupt on behalf of himself, his family, and his cronies, Yeltsin appointed Vladimir Putin as his successor in a bargain that exempted him from investigation into his affairs. The stealing goes on as before. Every year tens of billions of dollars are transferred abroad illegally, and whole countries like Cyprus and Slovenia lend themselves to money-laundering. The Russian government has difficulties holding the center together, paying wages, and collecting taxes.

Thousands of secret policemen, gulag camp personnel, and mass-murderers continue to receive pensions and wear their medals proudly. Not one has been brought to trial. To draw a line under the past, and once more to affirm the difference between right and wrong, the state ought to have initiated a judicial process for these criminals. The failure to do so leaves Communism like a virus in the bloodstream. The guilty have got away with their crimes. The concept of responsible citizenship goes by default. Decades will have to pass before Russia becomes a country under the rule of law, and even then the unaddressed legacy of Communism will haunt the collective memory.

Like Communism, nationalism did not bring freedom in the twentieth century but proved another instrument in the rule of the strong over the weak. Nationalism mobilized people, and contributed to the breakup of empires, European as well as Russian. Gamal Abdul Nasser, President Suharto, Kim Il Sung, Saddam Hussein, Colonel Mengistu, Mao Tse Tung, and the rest have sought legitimacy in Communism or nationalism, or more frequently in a blend of the two doctrines that allowed them the time-honored practice of establishing themselves as undisputed tyrants. For them, the Cold War was a blessed opportunity to maneuver by playing one side against another without scruple. Taken together, these tyrants have devastated whole peoples, and with them a great part of the world's stock of civilization and culture.

Africa, the Muslim and Arab world, almost all of Asia, are in the hands of one-man or dynastic rule, tyrannies made yet worse by the modern technology that holds them implacably in place. Of the two hundred or so states in the world, nearly half are failed societies, lawless arenas of war and civil war. Some self-proclaimed Beloved Leader and President for Life plunders the national wealth, and television screens worldwide show the victims of the resulting starvation and ethnic cleansing, if not genocide. Dissidents here and there analyze truthfully the condition of their society. As a rule, only the fortunate among them are able to find refuge somewhere in the West before they are imprisoned and killed.

Escape is the final choice for the Third World masses. A multi-billion-dollar industry has lately arisen of people-smugglers arranging for an extortionate price clandestine journeys to faraway places. In their millions, the poor and desperate are on the move. Sometimes their corpses are found suffocated in the heavy-duty vehicles in which they were hiding to cross frontiers, or washed up from unseaworthy boats onto Mediterranean beaches. In their failed societies, there is no intimation of how some political process might start that would give these victimized people a better choice or some say in deciding their fate.

The 1968 generation is now in power throughout the West. President Clinton dodged the Vietnam draft but did not inhale his marijuana joints. Prime Minister Blair explains, "I am a modern man. I am part of the rock-and-roll generation: the Beatles, color TV." A high proportion of his cabinet, including himself, belonged to the Campaign for Nuclear Disarmament and opposed the stationing of NATO cruise missiles in Europe. The French Prime Minister Lionel Jospin was a Trotskyite activist and anti-American agitator. Joschka Fischer, the German foreign minister, was a left-wing extremist, closely associated with terrorists and photographed at the time attacking policemen. Daniel Cohn-Bendit came to prominence for his leadership in the Paris rioting of 1968, and is now a member of the European parliament. What these contemporaries have in common is a self-righteous certainty that the world begins anew with them, that they know all that's worth knowing, and therefore whatever they do is virtuous by definition.

High culture once vitalized the necessary link between freedom and the institutions guaranteeing that freedom.

Replacing high culture, contemporary popular culture has instead introduced the debased belief that freedom is only "doing your thing," detached from morality and even more remote from the institutions that protect morality. President Clinton, to give the outstanding example, disgraced his office. Any previous president would have resigned in the wake of revelations about his relationship with a young intern and his public lies about it. Clinton ignored the moral dimension, and the public humored him as though he were a wayward teenager. Clinton seems set to enter the history books as a moral curiosity. His conduct damaged himself, and by association his party, in the subsequent election, rather than the office of presidency. American democracy, in other words, still retains sufficient vitality to overcome the personal defects of those who represent it.

In Europe, the Sixties generation is attempting to consummate a process begun half a century ago, namely the construction of a transnational and ultimately federal union. The United States has backed the construction of such a Europe since its inception. A federal Europe, it was safely assumed, would be the Siamese twin of a federal United States, all the more valuable an ally as a bloc than as individual states. The reality is turning out very differently. Henry Kissinger is only one among a number of influential voices now warning that the emergence of a unified Europe is "one of the most revolutionary events of our time." There were always some Europeans ungrateful that America rescued them from Nazism and Communism, and others who suffered from an assortment of superiority or inferiority complexes. Subterranean resentments of the kind are now evolving into an ideology that pits the European Union against the United States in another bipolar world. Just as the Soviet bloc fragmented after the collapse of Communism, so now the democratic world is sundering.

In contrast to the American precedent in the eighteenth

century, this European federation of states has grown opportunistic step by opportunistic step, as its leaders seized every opportunity to promote their project. The fifteen constituent members are due to take in another twelve countries, including Greek Cyprus (at the expense of Turkey), Malta, and countries in central and eastern Europe right up to the Ukrainian and Russian borders. Whatever the intentions of the European founding fathers, further treaties in recent years have endowed the European Union with the clear contours of empire.

IN BRUSSELS, its capital, the EU today has a bewildering structure in which there is no link between its institutions and the freedom they are supposed to ensure. At the apex are a president and twenty commissioners, appointed to office by national governments in a process invisible to the public. Not elected, they cannot be dismissed. The commission, and its subordinate councils of ministers drawn from national countries, have executive and legislative powers, and some judicial ones as well. These politicians are accountable to nobody but themselves. Here is the only legislative body in the democratic world that meets and deliberates in secret. A European court of justice was established with the political mission of granting legal force to the commission's work; its members are also appointed and may not be removed; there is no right of appeal. Commission and court combine to impose throughout the continent whatever they decree. A variety of instruments are available, including regulations that are binding, directives open to interpretation, recommendations, opinions, and resolutions. Nearly thirty thousand civil servants are employed, spread over two hundred buildings, with no fewer than seven hundred standing committees. The paperwork is overwhelming. Already in force, something on the order of eighty thousand resolutions have changed the daily routines and realities in every sphere of work and play in

Europe. The so-called European parliament of more than six hundred members is a token with no legislative or revisory powers. No speech there may last more than two minutes.

Empire-building is far advanced. The commission collects taxes and wants more. A European central bank exists, with the euro as common currency for the majority of members. A Growth and Stability Pact supposedly prevents one country from borrowing or incurring debts that the others will have to pay. There is a European defense force, and a police force, Europol, with powers of arrest and deportation not answerable to habeas corpus. A European legal code is forming. An immense range of goods and services and industries has been centralized and homogenized—in the cases of agriculture and fishery with disastrous commercial and ecological effects for producers and consumers everywhere in the continent.

GOVERNMENT NOW concerns itself with whole areas of public and private life where by common consent it has had no previous business. Some of these are no less onerous because they are absurd. Committees have been discussing the permissibility of British milk chocolate for thirty years; deciding on the circumference of home-grown peaches; contemplating which variety of tree may be planted on road verges. As European and national regulations gather into an avalanche, nothing is too trivial to escape attention. Without a specific license, as one critic has pointed out, a rural property owner in Britain "is not allowed to build a house, convert a barn, fell a wood, plant a copse, sow a field of corn, breed a calf, catch a trout, dredge a pond, move a footpath, drill an oil well or alter a hedge line." A joyless gray pall of uniformity is squeezing out the choices and energies of hitherto free people.

The experiment runs counter to the historic thrust of democracy. The central institution of democracy has been the nation-state, and Nazism and Communism consequently made sure to attack it. Imperfect as it often was in relation to minorities within its borders, the nation-state brought to-gether and enfranchised populations under the rule of law, thus defining their identity. Sovereignty was genuine in the sense that it was a two-way contract whereby citizens fulfilled their social responsibilities under the law because they had had a say in choosing those acting in their name. In perhaps unwitting or unconscious emulation of Nazism and Com-munism, the commission in Brussels is deconstructing the nation-state, draining the meaning out of national identity, destroying the sovereignty without which obedience to the law of the land becomes derelict. Parliamentary proceedings are everywhere reduced to rubber-stamping the tide of regulation and decree sweeping in from Brussels. Except under duress in Vichy in 1940, there is no previous example of elected parliamentarians surrendering of their own free will the duty of representation that their own electors granted them.

An alternative sovereignty is under construction, one that requires a European identity. There is no such thing, never has been, nor could there be, granted the differences in languages, religion, law, and national histories. The past and its achieve-ments, both good and bad, are vanishing. In the wisecrack of a character in a Tennessee Williams play, "Europe is just a fire-sale." In the absence of any non-residual traces of high culture, the commission is spending huge sums concocting the new fictitious identity, complete with what are known as European values, which turn out to be fantasies about Charlemagne or a common popular culture. On inspection this proves a matter of soccer matches, transnational golf teams, and pop concerts. Social or cultural unity is at the level prescribed by the Beatles: "All you need is love."

The EU is best described as a command-bureaucracy, and as such it is a mutation of previous totalitarian systems. It pays the usual lip-service to human rights but has already passed, or is in the process of passing, decrees that will outlaw political parties opposed to it, and that will constrain freedom of speech. In Austria, Jörg Haider's Freedom Party has rather mild reservations about the EU, but its success in a free election provoked the EU as a whole to boycott Austria. As one among many confusing features of the system, each country has its turn setting the European agenda. It was Sweden's turn when Haider was elected, and its then prime minister Goran Persson led the pack on the grounds that Austria was "out of line with EU values." Critics of the EU have already been penalized by laws concerning blasphemy. Bland words about human rights cloak a formidable machinery for future coercion and repression.

Totalitarian systems exist to privilege those who run them. The EU is no exception. Kohl and Mitterand oversaw the treaties that finalized the empire-building. In pursuit of their political goals, they engaged in all manner of illegal deals and payments that somehow escape full investigation. President Chirac of France claims that his status permits him not to answer charges of corruption. Roland Dumas, the head of the French constitutional court, no less, has been found guilty of bribery and corruption. An astonishing range of French, Italian, and Spanish politicians and their business associates have been charged with corruption, and a few are even in prison. Year after year, auditors refuse to certify EU accounts, because too much of its budget—up to $10 billion a year, by some estimates—goes missing. So great are the vested interests that a blind eye is turned to all manner of fraud and malpractice, even when identified in the media. To complete the comparison with the former Soviet Union, the commissioners and their bureaucrats award themselves huge salaries, allowances, expenses, subsidized food and drink—all tax free. Absolute power once more is corrupting absolutely. None of the statesmen or public servants of pre-1914 Europe would have considered, let alone actually profited from, any such plundering of the public purse.

Machiavelli wrote that "principalities are liable to danger when they are passing from the civil to the absolute order of government." It may be that people will rise up as their forebears did in defence of the institutions embodying the freedom for which they once fought, and trample down the command-bureaucracy now enveloping them. Confident in its Sixties-style self-righteousness, the EU leadership appears unaware that it is fostering the malign nationalism that it supposedly exists to cure. Opinion polls in every European country reflect a rising sense of dismay and outrage. Norwegians, Danes, Irish, and the Swiss have voted against further integration. Germany pays by far the largest net contribution to the EU budget, with the result that Germans see themselves obliged to carry other people towards whom they have no obligation. No German leader has ever risked a vote or referendum on the subject, out of well-founded fear that the result might blow apart the EU.

THE EUROPEAN PRESIDENT, Romano Prodi (against whom corruption charges were levelled in his native Italy), has complained that alienation from the EU is "a malaise that affects people in all states," but in the next breath adds that "The objective of an enlarged Europe must be realized." In response to reasoned objections, Wim Duisenburg, head of the European Central Bank, spoke for the nomenklatura: "I hear but I do not listen." At a moment when Denmark rejected the euro in a referendum, it was Belgium's turn to set the European agenda, and its foreign minister Louis Michel gave a definitive statement of the consideration Brussels has for public opinion. "I personally think it's very dangerous to organize referendums when you're not sure you're going to win them. If you lose it that's a big problem for Europe." Insulated from reality, these would-be absolute rulers are offering people the choice between submission and a revolution likely to have the form of a nationalist—even a fascist—backlash.

Between the wars, the Czech writer Karel Čapek visited Britain to write a book, published shortly before his death at a time when the Germans marched into Prague. "Wherever on this planet ideals of personal freedom and dignity apply," he wrote, "there you will find the cultural inheritance of England." This was once a judgment common to Britain's friends, as well as to opponents of its ideals of freedom and dignity. Now the British must look to themselves to weigh the value of this inheritance, which amounts to deciding what kind of people they are. Their culture provides little help. The political and intellectual elite—heirs of E. M. Forster and Ramsay Muir—has long since accepted that right and wrong are relative, neither absolute nor worth fighting for. Britain has already handed jurisdiction of its affairs in many fields to the commission in Brussels. Decisions affecting its social, commercial, and business interests, even its defence and foreign policy, are now taken abroad by people of other nationalities. In several areas, European law takes precedence over British law.

Opinion polls in Britain, however, show the picture of a rising majority against the EU, with a fast-growing minority who wish to repatriate the powers handed over to Brussels and to quit the EU altogether. Historical experience has bred deep in the bone the Churchillian sense that they have to go it alone—against the whole continent if need be, as so often before—on the grounds that it is better to be poor but free than rich and not responsible for yourself. When Tony Blair won the 1997 election, one of his closest cabinet associates (later disgraced for corruption) warned that "the era of representative democracy may be coming to an end." Blair believes that he will be able to persuade the British to redefine the independence and freedom they have for so long taken for granted and acquiesce in full political and economic integration with the EU. It would be an ironic coda to a long and on the whole successful history if the prime minister who could so recast British identity were to be rewarded with the presidency of Europe.

The suicide attacks of September 11 on the United States served to rally democratic states, postponing any sundering into potentially divided blocs, at least for the short term. Affirming that Britain stood "shoulder to shoulder" with the United States, Blair at once provided military support. Other European countries have preferred to remain spectators cheering from the grandstand. When the Italian Prime Minister Silvio Berlusconi stated the obvious—that Western civilization might in some ways be better than Islam because it is more free—he was forced to backpedal all round for what the British Home Secretary called "offensive, inappropriate and culturally inaccurate remarks." Moral relativism bears such fruit.

Islamic extremists have proved themselves the latest in the series of external enemies of democracy capable of doing great damage. Their primary strategic objective is to replace targeted regimes in the Muslim and Arab world, and no mechanism exists for the purpose except force. In the event that Islamic extremists were to seize power, one absolute system would replace another, in the manner of Ayatollah Khomeini's coup against the former Shah of Iran. So multiple are the motives and emotions in play that the focus of the threat is variable. For a long time now, Muslims have been encountering the West with ambivalence. On the one hand, the West brings material wealth, medicine, education, communications. On the other, these desirable things call into question the Muslim order that does not deliver them. An intolerable sense of humiliation and impotence arises. Opposed as they are in their declared view of what a Muslim state ought to be, Saddam Hussein and Osama bin Laden deploy the same vocabulary of Western "arrogance" and a countervailing need to rescue Muslim honor and pride. Within this framework jostles an immense range of age-old sectarian, ethnic, and tribal struggles, each with its appeal to ancestral loyalties.

The United States appears to influence or to block any outcome of these various regional struggles that would favor extremists, whether Islamic or secular. What looks to the West like the hindrance of civil war and the pursuit of stability looks to the extremists like the wanton frustration of their political ambitions. The more incomplete this perception of reality, the more Islam becomes a fulfilling identity for the extremists, a call for mobilization, and the unfailing source of fanaticism and hate. So they strike at the United States as a tactic in the strategy of reclaiming the whole Muslim world.

In terms of numbers and weaponry, Islamic extremists are not the Red Army. In terms of politics, though, they are quite as baleful as the Soviet Union. As usual, murder runs deep. Their absolute hostility to America presents the Muslim world with difficult, polarizing choices: whether to be for or against the war on terror; whether to prevaricate or to dissemble in the old non-aligned game of saying one thing and doing another; whether to play both sides off against each other. In short, the Muslim world must decide whether democracy and Islam are two beautiful but incompatible ideals. The Cold War lasted for a good four decades, and during its course countries shifted allegiance one way and the other. Should the war on terror extend over a period of years, any country that already faces an extremist challenge—Saudi Arabia, Pakistan, Egypt—risks civil war and collapse. Profit and loss considerations might also impel a country that is anti-American by definition—Iran, Iraq, Syria—to recalculate. Opportunists are many, but those who prefer to end on the losing side are few and far between.

It is time to reappraise the climate of defeatism and guilt that intellectuals have spread so far and wide throughout the West. Some still do so, continuously alienated from their own civilization and its values. Whatever contempt they feel for themselves and the democracy in which they live and work, though, none go so far as to advocate the adoption of a Taliban regime, as their forerunners in the Thirties used to agitate on behalf of the Soviet system. Terror and terror-states challenge even the most self-righteous among us.

A new organizing principle is emerging. The Anglo-American concept of freedom is incompatible with the Islamic conception of freedom put forward by Muslim extremists. Compromise is impossible between absolutism and democracy, between the state's imposed decree and the individual's need to be responsible for himself. What is freedom to the Muslim extremists looks in the West like subjection and slavery. People everywhere will be compelled to decide what exactly freedom means to them. To refer again to Truman, nations must choose between alternative ways of life. Here is the making of another Cold War, to be waged across an ideological divide. It is a measure of geopolitical change that Russia in this new perspective is an ally of democracy.

Resolve, the will to see things through to a right ending, is the end-product of the choices of the millions of individuals whose biographies make up the culture and the identity of a democratic state. Unquantifiable and fashion-tossed as resolve may be, the survival of the culture depends on it.

The Cultural War
on Western Civilization
by Keith Windschuttle

I N THE LAST WEEK of September 2001, shortly after the
terrorist assaults on the World Trade Center and the
Pentagon, the Prime Minister of Italy, Silvio Berlusconi, made
an extraordinary statement. During a visit to Germany, he
declared Western civilization superior to Islam. He said:

> We must be aware of the superiority of our civilization, a sys-
> tem that has guaranteed well-being, respect for human rights,
> and—in contrast with Islamic countries—respect for religious
> and political rights.

The minute he had uttered these words, a bevy of European
politicians rushed to denounce him. The Belgian Prime Minister, Guy Verhofstadt, said: "I can hardly believe that the
Italian Prime Minister made such statements." The spokesman
for the European Commission, Jean-Christophe Filori, added: "We certainly don't share the views expressed by Mr. Berlusconi." Italy's center-left opposition spokesman Giovanni
Berlinguer called the words "eccentric and dangerous." Within
days, Berlusconi was forced to withdraw.

It is true that the statement could have been more
diplomatically timed, made as it was while American officials
were trying to put together an anti-terrorist coalition of Islamic allies. But there is little doubt it would have generated

just as many denials no matter when it was uttered. The statement was extraordinary because, although Western superiority in every major area of human endeavor, especially in political and individual liberty, is patently obvious to everyone, it has become a truth that must not be spoken.

The chief reason is the prevailing ideology of the Western intelligentsia. For the past two decades and more, the leading opinion makers in the media, the universities, and the churches have regarded Western superiority as, at best, something to be ashamed of and, at worst, something to be opposed. Until thirty years ago, when Western intellectuals reflected on the long-term achievements of their culture, they explained it in terms of its own evolution: the inheritance of ancient Greece, Rome, and Christianity, tempered by the Renaissance, the Reformation, the Enlightenment, and the scientific and industrial revolutions. Even a radical critique like Marxism was primarily an internal affair, intent on fulfilling what it imagined to be the destiny of the West, taking its history to what it thought would be a higher level.

Today, however, such thinking is dismissed by the radical intelligentsia as triumphalist. Western political and economic dominance is more commonly explained not by its internal dynamics but by its external behavior, especially its rivalry and aggression towards other cultures. Western success has purportedly been at their expense. Instead of pushing for internal reform or revolution, this new radicalism constitutes an overwhelmingly negative critique of Western civilization itself.

According to this ideology, instead of attempting to globalize its values, the West should stay in its own cultural backyard. Values like universal human rights, individualism, and liberalism are regarded merely as ethnocentric products of Western history. The scientific knowledge that the West has produced is simply one of many "ways of knowing." In place of Western universalism, this critique offers the relativism of multiculturalism, a concept that regards the West not as the pinnacle of human achievement to date, but as simply one of many equally valid cultural systems.

Although originally designed to foster tolerance and respect for other cultures, these sentiments were subsequently captured by the radical left and manipulated to the point of inconsistency. Their plea for acceptance and open-mindedness does not extend to Western culture itself, whose history is regarded as little more than a crime against the rest of humanity. The West cannot judge other cultures but must condemn its own.

Though commonly known as multiculturalism, this position is defined by its supporters with a series of *post* prefixes: postmodernism, poststructuralism, postcolonialism. It is best understood, however, as an *anti* phenomenon because it defines itself not by what it is for, but by what it is against. It is entirely a negation of Western culture and values: whatever the West supports, this anti-Westernism rejects.

The aftermath of September 11 provided a stark illustration of its values. Within days of the terrorist assault, a number of influential Western intellectuals, including Noam Chomsky, Susan Sontag, and their youthful counterparts, such as Naomi Klein of the anti-globalization protest movement, responded in ways that, morally and symbolically, were no different to the celebrations of the crowds on the streets of Nablus and Islamabad who cheered as they watched the towers of the World Trade Center come crashing down. Stripped of its obligatory jargon, their argument was straightforward: America deserved what it got.

This intellectual response was not couched in terms of Western humanist values. Instead, it represented a descent into the kind of relativism not seen since the days of Lenin and Hitler when class-based and race-based hatreds were morally sanctioned by radical politics. The major difference today is that this time it is not class or race but the whole of Western society that has been relativized.

Anti-Westernism constitutes a true ideology: it sees the world as an arena of conflict and has a political program to change the world for its own ends. It is formidable in its comprehensiveness and in the number of intellectual fields it encompasses. They include history, literature, the arts, the social sciences, the physical sciences, and the law. It is also formidable in the number of professional and public institutions it has successfully captured and whose agenda it now controls. Since the demise of Marxism, it has emerged as the major ideological successor. What follows is a summary of the creed, coupled with some of the more obvious objections to it.

"WESTERN CULTURE was founded on aggression towards others": Despite being employed for the purpose of transmitting culture, most of the writers, editors, and teachers who advocate this cause are united in their hostility to the cultural traditions that have nurtured them from birth. They see the whole of Western culture since the ancient Greeks as something to be disowned.

The person who did most to establish this interpretation is Edward Said, the Arab-American literary critic employed by Columbia University and a long-time activist for the Palestinian cause. His influential 1978 book *Orientalism* claimed that, from its classical origins, Western culture had been defined not by its own internal development, but by its long history of antagonism to "the Other," that is, to non-Western cultures.

This motif persists, Said claims, from its origins in Homer right down to the modern period. The desire to rule distant peoples has had a "privileged status" in the West. There has been "something systematic" about its imperial culture that was not evident in other empires. Moreover, while Europe's ability to take over and rule distant colonies might now be a thing of the past, the imperialist imperative lives on today in American foreign and economic policy, where it is validated by Western culture and ideology. Said claims it is still driven, as it was in the nineteenth century, by the West's "untrammelled rapacity, greed, and immorality."

In particular, he argues, Western oriental scholarship led Europeans to see Islamic culture as static in both time and place, as "eternal, uniform, and incapable of defining itself." This gave Europe a sense of its own cultural and intellectual superiority. It consequently saw itself as a dynamic, innovative, expanding culture and rationalized its imperial ambition not as a form of conquest but as the redemption of a degenerate world.

Said has spawned a school of followers from a variety of intellectual disciplines. One of them is Richard Waswo, who, in his 1997 book *The Founding Legend of Western Civilization*, traces how the story of the fall of Troy and the founding of Rome by the Trojan survivors has been represented in Western literature. He calls the story a "legend of perpetual colonization" that "became the rationale for imperialist attitudes from ancient Rome to Vietnam." He examines the legend from its first expression in *The Aeneid* to *The Faerie Queene* to the fiction of Joseph Conrad and E. M. Forster, its manifestations in the films of John Ford, in the defoliation of Vietnam, and in the current policies of the World Bank.

Waswo is not an historian but is Professor of English at the University of Geneva. This has not, however, prevented him from receiving the endorsement of some of America's most celebrated academic historians, such as Hayden White, who praised him for having written "a counter-history to the official version, a complete re-reading of the Western canon," and "an indictment of the whole of Western civilization." This last phrase summarizes the appeal of the book, not only for aging radicals like White but also for a younger generation of middle-class student protestors. The most prominent among the student rioters against globalization in Seattle, Washington, D.C., and Genoa in the past two years were those who learned their version of Western cultural history at the feet of teachers inspired by authors like Said, Waswo, and White.

The claim that Western culture has always defined itself in opposition to others is an assumption that usually goes unquestioned in academic debate today. There is, however, very little to recommend it. Although they have long distinguished themselves from the barbarians of the world, Europeans do not primarily draw their identity from comparisons with other cultures. Instead, identity comes from their own heritage. Western identity is overwhelmingly defined by historical references to its earlier selves, rather than by geographical comparisons with others. To claim otherwise is to deny the central thrust of Western education for the past thousand years.

The argument also displays a highly selective view of imperial history in that it ignores empires other than those of Europe. The truth is that all great civilizations have absorbed other peoples, sometimes in harmony, sometimes by the sword. The Islamic world that this thesis defends is no different. The Ottoman Turks ruled most of the Middle East for a thousand years, largely with the concurrence of their Arab subjects. The British and the French displaced them in the nineteenth century, again with the approval of the Arabs, who by then wanted liberation from Ottoman rule. The Arabs themselves were not indigenous to most of the regions they now populate. Before the Turks, they were an imperial power who arose out of the Arabian Peninsula in the seventh century to conquer the Middle East, North Africa, South Asia, and Southern Europe. None of this history provokes any censure from the critics of imperialism today, who reserve their reproaches exclusively for the European variety.

"WESTERN LITERATURE AND ART endorse imperialism": Until the last two decades, most people brought up within Western culture believed that its literature, its art, and its music were among the glories of its civilization. Western literary criticism once aimed to seek out the genius of its authors and to extol their contribution to defining the human condition. Today, much of the academic debate about the Western literary heritage claims that it is politically contaminated. Some of these charges have long been well known because they offended against the post-1970s ideological triumvirate of gender, race, and class: *Othello* is ethnocentric, *Paradise Lost* is a feminist tragedy, *Jane Eyre* is both racist and sexist.

Western literature is today, however, most severely rebuked for its support of imperialism. The theorist making this accusation is, again, Edward Said. He claims the flowering of European literature since the sixteenth century either directly endorsed or provided a supportive environment for the expansion of Europe in the same period. Said draws on the thesis of the French Nietzschean theorist Michel Foucault that all knowledge serves the ends of power and that all intellectual disciplines, including literary and art criticism, are politically motivated.

Said argues this has been especially true of the novel, an art form born and reared in the period when European expansionism knew no boundaries. In his 1993 book *Culture and Imperialism* he claims that, of all modern literary forms, it is the novel that has been most culpable in reproducing and advocating the power relations of empire. His critique encompasses not only novels that are overtly about imperial affairs, such as those of Joseph Conrad and Rudyard Kipling, but even the work of such apparently domestic writers as Jane Austen and Charles Dickens. One of Austen's characters in *Mansfield Park*, Sir Thomas Bertram, owns a sugar plantation in the Caribbean, so this implicates her in support of slavery, Said claims. In *Great Expectations*, Charles Dickens dispatches one of his characters to Australia and another to Egypt, so this makes him an imperialist author, too.

Said extends his critique to opera, which he describes as an art form "that belongs equally to the history of culture and the historical experience of overseas domination." Because Giuseppe Verdi's *Aida* is set in ancient Egypt, Said claims it fosters military aggression towards the Orient. It contains "imperialist structures of attitude and reference" that act as an "anaesthetic" on European audiences, leading them to ignore the brutality that accompanied their conquest of other countries.

Equally culpable are European paintings of the Orient, even those of Delacroix and Ingres, which critics once thought portrayed the region in romantically admiring terms. Instead, art critics who follow Said, such as Linda Nochlin, now use them as examples of subtle and persistent Eurocentric prejudice against Arab-Islamic peoples and their culture. They purportedly exhibit the aggressiveness necessitated by the colonial expansion of the European powers. These paintings are primarily a reflection of European arrogance and Western prejudices: "the idea of Oriental decay, the subjection of women, an unaccountable legal system—pictorial rhetoric that served a subtle imperialist agenda."

Presented like this, stripped of their theoretical obfuscation, the ideas are transparently crude. They resemble the reductionism of one-time Marxist criticism, which invariably saw Western art and literature as expressions of "nothing but" the venal interests of the ruling class, the bourgeoisie, or some other culpable social class. They also stretch interpretation beyond credulity. To believe that because Jane Austen presents one plantation-owning character, of whom heroine, plot, and author all plainly disapprove, she thereby becomes a handmaiden of imperialism and slavery, is to misunderstand both the novel and the biography of its author, who was an ardent opponent of the slave trade. Similarly, to argue that because Charles Dickens uses some overseas locations as convenient off-stage sites to advance his plots, he thereby becomes an advocate of empire is to give him attitudes he never expressed. To claim that the art form of opera or the romantic indulgence of the nineteenth-century Orientalist school of painting derives from the European experience of overseas domination is to make an ideological misreading of them all.

Yet such is the authority of the dominant thesis that contemporary writers rush to praise these kinds of analytical crudities. "Readers accustomed to the precision and elegance of Edward Said's analytical prowess," wrote the Nobel laureate Toni Morrison for the cover blurb of *Culture and Imperialism*, "will not be disappointed." In return, not surprisingly, Morrison herself earns equally lavish compliments from the same school of criticism.

Of greater concern is the penetration this thesis has achieved in the higher education system. Edward Said is the immediate past president of the Modern Language Association, the principal professional association for teachers of literature at American universities. Publishers of books set for these courses now routinely commission the advocates of such theories to edit and introduce the literary texts that students will study. Penguin Books, for instance, engaged Said himself as editor of its latest edition of Rudyard Kipling's masterpiece *Kim*. A like-minded critic was commissioned to introduce the Penguin Classics edition of Austen's *Mansfield Park* and to endorse Said's thesis that this quintessentially domestic author was implicated in British imperial expansion.

"THE WESTERN ECONOMIC SYSTEM exploits the rest of the world": According to this ideology, Western prosperity is based on ill-gotten gains. Globalization, its adherents claim, is a euphemism for American imperialism. The poverty of the Third World is purportedly entrenched by debts to the International Monetary Fund and by the free market policies of the World Trade Organization. Hence, students and trade unionists riot outside the meetings that decide these policies, and church leaders sermonize us to forgive the debt.

Some of this argument is made in historical terms. The capital that funded the industrial revolution, some authors claim, derived from the twin exploitations of colonialism and slavery. Edward Said still cites the work of the Trinidad Marxist Eric Williams, who argued in *Capitalism and Slavery* (1944) that profits from the transport and sale of slaves made a substantial contribution to financing the industrial revolution in Britain. Hence, all those subsequent generations of Europeans who have enjoyed the standards of living provided by industrialism have done so from capital accumulated on the backs of black slave labor.

Another celebrated author in the same genre is Andre Gunder Frank, whose book *ReOrient: Global Economy in the Asian Age* (1998) rejects the thesis that European entrepreneurship, ingenuity, and technological innovation were responsible for the commercial and industrial revolutions between the seventeenth and nineteenth centuries. "Europe did not pull itself up by its own economic bootstraps," Frank writes, "and it was certainly not thanks to any kind of European 'exceptionalism,' of rationality, institutions, entrepreneurship, technology, geniality, in a word—of race." Instead, he claims: "Europe climbed up on the back of Asia, then stood on Asian shoulders—temporarily."

Both these arguments, however, are untenable. Some revisionist historians of British colonialism have recently overturned them. In the newly published *Oxford History of the British Empire*, for instance, David Richardson analyzes the contribution of the slave trade to industrialism in Britain and finds that profits from slaving voyages contributed less than 1 percent of total domestic investment in Britain at the time. In other words, slavery was irrelevant to the industrial revolution.

Similarly, the profits from British investments in its empire in the nineteenth century were not exploitative. Historians such as P. J. Marshall, P. G. Cain, and A. G. Hopkins have shown that British investment benefited India, Africa, and South America considerably. It provided the infrastructure of ports, roads, railways, and communications that allowed them access to the modern world.

European imperialism ended in the 1940s and 1950s. The non-West has now had half a century to try its own economic prescriptions. The fact that many of these countries have not progressed beyond the kick start provided by European colonial investment can no longer be blamed on the West. Those who have chosen to emulate the Western model, such as Japan, South Korea, Taiwan, and Singapore, have shown that it is possible to transform a backward Third World country into a prosperous, modern, liberal democratic nation in as little as two generations. In Japan's case, the model allowed it to rise from the ashes of total defeat to become a world power in less than forty years.

Those countries that still wallow in destitution and underdevelopment do so not because of Western imperialism, racism, or oppression, but because of policies they have largely chosen themselves. For example, after independence in 1947, India's flirtation with the Soviet bloc and with socialist economics needlessly condemned the country to Third World status, and consigned much of its population to humiliating poverty. Had India chosen the Japanese path, it could have been by now a much greater power than China. It is only in the past decade, with the partial adoption of the liberal economic policies of the capitalist West, that its fortunes have begun to turn around.

Elsewhere in the Third World, American policies of granting and lending money, of setting up factories there, and of importing the goods they produce cannot plausibly be regarded as imperialist exploitation. If it were, the countries involved would hardly be holding out their hands for more. Nor would they be recording the economic growth rates that are the envy of all those who lack the same American investment.

"VICTIMHOOD SHOULD PREVAIL over individualism": Western individualism is another of the targets of this ideology. It regards individualism as both the cause and effect of capitalism, which in its turn produced the imperialism that now oppresses the wretched of the earth. Individualism is also regarded as deriving from such ethnocentric Enlightenment constructs as human rights. It is the one great barrier to a collectivist solution for humankind. So individualism has to go.

In its place, the creed offers victimhood. Its political constituency comprises those it defines—by whatever stretch of the imagination this might take—as the underdogs and the marginals of society. Within Western countries, this includes ethnic and racial minorities, women, homosexuals, indigenous peoples, the exiled, the poor, the incarcerated, and the insane. Beyond Western society, it includes the masses of the Third World.

It is in pursuit of this political objective that much of the recent revision of the history curriculum has been done. Western history is no longer to be judged by the record of its achievements. Instead, it is to become a story of the struggle of its victims against oppression and discrimination and of how they have risen to challenge their exploiters. Consequently, the purpose of teaching history becomes to "empower" its victims.

One of the key intellectual concepts of victimhood is that of exile. As the number of refugees, asylum seekers, and illegal immigrants around the world mounts, so does the number of exiles. In fact, this is one quality many Western academics believe they have in common with those who now crowd their borders. There are two dimensions to this identification. These intellectuals assume for themselves the role of spokesmen for the poor, the weak, and the disadvantaged. They denounce the governments and powerful interests they claim have produced the desperation of the exiles. Intellectuals, moreover, can share their trauma because, deep down, they are exiles too. Radical intellectuals claim to know what it is like to be psychically banished, to feel displaced, uncertain of their identities, uncommitted to any location. These feelings even extend to those who still live in the country of their birth but who, because of their ethnic or sexual identity, sense they do not quite belong. One fashionable feminist book about a number of Australian women writers is entitled *Exiles at Home*.

Edward Said claims exile is the real condition of the modern intellectual. Indeed, he says, he knows it firsthand. "My own experiences of these matters," he says in *Orientalism*, "are in part what made me write this book." Like many of his kind, however, Said's claims are self-indulgent fabrications. He is the son of a wealthy Arab-American businessman and grew up in Cairo in a household with a butler, two drivers, and a bevy of servants. He spent his teenage years at an exclusive American private boarding school. He later invented an identity as a Palestinian refugee, a persona that allowed him full exile status:

> The life of an Arab Palestinian in the West, particularly in America, is disheartening. There exists here an almost unanimous consensus that politically he does not exist, and when it is allowed that he does, it is either as a nuisance or as an Oriental. The web of racism, cultural stereotypes, political imperialism, dehumanizing ideology holding in the Arab or the Muslim is very strong indeed, and it is this web which every Palestinian has come to feel as his uniquely punishing destiny.

Similarly, the Parisian poststructuralist feminist celebrity Hélène Cixous complains in a memoir about her adolescent travails as an Algerian Jewish girl in the French colony:

> I saw how the white, superior, plutocratic, civilized world funded its power on the repression of populations who had suddenly become "invisible," like proletarians, immigrant

workers, minorities who are not the right "colour." Women. Invisible as humans. I saw that the great, noble, "advanced" countries established themselves by expelling what was "strange."

Despite the discrimination and oppression Said and Cixous claim to have suffered, they fail to mention that this same white plutocracy gave both of them tenured university posts that put them among the most materially and occupationally privileged human beings on the planet. Nor do they acknowledge that both enjoy the added indulgence of the freedom to make whatever criticisms they fancy of the countries that sustain them.

The careers of Said and Cixous demonstrate that while it is one thing for a Western academic to pretend to speak on behalf of the wretched of the earth, it is an even smarter tactic to claim to *be* one of the wretched yourself. This way you not only become an articulate symbol of all that suffering but you also disarm your critics. Your words become sacrosanct. Anyone who doubts you or dares to challenge your claims thereby reveals himself as bigoted and uncaring. You are beyond censure.

"THE WEST MUST BE 'provincialized'": One of the most prominent fields of study produced by the ideology I am describing is postcolonialism. This is an intellectual movement focused primarily on the study of history and literature, although it is usually conducted at such an arcane level of theory that former students of either history or literature would find their subjects unrecognizable. Postcolonial social theorists and critics have gained a major foothold in academic life in the United States.

One of the leading tendencies within postcolonialism is the Subaltern Group of Indian historians or, more accurately, theorists about history. In 1994, the *American Historical Review*, the journal of the leading professional association, devoted an issue to them. The Subalterns took their name from terminology used by the Italian Marxist theorist Antonio Gramsci. Their origins lay in the 1960s Indian middle-class Marxist movement, the Naxalites, who emulated the Red Guards of Mao Tse-tung's China by assassinating landlords and police in Bihar and West Bengal. A number of the movement's members subsequently moved to America and Australia, where they gained academic positions teaching history.

Although they address historical topics, the Subalterns offer a radical critique of the discipline, which they see not as a methodology that can be applied to any society but as an ethnocentric product of European culture. History, they assert, is an artifact of the Western nation-state. Contesting the imperialism of the West involves contesting its version of history as well. India, of course, gained its independence fifty years ago so one might have thought there has since been plenty of opportunity for its historians to go their own way. The Subalterns insist, however, that they still need to struggle to liberate themselves from European modes of thought, especially English historiography.

Rather than arguing the point at home in India, these theorists choose to do it in the Western education system. Indeed, one reason why there are now so many Indian academics employed in the humanities departments of American universities is because of the network of influence provided by the postcolonial movement.

The aim of their project is to use postmodernist and poststructuralist literary analysis to deconstruct historical documents to recover the voice of the colonial oppressed who, because they were illiterate, left no documents of their own. They want to recover the authentic voice of Indian peasants, bandits, and others of low caste and to rewrite them into history. While English historians have generally regarded Mohandas Gandhi and the Congress Party as the leaders of the nationalist struggle against British imperialism, postcolonial historians want to argue that it was actually the work of the Indian lower orders.

The postcolonialists have adopted the theoretical tools used by comparable radical ideologues. Their political alliances and connections were described in the journal *Postcolonial Studies* thus,

> Postcolonialism has much in common with other related critical endeavors—such as women's studies and gay/lesbian studies—classified under the rubric of the "new humanities." Marked by an underlying scepticism, these closely aligned projects find their shared intellectual vocation in a determined opposition to coercive knowledge systems and, concomitantly, in a committed pursuit and recovery of those ways of knowing which have been occluded—or, in Foucault's terminology, "subjugated"—by the epistemic accidents of history. Given its particular inheritance, postcolonialism has directed its own critical antagonism toward the universalizing knowledge claims of "western civilization."

In other words, although it claims to eschew Western culture, the methodology of the postcolonial critique derives from one radical stream of the West itself. The members of this movement want to reject the West but all they are doing is choosing one aspect of its intellectual culture, European post-structuralist theory, over another, English historiography.

Some of them do recognize this dilemma. Dipesh Chakrabarty, a Subaltern historian recently appointed to a personal chair at the University of Chicago, has written a book called *Provincializing Europe* (2000), whose title neatly summarizes the intellectual ambitions of the movement. Provincializing means to "re-read the European philosophers of modernity in order to show up the parochialism of their imagination."

Chakrabarty also wants to transcend the limits of the methodological assumptions of European forms of investigation. For instance, he wants to incorporate the magical beliefs of traditional India into its history, not as categories to be observed skeptically but as living historical presences. He is too committed, however, to the modern intellect to believe in magic himself so the best he can do is revert to the language of the German Nietzschean philosopher Martin Heidegger and recommend his hermeneutic analysis of "particular ways of being-in-the-world." In short, Chakrabarty would rather withdraw into arcane and largely irrelevant theoretical speculation than adopt the contaminated tools of English historiography.

Despite the substantial academic and publishing resources now being invested in it, and despite its claim to be showing both Indians and other oppressed peoples how to recover their own epistemological independence, postcolonialism is a profoundly backward intellectual movement. There is nothing about it that is innovatively non-Western or, indeed, original in any way. To use a favorite term of one of its other gurus, the Harvard literary theorist Homi Bhabha, it is yet another example of colonial "mimicry" of the West. Only in this case it shuns the most positive aspects of the Western intellectual tradition in order to mimic the worst.

"WESTERN VALUES are culturally relative": In 1987, the American philosopher Allan Bloom opened his withering dissection of the faults of the higher education system, *The Closing of the American Mind*, with an observation on the triumph of relativism. "There is one thing a professor can be absolutely certain of," he remarked, "almost every student entering the university believes, or says he believes, that truth is relative." In the face of the various claims to truth and the divergent ways of life that characterize modern society, higher education had responded, Bloom argued, by promoting the idea that the real danger was the true believer. This, he noted with bitter irony, was "the great insight of our times."

The study of history and of culture teaches that all the world was mad in the past; men always thought they were right, and that led to wars, persecutions, slavery, xenophobia, racism, and chauvinism. The point is not to correct the mistakes and really be right; rather it is not to think you are right at all.

More than a decade on, not only does Bloom's observation continue to be true, but relativism has also become institutionalized in the higher education sector and is now taught as a formal doctrine. This is accomplished through broad intellectual tendencies such as postmodernism and poststructuralism as well as in particular curriculum areas such as cultural studies, anthropology, literary theory, women's studies, the sociology of science, and the history and philosophy of science.

One of the intellectual devices by which this has been accomplished is through a change in the meaning of the term "culture." Until recent decades, this term was widely used in the sense established by Matthew Arnold in his great nineteenth-century tract *Culture and Anarchy* where it meant "the best that has been thought and said." His concept of artistic excellence and of its critical appreciation by an educated elite provided the principal rationale for the teaching of the humanities for the first two-thirds of the twentieth century.

At the same time, however, the discipline of anthropology had its own meaning for the term. Anthropologists used culture in the sense defined by the nineteenth-century German romantic movement, by which it meant the whole way of life of a distinct people. As academic politics after the 1960s succumbed to a fierce kind of egalitarianism in which excellence and elitism became pejorative terms, the Arnoldian definition lost its position. The belief that all cultures were equal took its place.

This notion of cultural relativism entailed a radical rethinking of Western intellectual life. In aesthetic criticism, it meant traditional standards had to be jettisoned. Italian opera could no longer be regarded as superior to Chinese opera. The theater of Shakespeare was not better than that of Kabuki, only different. In political thought, the pursuit of universal values such as human rights became suspect. Rather than principles that were eternal or self-evident, cultural relativists said these values were bound by their own time and space. They were simply the ethnocentric products of the eighteenth-century European Enlightenment. Instead of human rights, the fashionable term became "social justice." Human rights have been written down in declarations and laws, so it is possible to check what they mean. Social justice lacks this quality but this gives it the advantage of meaning whatever you want it to. There is no way of ever telling when it is satisfied. Social justice thus offers an unlimited vista of political appeal.

The major problems for the acceptance of cultural relativism have come from its source in anthropology. Cultural practices from which most Westerners instinctively shrink, such as cannibalism, human sacrifice, the incineration of widows, and female genital mutilation, have had to be accorded their own integrity, lest the culture that produced them be demeaned.

This has not been easy but the feminist movement has been the leader in coming to the rescue. Although they initially found the overt misogyny of many tribal cultures distasteful, feminists in recent years have come to respect practices they once condemned. Feminist academics now deny that *sati* is barbaric. Gayatri Chakravorty Spivak gives it an honorable place in Indian culture by comparing it to the Christian tradition of martyrdom. Female genital mutilation has been redefined as genital "cutting," which Germaine Greer argues should be recognized as an authentic manifestation of the culture of the Muslim women concerned. Similarly, the Parisian literary theorist Tzvetan Todorov, in *The Conquest of America* (1985), compared cannibalism to the Christian Eucharist, and the Australian postmodernist historian Greg Dening, in *Mr. Bligh's Bad Language* (1992), declared human sacrifice to be the ritual equivalent of capital punishment.

To any outside observer, something is obviously going terribly wrong here. The logic of their relativism is taking Western academics into dark waters. They are now prepared to countenance practices that are obviously cruel, unnatural, and life-denying, that is, practices that offend against all they claim to stand for.

The reality is that if all cultures are relative then we are faced with moral nihilism. If values are always expressions of something called culture, and there are no universal moral principles, then no culture can itself be subjected to any values, because there could be no transcultural values to stand in judgment over any particular culture. Cultural relativism, in short, approves any cultural practice at all, no matter how barbaric. It is a philosophy of anything goes.

Cultural relativists, moreover, are faced with two other unresolvable dilemmas. They endorse as legitimate other cultures that do not return the compliment. Some cultures, of which the best known is Islam, will have no truck with relativism of any kind. The devout are totally confident of the universalism of their own beliefs, which derive from the dictates of God, an absolute authority who is external to the world and its cultures. They regard a position such as cultural relativism as profoundly mistaken and, moreover, insulting. Relativism devalues their faith because it reduces it merely to one of many equally valid systems of meaning. So, entailed within cultural relativism is, first, an endorsement of absolutisms that deny it and, second, a demeaning attitude to cultures it claims to respect.

"WESTERN KNOWLEDGE is culturally relative": Despite the overwhelming success of the scientific methods developed in Europe from the sixteenth to the eighteenth centuries, the critics of Western culture still insist that truth is relative.

Western knowledge is only one kind of knowledge and Western methodologies are only one of the "ways of knowing."

There are a number of sources of this cognitive relativism but the most popular is that of Michel Foucault, who argues that truth and objectivity are Western conceits. All knowledge is bound by culture, he claims. Within each culture, knowledge is generated for political purposes. Hence, Western knowledge is politically beholden to the powerful. To signify this interconnectivity, Foucault calls it "power/knowledge."

This is a congenial argument for postcolonial historians. They believe that Western empirical methods were among the forces that subjugated the Orient, so they regard empiricism and its quest for objective knowledge as a form of imperialism. This is why they are so enamored of the subjective hermeneutics, or literary interpretations, that prevail in postmodernism and cultural studies. Objectivity equals domination; subjectivism equals intercultural equality and respect.

If taken seriously, this means that science can no longer be regarded as a universal method for discovering truths. It means, moreover, that any reasonably coherent doctrine or body of beliefs can produce "truths" of its own. Science is thus reduced to one belief system among many. This view is especially popular within the fields of cultural studies and the sociology of knowledge where science is invariably termed "Western science," in order to differentiate it from its ostensible competitors. As one of Australia's leading academic sociologists, R. W. Connell, has put it:

> The idea that Western rationality must produce universally valid knowledge increasingly appears doubtful. It is, on the face of it, ethnocentric. Certain Muslim philosophers point to the possibility of grounding science in different assumptions about the world, specifically those made by Islam, and thus develop the concept of Islamic science.

This claim, however, is no different from some of the more grotesque historical examples of relativism in science: for instance, the conflict between "Aryan" and "Jewish physics," which set back German science under the Nazi regime, and the claims by the Marxist plant geneticist T. D. Lysenko to have developed a "proletarian" approach to science, in opposition to "bourgeois" science. The application of Lysenko's methods to agriculture not only produced a series of disastrous crop failures in the USSR in the 1930s and 1940s, but was partly responsible for the Chinese famine of 1958–62, the worst in human history, which caused the deaths of between thirty and forty million people during the so-called Great Leap Forward.

One can only wish that, instead of deploying armaments produced by Western technology, the present armed forces and terrorist cells of some Islamic countries heed the advice of the postcolonial theorists and adopt the inventions of Muslim science instead. The most recent Muslim innovation in armaments was the Mameluke curved sabre of the fourteenth century.

The truth is that the scientific method developed by the West *is* a universal method and its success is sufficient to refute any theory about the relativism of truth. Western science makes genuine discoveries. Western knowledge works, and none of the others do with remotely the same effectiveness. To say this, however, is not to be ethnocentric. Western knowledge has nothing whatever to do with racism, or the elevation of one segment of humanity over another. It endorses a style of knowledge and its implementation, not any particular race of people or ethnic group. This style of knowledge did, of course, have to emerge somewhere and at some time, and to this extent it certainly has links with the Western intellectual tradition. It emerged in this social context, but it is clearly accessible to people of any background. Far from being bound by Western culture, Western science belongs to the whole of humanity.

"CULTURE PREVAILS over civilization": When Silvio Berlusconi spoke of Western civilization rather than Western culture, he was reviving terminology that cultural relativism has rendered uncomfortable. The term "civilization" is not archaic but is actually a concept from the modern era. The word did not come into use until the 1770s. The first time it entered Dr. Johnson's English dictionary was the fourth edition of 1772, and it was accepted by the dictionary of the French Academy only in 1798.

Civilization was a concept born in the European Enlightenment and was identified principally with societies that were based on reason, that were open to new ideas, and that looked to the wider world for inspiration. In Germany at the same time, the romantic movement arose in opposition to this. Instead of reason as the basis of social organization, romanticism emphasized organic connections to the land and the virtues of closed rather than open communities. Civilization implied there was a hierarchy of human societies and that there were some that had not made the grade. Civilization meant establishing a polity on rational principles like liberalism and democracy whereas romanticism emphasized the bloodlines of ethnicity and race.

"Civilization" was in common use for the next two centuries. However, it became one of the first casualties of the culture wars of the post–Vietnam War era. After the 1970s it was widely regarded as politically incorrect. Subsequently, it took on an embarrassed and apologetic demeanor and was retained primarily as token usage.

In its place, the romantic concept of culture as a whole way of life came to prevail. Such a view was a direct result of the rise to intellectual prominence of the anti-Westernism identified here. Its version of culture recognizes no hierarchies and no excellence. Western civilization is just another culture. Cultures are beyond good and evil. Accordingly, "cultural studies" is the field that now dominates academic teaching and research in the humanities, in triumph over its adversary, the cultivation of civilization.

Ultimately, this is why Silvio Berlusconi's reference to the superiority of "our civilization" was so shocking, and why so many of his European peers reacted in horror. He threw aside the conceptual shroud that had smothered these issues for so long. While Berlusconi's usage was striking, however, it was not original. He was echoing words already used by the American president. In the immediate aftermath of September 11, George W. Bush described the terrorist assaults as "an attack on civilization." This instinctive response was the real breakthrough and is one positive cultural outcome of those terrible events. The assaults left anyone who could think for himself with a sudden clarity of vision about what was at stake. This is why radicals like Susan Sontag went out of their way to mock and subvert Bush's usage, by putting terms like "civilization" and "liberty" within scare quotes to undermine their authority, thereby trying, unsuccessfully, to restore the ideological shroud.

We are fortunate there is still a generation that understands the term "civilization" and is prepared to use it in all its connotations. For it still signifies the yawning chasm that exists between open societies based on universal principles and closed, self-absorbed communities based on relativist, tribal values. If the Western intellectual left had its way, the word would be expunged from memory. If that ever happened, it would be that much harder for the heirs of Western civilization to appreciate all it has achieved and, above all, to be prepared to defend it.

The Slyer Virus:
The West's Anti-Westernism

by Mark Steyn

For I dipt into the future, far as human eye could see,
Saw the Vision of the world, and all the wonder that would be;

Saw the heavens fill with commerce, argosies of magic sails,
Pilots of the purple twilight dropping down with costly bales;

Heard the heavens fill with shouting, and there rain'd a ghastly dew
From the nations' airy navies grappling in the central blue;

Far along the world-wide whisper of the south-wind rushing warm,
With the standards of the peoples plunging thro' the thunder-storm;

Till the war-drum throbb'd no longer, and the battle-flags were furl'd
In the Parliament of man, the Federation of the world.

There the common sense of most shall hold a fretful realm in awe,
And the kindly earth shall slumber, lapt in universal law.
—Alfred, Lord Tennyson, "Locksley Hall" (1842)

IN THE FIRST WEEK of September 2001, the kindly earth, lapt in universal law, was gathered in South Africa, yakking incessantly, shrieking hysterically, but slumbering nonetheless. In a novel or a movie, it would have seemed too pat, the juxtaposition too obvious. But real life is not so squeamish as the professional scenarist, and so the weekend of September 8, 2001, found the representatives of the civilized world locked in intense negotiations with the planet's preeminent thugs over what recompense the West should make for its evil legacy.

Underneath the surface controversy, the United Nations Conference Against Racism, Racial Intolerance, Xenophobia and/or Related Intolerance in Durban had an impressive unanimity on the key points. Everyone agreed that the West was guilty as charged, disagreement being confined only to the appropriate remedy. Dismissing apologies for colonialism and slavery as a pathetic attempt to cop a plea, Robert Mugabe's government—taking time out of its hectic schedule of terrorizing white farmers—called on Britain and America to "apologize unreservedly for their crimes against humanity." There was a big split on the slavery-reparations front between the African-American bloviators, who wanted whitey's payments to go to individuals, and the African presidents, who thought it would be more convenient if the West just dropped off one big check at the presidential palace. The Organization for African Unity demanded that reparations for the Hutu slaughter of the Tutsis should be paid—by the Americans.

> But the jingling of the guinea helps the hurt
>   that Honour feels,
> And the nations do but murmur.

Instead of slapping their knees and weeping with laughter and wondering how the after-conference cabaret was ever going to top this, the Europeans and North Americans were at pains to agree with their chastisers. The British, French, Dutch, Italians, Spanish, Germans, and Portuguese were happy to concede European colonialism was wrong, but unhappy at having their case formally presented by the Belgians as current holders of the EU's rotating presidency. Having been remarkably inept and corrupt imperialists, the Belgians understandably find consolation in the leftist theory that the murkier bits of their history owe more to the general, inherent iniquities of colonialism rather than to their specific failure to be any good at it. Prostrate as they were, their European colleagues had enough residual rump professional imperialist pride to resent Brussels's willingness to overegg the self-abasement pudding.

Otherwise, the West's current leaders—Britain's Tony Blair, France's Lionel Jospin, Canada's Jean Chrétien, et al.—side with their tormentors on the sins of their fathers, but feel that, as impeccable multiculturalists, they themselves should be cut some slack. Mr. Chrétien was all for the conference shining a useful spotlight on the most wicked racist sexist societies on earth but was a bit taken back to find that the first country caught in the beam was his own. Matthew Coon Come, chief of Canada's "First Nations," told UN delegates that he and his fellow natives were victims of a "racist and colonial syndrome of dispossession and discrimination" and only last year had been savagely attacked by "white mobs" acting on the behest of the government in Ottawa. The crowd applauded wildly. Needless to say, the Canadian government had paid for Mr. Coon Come to fly to Durban to explain how oppressive it is. In Britain, your average Tory backbencher likes to spend his lunch hours hanging upside down in a bondage dungeon being flayed by Miss Whiplash for fifteen quid plus a small tip. Enlightened opinion has, as in so many other areas, "federalized" this important adjunct to government. Mr. Coon Come provides essentially the same service as Miss Whiplash, though at rather greater cost. The United States, though it had spent years being damned by *biens-pensants* for refusing to pay its UN dues, was happy to pony up 25 percent of the tab for Durban.

And it was cheap at the price. As the conference bogged down in the precise degree and number of anti-Israeli slurs the final communiqué could accommodate ("Okay, you can have two 'racist Zionist murderers' but take out the 'Jew bloodsuckers'"), the chancelleries of the West devoted most of their attention to calibrating the status of their emissaries, like a dowager duchess obsessing over placement at dinner. Though many nations were represented at the highest level— "Today the Presidents of Nigeria, Latvia, Togo, and Cuba, among others, addressed delegates on the topics of racism, slavery, and reparations," reported *The New York Times* without giggling—some European nations downgraded their delegations to "mid-level." Canada toyed with downgrading from "mid-level" to "low-level," but eventually decided against it: the low-level diplomat is the gunboat of modern international relations and not to be deployed lightly.

The United States, for its part, downgraded from low-level to complete withdrawal, much to the regret of other delegates such as the Reverend Jesse Jackson, President-for-Life of the People's Republic of Himself. According to Jesse and Co., only by remaining at the table can we "influence the debate." Take the Syrian Foreign Minister, whose position is that the Holocaust is "a Jewish lie." Okay, we can probably never get him to accept that six million Jews were murdered but, if we'd joined the Norwegian delegation in all-night negotiations, we might have been able to persuade Damascus to accept a compromise position acknowledging that, oh, eight or nine hundred may have died, mostly troublemakers who were asking for it. This would represent what the Rev. Jackson, the UN bigwigs, and Norway call "progress."

Fortunately, it wasn't all negative. The delegates came up with a delicious new term for advanced capitalism— "techno-racism"—and there was a rapturous ovation for Fidel Castro, who was introduced as the leader of "the most democratic country in the world." Late on Saturday, the UN's Mary Robinson declared the Conference a grand success and everyone went home. A little over forty-eight hours later, three hijacked airliners were flown into the Pentagon and the World Trade Center.

The left were the first to draw the connection between the UN Conference and Ground Zero, even before the dust had settled. What happened, said various professional grievance-mongers, was a reaction to America's decision to walk out in Durban. It then emerged that the nineteen wealthy Arabs, mostly Saudi, had been planning their attack for years, while living openly in the United States and other Western societies.

But, of course, in broader terms the left is correct: Durban leads inevitably to the rubble of lower Manhattan. If we are as ashamed as we insist we are—of ourselves, our culture, and our history—then inevitably we will invite our own destruction. If Western civilization is really something to apologize for, then surely the sooner all our cities are flattened the better it will be for the world. In that sense, aside from anything else, September 11, 2001, was a call to moral seriousness. We know now what is at stake.

AROUND THE WORLD, there are certain societies that function and those that don't. The ones that work have certain things in common. The ones that don't reject some or all of those features, disdaining explicitly the rule of law, property rights, free expression, and representative government, thereby additionally depressing economic activity, technological innovation, foreign investment, education, and the arts. For the people running these loser states, this grim, soiled laundry list is necessary to maintain the regime. For those observing from the West, it is in the nature of multicultural man, generous to a fault, to regard these aberrations as just another "alternative lifestyle"—lesbianism, vegetarianism, totalitarianism, whatever. I recall the Duke of Edinburgh being lectured by some or other African President-for-Life, explaining how his country had learned from the mistakes of the British: having a lot of different parties simply meant you wasted too much time arguing with each other. Under his nation's evolved form of democracy, lots of different views were still allowed, but now they were brought together within one party, which was much more effective. How seductive it sounds: for many starry-eyed Western progressives, the Afro-Marxist economic illiterate is the latter-day version of Rousseau's noble savage, his very inability to master the rudiments of competent public administration a triumphant confirmation of his cultural integrity. For the real-politik crowd, it's all you can expect from these countries. And, for a vast mass of others in between, Tennyson's "Parliament of man" and "Federation of the world" are so worthy in and of themselves, such a restrained vision of an attainable Utopia, "the common sense of most," that we are willing to pretend the Foreign Minister of Syria is no different from the Foreign Minister of Luxemburg or New Zealand. If this polite fiction was ever worth observing, it is so no longer.

The good news was that, in the immediate aftermath of September 11, it quickly became clear that there was no serious antiwar movement—just a few aging Ivy League slogan-parroters whose tired tropes failed to spark even on campus. Noam Chomsky will never be a threat to anyone because, when he warns that the Pentagon programs are being "implemented on the assumption that they may lead to the death of several million people in the next couple of weeks," he's being too self-evidently ridiculous for all but his most gullible patrons. Week after week, poll after poll showed that those opposed to the war numbered no more than 5 percent. True, they were overwhelmingly concentrated in our most prestigious institutions—Berkeley, National Public Radio—but the inability of the elites to rouse the masses to their tattered banner speaks well for Tennyson's "common sense of most," at least in the United States. Not for the first time, one appreciates the importance of the popular will as a brake on the inclinations of the elite.

This is one of the great strengths of . . . well, not democracy per se, but of our culture and its particular kind of political temperament. In the Middle East, the nominally pro-American sewer regimes sell themselves to the state department on the basis that they're a restraint on the loonier inclinations of their people. And there's a measure of truth in that. Insofar as public opinion can be determined in the Arab world it seems that the majority believe that it was Mossad that destroyed the World Trade Center. "Only the Jews are capable of planning such an incident," Imam Muhammad al-Gamei'a said, "because it was planned with great precision of which Osama bin Laden or any other Islamic organization or intelligence apparatus is incapable." This sounds like what the Great Satan's grade-school teachers might call a self-esteem issue: we Muslims just aren't smart enough to pull off a Jew stunt like this.

Not so, say 30 percent of Greeks. It was the American government that destroyed the World Trade Center, *because* it was looking for an excuse to invade *Afghanistan*! Of course! Washington was just waiting for an opportunity to seize a country uniquely blessed in supplies of premium-grade rubble.

The Greeks! The font of our civilization! Evidently, it'll take a lot more than the British Museum returning Lord Elgin's plunder to get them their marbles back. But we forget that Greece, like Spain and Portugal, was a dictatorship a quarter-century ago. When Americans look back on the Seventies, it means Jimmy Carter, the Partridge Family, flared pants. In Southern Europe, it means Franco, Salazar, and the Colonels. The exceptionalism of the American experience can be measured against not just Cuba, Rwanda, and Iraq, but also Greece and Austria and France. Continentals, for their part, are happy to acknowledge America as an aberration, though in their own snide way: if you talk to the French, for example, the fact that America had Prohibition seems far more bizarre to them than that Italy had Fascism; it's apparently more irrational to have a Communist scare (America) than Communism (East Germany).

In 1999, Thomas Friedman of *The New York Times* unveiled his "Golden Arches" theory of history—that no two countries in which McDonald's operated had ever gone to war with each other. A few weeks later, NATO began bombing Belgrade, though narrowly missing the local McDonald's franchise. Friedman's thesis is insufficient: today, Europeans eat Big Macs and listen to Britney Spears, just as a century ago Americans listened to Caruso and flocked to *The Merry Widow*. Or to put it more bluntly: even under the Taliban, the Afghans played cricket. But a common taste isn't the same as a common culture, as Friedman should have known. Given the choice between its booming westernized economy or a blood-soaked wasteland, Yugoslavia eagerly chose the latter. The critical soundtrack is not Britney, but the deeper rhythms of the culture playing underneath.

The rest of the world is reluctant to acknowledge this. Mr. Mugabe says Britain is to blame for Zimbabwe. The Arabs say America is to blame for the Middle East. And Britain and America don't disagree, not really. The Durban Syndrome— the vague sense that the West's success must somehow be responsible for the rest's failure—is a far slyer virus than the toxic effusions of the Chomsky-Sontag set, and it has seeped far deeper into the cultural bloodstream.

At its most benign, Durban Syndrome manifests itself in a desire not to offend others if one can offend one's own instead. We saw this after September 11 in the incessant exhortations from government, public service announcements, the nation's pastors and vicars, etc., that the American people should resist their natural appetite for pogroms and refrain from brutalizing Muslims. Ninety-nine-point-nine-nine-nine percent of Americans had no intention of brutalizing Muslims but they were sporting enough to put up with being characterized as a bunch of knuckle-dragging swamp-dwellers, understanding that diversity means not just being sensitive to other peoples but also not being too sensitive about yourself. Similarly, at airports across the continent, eighty-seven-year-old grannies waited patiently as their hairpins were confiscated and their bloomers emptied out on the conveyor belt, implicitly accepting this as a ritual of the multicultural society: to demonstrate that we eschew "racial profiling," we go out of our way to look for people who don't look anything like the people we're looking for.

This is what we're fighting for—the right not to tolerate any intolerance of our tolerance. As Keith Windschuttle pointed out earlier in this volume, Silvio Berlusconi, the almost implausibly pro-American media magnate currently serving as Italy's prime minister, wandered deplorably off-message when he suggested that "we must be aware of the superiority of our civilization, a system that has guaranteed well-being, respect for human rights and—in contrast with Islamic countries—respect for religious and political rights, a system that has as its values understandings of diversity and tolerance." Poor old Berlusconi found himself scorned as a pariah by his chums in the EU, though no one seemed able to single out anything in his statement that was not, in fact, true. Nevertheless, the Belgian Prime Minister apologized pro-fusely to Islam and promised to send the guy for sensitivity training. Despite including the multiculti buzz-words of "diversity" and "tolerance," Berlusconi had made the mistake of assuming said diversity and tolerance derived in some way from our Western heritage. Best to keep it simple: our tolerance derives from our diversity, our diversity from our tolerance, that is all ye know and all ye need to know. And so Her Majesty's viceroy, the Rt. Hon. Adrienne Clarkson, Governor-General and Commander-in-Chief of Canada, stood on the deck of HMCS *Preserver* a few weeks after Sep-tember 11 and told her forces, as they set sail for the Gulf, that they were fighting not for queen and country—perish the thought—but for "tolerance" and "multiculturalism."

As it turns out, even these virtues may be somewhat *vieux chapeau*. Helena Kennedy is a left wing thinker, celebrity lawyer, and Chair of the British Council who goes under the stage name Baroness Kennedy of the Shaws, QC. Promoting a forthcoming lecture called "Cultural Conundrums in the Brave New World," Lady Kennedy opined that it was too easy to go on about "Islamic fundamentalists." "What I think happens very readily," she said, "is that we as Western liberals too often are fundamentalist ourselves. We don't look at our own fundamentalisms." Her interviewer asked what exactly she meant by Western liberal fundamentalism. "One of the things that we are too ready to insist upon," replied Lady Kennedy, "is that we are the tolerant people and that the intolerance is something that belongs to other countries like Islam. And I'm not sure that's true."

If Lady Kennedy is saying that we're too tolerant of our own tolerance, she might be on to something: there is something a little preposterous about a world in which the Western politician's first reaction to the slaughter of thousands by Islamic fundamentalists is to buzz his secretary and demand she find him a mosque to visit so he can demonstrate his respect for Islam. But in fact Lady Kennedy seems to be saying that our tolerance of our own claims to tolerance is making us intolerant of other people's intolerance: when we moan about Islamic fundamentalism, we forget how offensive our own fundamentalisms—votes, human rights, drivers' licenses for women—must be to others. The baroness says we're too tolerant of ourselves, and she'll tolerate anything but that.

THE BRITISH COUNCIL was founded to promote British culture around the world, but that was then and this is now. Today, explained Lady Kennedy, it's all about "mutuality—an exchange without anybody saying which set of values is more important." In the multicultural West, our values are that we have no values: we accord all values equal value—the English feminist concerned that her tolerance is implicitly intolerant or the Sudanese wife-beater and compulsory clitorectomy scheduler. That's why Lady Kennedy likes "globalization." It gives her "warm feelings that are about sharing," she said. "I feel often when I meet with women, you know, from other parts of the world a shared sense of, somehow an experience of . . . of . . . womanhood."

Baroness Kennedy has got her priorities right. I am woman, hear me roar! Say it loud, I'm black and proud! We're here, we're queer, get used to it! The one identity we're not encouraged to trumpet is the one that enables us to trumpet all the others: our identity as citizens of a very particular kind of society, built on the rule of law, property rights, freedom of expression, and the universal franchise. I am Western, hear me apologize! Say it loud, I'm Canadian and cowed! We're Brits, we're shits, awf'lly sorry about that!

As an example of how formalized this routine now is, consider the Congressional Resolution that came before the House of Representatives a couple of months after 9/11. On the face of it, it was an unexceptional measure to inaugurate "Native American Month." But, along with various unobjectionable platitudes, it included the observation that "Native American governments developed the fundamental principles of freedom of speech and separation of powers in government, and these principles form the foundation of the United States Government today."

This is a reference to the Iroquois Confederation, which, according to the multiculturalists, America's Founding Fathers used as the blueprint for the U.S. Constitution. It's not just that the white man stole the red man's land but his very system of government, too. To call this a revisionist theory would be to credit it with a degree of scholarship. There's not the slightest evidence that consideration of how any particular group of Indians governed themselves had any bearing on how the American colonists wished to govern themselves— nor, come to that, that the Indians in question even formulated for themselves any such "separation of powers." The principal Indian contribution to the founding of the American Republic was, sad to say, getting whupped in the French and Indian Wars. The New England colonists who fought under

Lord Amherst stood in Montreal on September 8, 1760, and watched the French flag come down the flagpole and half a continent change hands; they returned to their towns with a new sense of themselves and their potential. In Japan after the war, the Americans were insistent that Emperor Hirohito cut out all that nutty stuff about being a direct descendant of the sun goddess. But it's no more irrational than our determination to pretend that a group of Anglo-Celtic settlers who'd been governing themselves for a century deliberately chose to adopt an Iroquois constitution.

The republic's founders were, I'm afraid, British subjects animated by certain eighteenth-century English theories about liberty, themselves deriving from the principles of common law and Magna Carta. It is not "Eurocentric" to make such an obvious point. Indeed, "Europe" was noticeably antipathetic to these ideas and in many ways still is. That's why, while America still has only the same yellowing parchment it started out with two centuries ago, the continent has lurched through its Third Reichs and Fourth Republics and wholesale constitutional rewrites every generation. The U.S. Constitution is not only older than the French, German, Italian, Belgian, Greek, and Spanish constitutions, it's older than all of them put together. The ideas of a relatively small group of Englishmen on the rule of law and responsible government have been responsible for centuries of sustained peaceful constitutional evolution in America, Britain, Canada, Australia, New Zealand, India, Barbados, Mauritius. True, of those Englishmen, America got the exceptional talents, as is clear from a casual comparison of *The Federalist Papers* and an equivalent opus called Canada's Founding Debates. But generally, around the world, the likelihood of living your life unmolested by the arbitrary cruelties of government is inversely proportional to how far the state departs from Anglo-American theories of liberty.

This is not an argument about "Englishness," whatever that

is. I doubt whether more than one in a thousand Americans could name England's "national day"—St. George's Day is unobserved even in dear old Blighty—and certainly no New Yorker has ever seen an English parade wending its way up Fifth Avenue in national dress. English nationalism is very nearly an oxymoron (at least anywhere outside the soccer terraces): the English have traditionally preferred to submerge their own ethnic identity within larger forces, inventing Britishness as a means to make the Scots, Irish, and Welsh feel more at home—and eventually the Indians, Basutos, and Fijians, too. By the late 1940s, a quarter of the world's population were "British subjects" and, formally, no distinction was made between a Londoner and a Malay. *"Civis Britannicus sum,"* as Lee Kuan Yew, the former Prime Minister of Singapore, likes to say, not entirely tongue in cheek. American and British nationality were the first non-ethnic citizenships of the modern world, a concept other countries have adopted only recently and reluctantly: until a few years ago, third-generation Turkish workers in Germany were unable to become citizens.

Every revolution—France's, Russia's, even Iran's—claims to be exportable, but some values seem more universally applicable than others. That's why the framework that the Founding Fathers devised to unite a baker's dozen of small homogeneous colonies on the Atlantic coast proved strong enough to expand across a continent and halfway round the globe to Hawaii. That's why the British have successfully exported Westminster constitutions to Belize, Papua New Guinea, and India, the world's largest democracy, mainly Hindu but with a minority population of 150 million Muslims (that's some minority) who, to their credit, have no interest in the fetid swamp of militant Islamism in which so many of their co-religionists elsewhere are festering. Of the world's fifty most free nations, half were once ruled by Britain. That's the sort of thing most countries would boast about, not teach in schools as a shameful legacy of oppression.

That said, this is not an argument in favor of the "Anglosphere," a concept that is much promoted by John O'Sullivan and others but that these days is confined mainly to the battlefield. The "Partnership of Nations," as America and its allies were billed in Afghanistan, consisted on the ground of the United States plus the British, Australian, and New Zealand SAS (special forces commandos) and somewhere a little further back Canada's JTF2 (being semi-French, Canada is a semi-detached member of the Anglosphere). All these states are British-derived and, on the face of it, suggest a working version of Winston Churchill's dream of a grand reconciliation between the United States and the British Empire in some new configuration. But these days what these countries share is a common culture that, officially, recoils from the idea that they have a common culture. We're multiculturalists now, and the salient point about multiculturalism is that it's a unicultural phenomenon, existing almost entirely in the Anglo-American world.

Young Britons, we're told by Tony Blair and the other Europhiles, now think of themselves as European—they eat pasta, they drink Perrier, they like nothing better than to curl up with a good EU harmonization directive on the permitted curvature of bananas, they wear regulation Euro-condoms, etc.

Similarly, Australians, according to *their* new orthodoxy, think of themselves as Asians. This was the essence of the republican case in the 1999 referendum on the monarchy: it was inappropriate to have an English queen presiding over a country with so many Vietnamese restaurants. As it transpired, not all Australians were up to speed on the new orthodoxy and on referendum day Her Majesty won handily. Australians, the republicans assured us, wanted an elected head of state. Now they've got one. To paraphrase Tony Blair, she is the people's queen now.

CANADIANS, meanwhile, think of themselves as . . . well, they've yet to come up with a word for it, but it sure as hell isn't "British" or "American." In the last thirty years, no other country has worked so hard to upturn the realities of both history and geography.

And in America, Congress now wants us to believe that the U.S. Constitution is based on that of the Iroquois Confederation, but with "Iroquois" whited-out and "United States of America" scribbled on top by Ben Franklin. The Congressional Resolution is an unusually literal confirmation of a general rule: these days the surest sign that you share the Britannic inheritance is your willingness to reject it.

Since September 11, "the survival of culture" has been not just a theoretical proposition. Though the demolition of the Twin Towers was seen as an assault on Western modernity—on skyscrapers, Wall Street, jet travel—Islamofascism is no friend to Eastern antiquity, either. A few months earlier, the Taliban cheerfully blew to smithereens the great stone Buddhas that had loomed over some of the world's earliest trade routes for two millennia. Multiculturalism was invented to make amends for "cultural imperialism," for the idea that the West in taking its ideas to the world had somehow obliterated all the other cultures out there. But this couldn't be further from the truth.

Relaxed about its own middlebrow contributions—Wodehouse, Gilbert & Sullivan—English culture has been fascinated with the glories of the past. No other civilization has gone to such extraordinary lengths to reconstruct its predecessors—sending out professors to scramble in the dust for the pharaohs' tombs; reconstructing baroque instruments so that the music of the period can be heard as it sounded at the time; building an amphitheater in the English countryside so that schoolchildren can enjoy Euripides and Sophocles—in the original Greek. Much of what survives from the ancient world would have been lost forever without our respect for the past as the building blocks of our own culture. As it happens, willful cultural vandalism is more characteristic of the new age: crucifixes in urine, dung-smeared madonnas, yawn, yawn, been there, done that. Had some waggish Taliban scooped up the rubble from those Buddhas and entered it for Britain's Turner Prize, I've no doubt it would have won and been hailed by the judges for the way it wittily deconstructs traditional notions of religious iconography.

And, while it's not as dramatic as blowing statues sky-high, when Congress is willing to collude in a fiction about the foundation of America's institutions, it's embarking on the same process, removing some of those building blocks from our civilization. Once begun, selective demolition is hard to control. Until relatively recently in Canada, many natives went to "residential schools" run by the Christian churches on behalf of the federal government. They learned the same things children learned in other schools: there was a map on the wall showing a quarter of the globe colored red for the Queen-Empress's realms; there was Shakespeare and Robert Louis Stevenson, and "Dr. Livingstone, I presume"; there was not a lot about the Iroquois Confederation. No doubt, as in any other school system, there were a number of randy teachers and sadistic brutes.

In the Nineties, a few middle-aged alumni came forward to claim they'd been "abused" while at the residential schools. How did the churches react? Here is Archbishop Michael Peers, the Anglican Primate of Canada, making his first public statement on the matter in 1993: "I am sorry, more sorry than I can say, that in our schools so many were abused physically, sexually, culturally, emotionally."

At that point, there was not one whit of evidence that there was any widespread, systemic physical or sexual abuse in the residential schools. There is still none. But His Grace had lapsed reflexively into a tone that will be all too familiar to anybody who's attended an Anglican service anywhere outside of Africa or the Pacific isles in the last thirty years. In the Sixties, "Peter Simple," the great satirist whose work appears in *The*

Daily Telegraph, invented a character called Dr. Spacely Trellis, the "go-ahead Bishop of Bevindon," whose every sermon on the social issues of the day reached a climax with the words, "We are all guilty!" Riddled with self-doubt and an enthusiastic pioneer of the peculiar masochism that now afflicts the West, the Anglican Church has for years enjoyed the strange frisson of moral superiority that comes from blanket advertising of one's own failures. It was surely only a matter of time before some litigious types took them at their own estimation.

So, IN THE WAKE of Archbishop Peers's sweeping declaration of his own guilt, more victims spoke up—dozens, hundreds, totaling eventually some fifteen thousand "survivors" with some five thousand claims of damages. Though none has yet been tested in a court of law, by 1999 the costs merely of responding to the charges were threatening to bankrupt not just several Protestant and Catholic dioceses but the entirety of both churches throughout Canada. Yet still the clergymen felt it would be bad form to defend themselves. A United Church of Canada employee, John Siebert, spent six years researching the history of residential schools and their impact on native culture and pointed out several helpful facts:

- Native children were not forced to abandon their own beliefs and become Christians; in 1871, before the first residential school ever opened, 96 percent of Canada's Indians identified themselves as either Anglican or Catholic.

- When, over the years, the federal government and the churches wanted to close residential schools, it was the Indian bands (the tribal councils) that wanted to keep them open.

- . . . ah, but there's no point even going on. The defendants weren't looking for a defence, only a way to plea-bargain themselves into oblivion.

So Mr. Seibert's former employers at the UCC wrote to the papers, indignantly dissociating themselves from his position, facts notwithstanding: "It is the position of the United Church that the national residential schools system was an integral part of a national policy intended to assimilate First Nations people into the dominant Euro-Canadian culture," they said. "There are simply too many stories of the pain and cultural loss experienced by survivors of the residential schools system to conclude that this policy and its expression in the residential schools system represents anything but a profound failure in the history of the relationship between First Nations and non–First Nations peoples." With defendants like this, who needs plaintiffs? The Canadian government, a co-defendant, prepared for an optimistically priced out-of-court settlement of some $2 billion, split between fifteen thousand "survivors" of "crimes" never recognized by any court.

Nonetheless, "pain and cultural loss" are categories worth separating. Is it possible even the horniest vicars could sodomize fifteen thousand kids? Well, no. Ninety percent of claims are for the vaguer offence of "cultural genocide," a crime we'll be hearing a lot more of in the future. "Cultural genocide" is similar to traditional forms of genocide—such as being herded into ovens or hacked to pieces with machetes—but with the happy benefit, from the plaintiffs' point of view, that you personally don't have to be killed in order to have a case. All you need are blurry accusations, historical resentments, and a hefty dose of false-memory syndrome. Against craven clerics like the Anglican Church, that's more than enough.

"Follow me," said Christ, "and I will make you fishers of men." But that's a tad strong, isn't it? Much easier to concede that, yes, doing the Lord's work for over a century is, indeed, cultural genocide, and the only question is whether our victims will accept a postdated check. Residential schools did not forcibly "convert" their charges, most of whom had been

Christians for several generations. There have been Christian Indians on this continent for four centuries. The first complete Bible published in North America was a 1663 translation into Algonquin, for the Indians around Boston and Roxbury. In a theological sense, the essentially temporal expression of Christian spirituality has for the most part been complementary to rather than a displacement of the fundamentally spatial nature of Indian spirituality. The Iroquois may not have drafted the U.S. Constitution but they could easily have written the King James Bible. But Archbishop Peers and his chums not only have no interest in being fishers of men; they're desperate to unhook and throw back many of those reeled in centuries ago, preferring to abandon them to the secular hell of identity-group welfare.

Onward, Christian soldiers, retreating into oblivion. As for "cultural genocide," if there's any going on these days, it's the genocide of the Britannic inheritance—in North America, in the Antipodes, in Blair's Britain. A couple of generations back, governments thought they were doing native children a favor by teaching them the English language, the principles of common law and Magna Carta, and the great sweep of imperial history—that by doing so they were bringing young Indians and Inuit "within the circle of civilized conditions," enabling them to become full participants in the modern state. It's only half a century ago, but that's one memory the Government of Canada will never recover.

No civilized society legislates retrospectively: if you pass a seatbelt law in 1990, you don't prosecute people who were driving without them in 1980. Likewise, we should not sue the past for noncompliance with the orthodoxies of the present. We are the accumulations of our past, in its wisdom and folly, and to repudiate it is a totalitarian act, never more explicitly captured than in Pol Pot's proclamation of "Year Zero." The reason why the American Revolution succeeded and the French, Russian, and almost all others failed is precisely because it resisted the "Year Zero" approach. Today, though, almost every Anglo-American institution instinctively opts for Pol Pot Lite. The Anglican Primate of Canada is not saying he personally has done anything wrong, but is merely casually defaming the memory of generations of his predecessors. Tony Blair apologizes for the Irish potato famine, thereby slandering his predecessors, many of whom from Queen Victoria down acted with great compassion and generosity. And, as we know, Bill Clinton has for years been too busy apologizing for the sins of his predecessors to apologize for any of his own: "I cannot tell a lie. My slave-owning predecessor George Washington did cut down that cherry tree."

And once their authentic culture has been discredited, the Anglosphere governments are happy to spend time and money inventing an entirely different one. A decade ago, to counterbalance their membership of the (British) Commonwealth, Canada prevailed upon France to set up a French version of the organization. The Quai d'Orsay, for its usual devious reasons, was happy to oblige. The "Francophonie" does everything the Commonwealth does but in French. Or rather it would do it in French if enough of its members knew how to speak it. The Commonwealth is made up of former colonies of Britain, bound by ties of language, legal system, or, if all else fails, cricket. But Paris gave the old globe a spin and decided it didn't have enough former colonies, so the Francophonie was expanded to include nations that had a vague, unspecified connection with French. And not just nations. The Francophonie's members include Poland, the Czech Republic, Louisiana (really), and for all I know the express croissant shop at the Rockefeller Center subway station.

I CAN'T SPEAK for Louisiana, but otherwise many of the government leaders are of the genocidal strain. Real genocide, that is, not the "cultural" variety. I'm sure President Mutilata of Nogo enjoys his trips to Francophonie summits, even if the

Champs Elysées Wal-Mart has a disappointing range of machetes. But it's hard to see what Canada gets out of it. Discussions on the perennial problem of human rights proceed according to ritual. The Swiss suggest holding an open press conference at which the demonstrators could make their case. Burundi then files a countermotion suggesting the troublemakers should be clubbed and disembowelled and their genitals hung out on the balcony railings. Then, just when the summit seems hopelessly split from top to toe like a Tutsi villager, the Canadians draft an ingenious compromise proposing that they all leave quietly by the back door and return to their hotels for a quick shower and cocktail before the Acadian cultural gala. "Once again we see Canada acting as a force for good in its traditional role as honest broker," says the prime minister, and everybody goes home.

Comparing Quebec and Mauritius with Paris-administered territories such as Chad and Mali, you could make a compelling case that the best and least brutal guarantor of the French language and culture on the planet has been the British Crown. But the argument hardly seems worth the effort. The real question is why Canada feels it has to go to such expensive lengths as inventing a completely bogus international body to demonstrate its multicultural bonafides.

For the British, the European Union is scarcely less perverse. One day before September 11, the playwright Harold Pinter gave a speech at the University of Florence. After the usual stuff about America deliberately bombing civilian targets in Yugoslavia and rejecting Kyoto and the International Criminal Court and being "an authentic rogue state" and "the most dangerous power the world has ever known" and "a brutal and malignant world machine" that has to be "resisted," the great man tossed in a witticism that delighted his audience. A propos Mr. Bush's frequent references to "freedom-loving people," Pinter remarked, "I must say I would be fascinated to meet a freedom-hating people."

Actually, it's not that difficult. The chaps who run the EU, if not actively freedom-hating, certainly regard it as a frightful nuisance. The principle underpinning the EU is not "We, the people" but "We know better than the people"—not just on capital punishment and the single currency, but on pretty much anything that comes up. Not so long ago, Jean-Pierre Chevenement, then France's Defence Minister, insisted that the United States was dedicated to "the organized cretinization of our people." As a dismissal of American pop culture— Disney, MTV—this statement is not without its appeal, though it sounds better if you've never had the misfortune to sit through a weekend of continental television. But the reality is that no one is as dedicated to the proposition that the people are cretins as M. Chevenement and the panjandrums of the new "Europe." The EU is organized on this assumption. If, like the Danes and now the Irish, they're impertinent enough to tick the wrong box in referenda on deeper European integration, we'll just keep re-asking and re-re-asking the question until they get it right. It's not really about left or right in the sense of political alternatives so much as a permanent European governing class with very tight rules of admission.

After September 11, Tony Blair declared he had a twin-track commitment—to Mr. Bush's war on terrorism and to deeper integration within the EU. But the two are irreconcilable. Had Osama bin Laden waited till 2005 to attack New York and Washington, Mr. Blair could not have dispatched his task force: he would be bound into a common European foreign and defence policy. Would the EU offer frontline troops to Mr. Bush? In the Gulf War, Belgium refused even to fulfill its pre-existing contracts to sell the British ammunition because it didn't wish to fall out with Saddam. There is a level of basic incompatibility here which the British persist in deluding themselves about. To London's Europhiles, Britain is obviously "part of" Europe. But, in the age of jet travel, cell phones, wire transfers, and the internet, we're less bound by physical proximity than ever. Yet Britain for the first time in history has chosen to be imprisoned by geography and to disconnect itself from its culture.

If the hope is that small-time African losers like Robert Mugabe will stop beating up on Britain, I fear Mr. Blair is likely to be disappointed. As long as we are ashamed of ourselves, there'll always be something to apologize for. Touring Africa in 1998, Bill Clinton began by saying he was sorry for America's role in the Cold War. In what was described by aides as "a spur of the moment rumination," he said,

> Very often we dealt with countries in Africa and other parts of the world based more on how they stood in the struggle between the United States and the Soviet Union than how they stood in the struggle for their own people's aspirations to live up to the fullest of their God-given abilities.

Is that really what we did wrong in Africa? Isn't it the case that the only thing the West has to apologize for in the Cold War is that it was too indulgent of Kwame Nkrumah, Julius Nyerere, and postcolonial Africa's other founding frauds and simply stood by as they beggared the continent with their uniquely virulent strain of tribal Marxism?

But, of course, on the president's tour or at the Durban Conference, that's the one item that's never on the agenda. If Cold Warriors and old-school imperialists and Anglican missionaries were to take a leaf of Mr. Clinton's book and apologize for things they had nothing to do with, they might try this line: We apologize not for inflicting Western values but for inflicting all the anti-Western values, all of which, paradoxically, are also Western. Until Islamic fundamentalism came along, all the noisiest anti-Western ideologies were developed in the West, again mostly in Anglo-America. (Capitalism itself, as the French Eurocrats used to lecture Mrs.

Thatcher, is "an Anglo-Saxon fetish.") Whether you're a liberal democracy or a moribund dictatorship, you're operating to a Western template. Ever since Karl Marx sat in the Reading Room of the British Library writing *Das Kapital*, great Western thinkers have been obsessed with discovering the flaw in capitalism, a kind of negative Holy Grail for the knights of progressivism. For Marx, capitalism functioned only by exploiting the proletariat. But the proletariat got richer and bought homes in the suburbs. So the next generation of Marxists turned their attention to "colonialism": capitalism functioned only by looting the West's imperial possessions. But the West decolonized in the Fifties and Sixties, and it didn't get any poorer, only the colonies did. So the Marxists invented "neo-colonialism": capitalism functioned by informally exploiting the nominally independent developing world. But the dramatically differing rates at which developing economies developed in Asia, Africa, and Latin America seemed to have little to do with external forces and a lot more to do with obvious local factors.

By the time the UN met at Durban, the grievance-mongers were down to slavery: Europe and America had built their wealth on the slave trade. By this theory, the United Kingdom, which was first to abolish slavery—in the British Isles in 1772 and throughout the Empire in 1833—ought to be an economic basket case, while the Sudan, Mali, Niger, Sierra Leone, Ghana, and the Ivory Coast, to name just a few of the countries in which slavery is currently practiced, ought to be rolling in dough. Instead, of course, large parts of the post-colonial world are more impoverished than they've ever been. Fifty years ago, Uganda was a net food exporter. Today, it can't feed itself. The average Egyptian earns less now than he did when the British left—that's not adjusted for inflation, but in real, hard pounds.

Jesse Jackson and John Conyers have no interest in suing Mali for slavery reparations, because those poor chumps have a per-capita income of six hundred bucks. Like all the rest of the West's anti-Western theorists, they don't dispute that capitalism works but only *why* it works. To those of us of a less pathological bent, it seems obvious that, rather than "exploiting" people, it invites citizens to exploit their own potential. Some will develop computer software and become billionaires (Bill Gates). Some will make a nice living as professional race-baiters and corporate shakedown artists (the Rev. Jackson). Some will clean up cranking out ridiculous theses for lucrative niche markets (Noam Chomsky), all the while bemoaning the system that keeps them in the style to which they have become accustomed. Only our society generates enough cash to fund such a wide range of fatuities. Even Osama bin Laden owes his wealth to U.S. investment in Saudi Arabia. That the son of a spectacularly rich building contractor should have wound up literally digging himself his own personal hole in the ground in the Hindu Kush is in its way a poignant emblem of the Middle East's perverse misunderstanding of modernity.

THIS THEN is the paradox of the most successful culture in history: the "Anglo-Saxon fetish" and its attendant liberties have enabled more people to live their lives in freedom, health, and material comfort. Yet at the same time no other culture works so hard to deny its achievements and its heritage, to insist there must be a catch, there's gotta be an alternative. There isn't. The Anglophone culture has succeeded because it is in its way an anti-culture—a culture of individual rights, not collective rights or group rights (which the Euro-left have always been partial to) or identity politics (in which form collective rights have made a critical beachhead here). A "Federation of the World" is a nice fancy, but it will inevitably be a fretful, Durbanized, Jessefied world:

> Knowledge comes, but wisdom lingers, and
>   I linger on the shore,

And the individual withers, and the world is
  more and more.

Knowledge comes, but wisdom lingers, and
  he bears a laden breast,
Full of sad experience, moving toward the
  stillness of his rest.

Burke and Political Liberty

by *Martin Greenberg*

P OLITICS TODAY, though it must deal with the most
serious matters, is a great deal lacking in seriousness. This
is due partly to a lack of thoughtfulness among politicians: to
their inability, or refusal, to appreciate the questions of principle that are always involved, however unacknowledged, in
political action. We therefore need a strong (in Coleridge's
phrase) clerisy. But the majority of our "clerks" inherit un-
critically a utopianism whose origins lie far back in religious
dissent; they exhibit an ignorant political romanticism that
looks for innocence abroad and evil-doing at home. Today's
left-liberal intellectuals, and the troops of the enlightened who
trail after them in public and private life, are not moved by
ordinary emotions of fear and anger when their country
comes under deadly terrorist attack—they are full of *understanding*. Their moral vainglory would cut the throat of liberty
once again; and an endangered liberty in modern times means
an endangered culture. How well Edmund Burke understood
this, two centuries ago.

"Irish adventurer" is what Burke's detractors called him,
with some truth but more malice. He had come from Dublin
to London in 1750 at the age of twenty-one to acquire a law
degree and then return home. Instead, giving up the law, he
stayed on to make his way as a writer. To scribble for a living
was to inhabit the lower regions of respectability. Also there

were his Roman Catholic mother, sister, and less close kin. (He himself, following his father, adhered to the Established Church—Anglican—of Ireland.) Far from repudiating these questionable connections, Burke only added to them by marrying the Irish Catholic Jane Nugent.

He wrote *A Vindication of Natural Morality* and *A Philosophical Enquiry into the Origin of Our Ideas of the Sublime and Beautiful* in the late 1750s. He undertook to write a yearly chronicle of events, the *Annual Register*, his qualification being that he knew so much; so that he came to know even more. Burke always seemed to know more than anybody else about whatever the subject was. Early on he attracted notice by his literary endeavors and was much admired by his deep-dyed Tory friend Samuel Johnson. His life took a decisive turn in 1765 when he became private secretary to the Marquis of Rockingham, a high-minded leader of the Whig party. At the end of the year he became a member of Parliament for a pocket borough and was much applauded for his first speeches attacking the vacillating British policies on the American colonies.

Irish-born Burke soon established himself as an eloquent champion of the Whig cause—the Anglican cause that had imported a foreign king and army into England in 1688 to chase for all time all royal absolutism from England. The Glorious Revolution was the work of Whig noblemen who violated legitimacy so as to have a Protestant monarch who would be in sympathy with the feelings of the people ("people" meaning the small group of the propertied consisting first of all of the great landowning peers, then county gentry, city merchants, and a few others). Because they fought better for James in Ireland than he had fought for himself in England, the Irish Catholics were punished with long-lasting penal laws. This history (still very present) made for some inner strain in Burke. He never forgot—nor was he allowed to forget—his origins. It was not the only self-division that was to strain his spirit.

Chance may have steered Burke into the Rockingham camp; ambition, but also conviction, kept him there. He was not a Whig by chance. With his Whiggism went an admiration for the Whig aristocratic ideal, with whose embodiments he now became closely engaged. It doesn't seem, however, that he was ever an intimate of those indolent, fox-hunting, many-acred lords; their pleasures, their lives were not his. He was surely dazzled by the grandeur of the Whig magnates— for a while. Disabusement, however, didn't follow, but rather an appreciation sufficiently clear-eyed which measured the great ones against their own high conception of themselves. It is not surprising that the aesthetician of the sublime should have responded to the magnificence of the English lords.

Burke's commoner's admiration for the Whig grandees deepened into a profound political sentiment. He had "long considered men of honor and noble reputation," David Bromwich writes in the introduction to his fine anthology of Burke's speeches and letters (Yale, 2000), "as the steadiest resource of liberty, whether the threat to liberty came from the king or from the people. By their habit of reflecting on themselves in a line of succession, and the wish to deserve the pride that belongs to the character of their families, such persons are to be relied on more than any others for public spirit and self-sacrifice."

As Wordsworth in the *Prelude* saw Burke as oak-like, so Burke saw the Whig aristocracy. In a 1771 letter to the Duke of Richmond, Burke wrote that "persons in your station of life ought to have long views. You people of great families and hereditary trusts and fortunes are not like such as I am. . . . We are but annual plants that perish with our season and leave no sort of trace behind. You, if you are what you ought to be, are the great oaks that shade a country and perpetuate your benefits from generation to generation." There was some ambiguity, however, in his denominating "you people of great families" as great oaks. Oaklike stability might also be called oaklike stolidity. In the same letter he had written that "men of high birth and great property are rarely as enterprising as others"—as enterprising, for example, as the Jacobins in France, he was to say many years later, as enterprising as Burke himself, you think (and *he* thought).

Burke enjoyed Rockingham's high regard, deference to his abilities, and also his considerable financial help. Still, the high position a commoner might win for himself in pre-modern England was always open to being called an adventurer's prize. Merit was an ambiguous thing in a hierarchical society based on a hereditary governing class of noble landowning families, a church establishment, and a limited monarchy: what counted was family and rank. Burke in his political career until the 1780s was a Whig reformer of the English constitutional monarchy, all his concern being for the constitution and all his criticism being for the monarchy. However radical his criticism, he had no wish to alter the foundations of the existing system, which he accepted without question when young and hotly defended when old. Yet where was his own place in it? The brilliant protégé of a great lord thanks to his talents, he had a position, not a place. Early in his political life he bought an estate he couldn't afford and looked to become a titled lord, the Earl of Beaconsfield. "Burke remained caught," writes J. D. C. Clark in the introduction to his splendid edition of Burke's *Reflections on the Revolution in France*, "in the tension between the patrician ethic he sought to uphold and the claims of talent, which were his title to assimilation into the aristocracy."

When his much-loved only son died, that long-held ambition died, too. That, and his own approaching death, freed him to assert with less constraint the pride he took in the merit his abilities had earned him. In *Letter to a Noble Lord* (1796), Burke replied with a crushing force to two whippersnapper peers, obscenely rich enthusiasts of the *philosophes* and the French Revolution, who had attacked him for accepting a pension from the Crown. He set his lifetime of accomplishments against the nothing of their juvenile efforts, his defense of their inherited rank and acres against their coquetting with a power whose universal ambition, if it were able to reach across the water, would have swept away all that they were and owned with a grin. Burke's prose—sober-paced, weighty, powerful to the point of being overbearing—has always close behind its argumentation a reserve of poetic energy which now gleams, now flashes, and now, as in this letter, explodes in a fireworks of dazzling metaphors, a storm of epical-satirical language that tosses around the Duke and Earl, great galleons of the nobility, like little cockboats.

WHEN BURKE fell out of favor in post-Victorian times, the charge of adventurism turned into the blunter accusation of servility. He wore, an important historian wrote, the "livery" of his noble friends. After World War II the sneer was still being repeated, as I found in an essay by the distinguished historian of the eighteenth century, the late J. H. Plumb. Burke, said Plumb, was "the servant philosopher of the Rockingham Whigs." Was Aristotle the servant schoolmaster of Alexander the Great? I suppose he was. To be the political brains of a lord who owned immense tracts of land and who inherited with them without effort great political power according to the hereditary system of old England, when all you yourself owned was your talents, was, of course, to "serve" him. Without patronage, politics was closed to the likes of Burke. By Professor Plumb's time even dons (who continued to live like lords) had come around to being democrats and Burke was now regarded as a disgusting reactionary. He was deferential to aristocratic rank, yes. Deference, however, wasn't slavishness; it belonged to the general, largely unquestioned, acknowledgment of rank in pre-modern Britain. It allowed for some mutuality of respect. And it entailed no suspension of his critical faculties.

Burke scolded the peerage in order to bring them up to the measure of their station. He could become quite impatient with his ducal oaks for being planted too, too solidly. During the American crisis he wrote to Rockingham, saying that "the question, then, is whether your Lordship chooses to lead or to be led, to lay down proper ground for yourself, or stand on the ground which will be prepared for you." In his brilliant *Thoughts on the Present Discontents*, he wrote, as part of his attack on the "King's men," that

> The virtue, spirit, and essence of a House of Commons consists in its being the express image of the feelings of the nation. It was not instituted to be a control *upon* the people, as of late it has been taught. . . . It was designed as a control *for* the people [which was not a control *by* the people].

Burke's discourse enlarged a partisan defense of his party and an attack on the crown into an amplitude of observations about political society and human nature. Dr. Johnson said about him that "his stream of mind is perpetual." Oliver Goldsmith, more critical, regretted that Burke had "narrowed his mind / And to party gave up what was meant for Mankind." Time has proven witty Goldsmith wrong. Burke's political writings, delivered in a voice that seems to belong to some giant before the Flood, have become a general possession of our politico-literary culture. His was a reasonable, undogmatic politics: "All government, indeed every human benefit and enjoyment, every virtue, and every prudent act, is founded on compromise and barter. We balance inconveniences; we give and take; we remit some rights, that we may enjoy others; and we choose rather to be happy citizens, than subtle disputants."

A sardonic modern knowingness, confident of its better scholarship and better sentiments, dismissed as a myth the once orthodox tradition, which Burke had so large a hand in defining, of Whiggism as the great bulwark of English constitutional liberties. It is now held that what the Whig-landed oligarchy defended were its own class privileges. But the idea of class, and of class differences as constituting a fundamental struggle, is a modern one and did not exist yet. The ascendancy of the British aristocracy was a given: thus was the world constituted. Their privileges, which were also called their liberties, belonged to them by prescriptive right, the right conferred by ancient custom. The antiquity of customs was a sign of their enduring wisdom, not (as with us) of their superannuation. Upon the liberties of the aristocracy rested their independence, out of which grew a great tradition of public service. And by their service the constitutional powers of Parliament in an age of absolutizing monarchies were preserved and maintained for the nation. "Nation," the British nation, meant themselves, to be sure, but we must allow another time to have been itself and not scold it for stupidly (or wickedly) failing to be us. There lay in the word "nation" an inclusive significance which a later age would unfold and that the aristocracy, little as it liked it but in the end not intransigent, not *outrancière*, would find itself, somewhat bewilderedly, accepting. Across the Channel, the same class had been reduced by Louis XIV to the privileged impotence of Versailles courtiers.

Burke was a reformer but opposed "innovation," or drastic (revolutionary) change. He was one with the governing classes of his time in his opposition to democracy. Today we equate democracy and liberty. In fact, it's a loose equation; the two parted company often enough in the twentieth century. For Burke, democracy was the tyranny of the many-headed, as in the classical tradition. It might be respectable under certain conditions—he would "reprobate no form of government merely upon abstract principle"—but to him it smelt of, it was, the mob. His was one of the great voices of political liberty, and he found it upheld by ancient common-law traditions and the patriciate (when it was virtuous) of the hereditarian England to which he had come and lent his genius.

What, Burke asked, was the English constitution but the ancient customs, legislated into law, of the English people? Its "sole authority is, that it has existed time out of mind." Burke's term for such authority, prescription, is a legal, not an anthropological, biological, mystical, or any other kind of term. British experience, British history, the community of Britons had created the British body politic without calculation and without system by following "nature, which is wisdom without reflection and above it." Burke despised a speculative, abstract politics; retorting in the *Reflections* to the metaphysical schemers of revolution, English and French, he upheld the spontaneous, improvisatory way the British did things. His great follower in this was the patriot socialist George Orwell. (I have never seen a reference to Burke in Orwell. Are there any?) Writing about the English in 1940 (under Nazi bombs) Orwell said "they have a horror of abstract thought. . . . But they have a certain power of acting without thought." Imagination, feeling, heart play their part in improvisation; revolutionary rationalism excludes them. "In England," Burke wrote, "we have not yet been completely [dis]embowelled of our natural entrails, we still feel . . . those inbred sentiments which are . . . the true supporters of all liberal and manly morals." Orwell one hundred and fifty years later preferred his "God-save-the-King" upbringing to being "like left-wing intellectuals who are so 'enlightened' that they cannot understand the most ordinary emotions."

The British people, Burke wrote, didn't follow ideas. By following nature in its

> changeable constancy . . . of decay, fall, renovation, and progression . . . in what we improve we are never wholly new; in what we retain we are never wholly obsolete. By adhering in

this manner to our forefathers, we are guided not by the superstition of antiquarians, but by the spirit of philosophic analogy.

His traditionalism linked the present to the past, but also, just as importantly, to the future. It was rational, not sentimental.

Burke's argument that time was of the essence in political life, not as swift, decisive action but as slow, accumulated "habitudes," would prove as true for democratic as for aristocratic rule. In an age of revolution, custom was the enemy blocking the way to change. Yet in Britain's case it provided a link to the future as much as it blocked the way to it. Prescription of government, Burke said, is not

> formed upon blind unmeaning prejudices—for man is a most unwise, and most wise being. The individual is foolish. The multitude, for the moment, is foolish, when they act without deliberation; but the species is wise, and when time is given to it as a species it almost always acts right.

The English species (for he didn't mean the human) was indeed given time; it surely did not seize it. Over the nineteenth century and a good part of the twentieth, with much dissension, after peaceful mass meetings of the people and wild riots, after massacres by the authorities and concessions grudgingly allowed, after the formation of distinct (but not so very distinct) parties, slowly and reluctantly, by a second and third Reform Bill after the first, a Parliament still run by aristocrats conceded political rights to the (respectful, not revolutionary) manufacturing and business classes of the midlands and the north, to the less propertied, and to the propertyless, until an entire people possessed them. But "rights" isn't the right word if it suggests the Rights of Man. It was more a case of Parliament extending the privileges of the few to the many; step by step it privileged the entire British people.

THE EGALITARIAN IDEAS of the French Revolution had spread in Britain during its first years, but then were checked by stiff repression. They never penetrated deeply and they never would. (Egalitarianism, but not the angry French kind, came late to Britain, during World War II.)[1] Having established parliamentary rule on firm foundations at the end of the seventeenth century, the English aristocracy submitted to that rule when compelled to share its power and when ultimately forced to give it up entirely. The Duke of Wellington, after the passage of the 1832 Reform Bill, foresaw the end of "reverence for old authorities, even for the House of Commons, which will only change to become worse, will render government by royal authority impracticable. . . . [T]he result will be that at last we shall have a revolution gradually accomplished *by due form of law!*" (his emphasis). And so it happened.

The enfranchisement of the entire people, the idea of which Burke so abhorred, was accomplished as a purely British matter, in the spirit of Burke. "[I]t has been the uniform policy of our constitution," he famously wrote in the *Reflections*, "to claim and assert our liberties, as an *entailed inheritance* derived to us from our forefathers, and to be transmitted to our posterity as an estate specially belonging to the people of this kingdom without any reference whatever to any other more general or prior right." Such a purely British liberty, expressly dissociated from any sublime conception uniting the British people with all humanity, signalled a new sense of separation from the Continent. A gentlemanly England had been a part of the Europe of gentlemen. When the French Revolution

---

1 In recent times, however, a politically driven cultural egalitarianism has gone to lengths it would have needed a Swift to imagine. *"A la lanterne,"* the cry now is, "with all that old and honored stuff, the luxury of aristocrats and snobs! Judge not! Defending the superior and condemning the inferior is the last stand of the privileged."

made war on gentlemen, the English withdrew into insularity. This had its bad consequences. Its good consequence was that it saved them from being drawn too deeply into the hubbub and violence of European revolution and reaction. It allowed them to be a bulwark of liberty for the two centuries during which the guillotine, the gallows, and the death camp seized the rule successively at critical times in Europe.

The great democratic transformation of Britain being gradually accomplished, the hitherto excluded were now able to make their voices heard; life became more just. But admirable elements were lost, too, never to be recovered. Admirable, irrecoverable—such was "the age of high politics" as Bromwich calls it, that Burke "helped to invent," and represented. "High politics" is a good phrase, not least because it suggests a connection with high culture. The politicians of Britain in the eighteenth century (and in the nineteenth, but not in the twentieth) were cultivated men sharing, among many things, the same classical education. Gibbon illustrated this atmosphere in a report, so amusing, of a parliamentary exchange:

> Mr. Burke, in the course of some very severe animadversions which he made on Lord North for want of due economy in his management of the public purse, introduced the well-known aphorism, *Magnum vectigal est parsimonia*, but was guilty of a false quantity by saying *vectĭgal*. Lord North, while this phillipic went on, had been half asleep, and sat heaving backwards and forwards like a great turtle; but the sound of a false quantity instantly aroused him and, opening his eyes, he exclaimed in a very marked and distinct manner, "vectīgal." "I thank the noble Lord," said Burke, with happy adroitness, "for the correction, the more particularly as it affords me the opportunity of repeating a maxim which he greatly needs to have reiterated upon him." He then thundered out "magnum vectīgal est parsimonia." (Cicero: Thrift is a large income.)

In such an atmosphere of intimacy and common culture, bombast, vanity, sophistry, hypocrisy, and falsehood were no less active than usual, but perhaps it was harder to outface scrutiny.

Politics, a free politics, for Burke was the contest of principled parties for power. Men came together who had common interests but also common convictions about the common good. A "generous contention for power" was easily distinguished from "the mean and interested struggle" of factions. Politics today by comparison is shockingly low in the mostly lip-service it pays to the common good. Just as shocking is its economization. Today politicians offer themselves as agents of economic interests, political assemblies turn into marketplaces, the body politic into a body economic. A society with an enervated political and all-absorbing economic life is threatened by triviality, a life of jobs and cars, which threatens worse things in turn.

Burke's chief concerns before 1789 were Ireland, America, and India. The Protestant domination of his native country showing little of the skill, wisdom, and humanity that he thought might have won for it a measure of prescriptive right, he became more and more bitter. His own efforts on behalf of Catholic Ireland he reckoned of small account in the end. His second great concern, the American colonies, engaged his energies from his first day as an MP. It was a subject about which he came to know a great deal and the English knew little and cared less, except as the colonies were a source of wealth and pride of empire. British policy vacillated between rigor and retreat. Burke urged a policy of generosity.

I first read his speech *On Conciliation with the Colonies* in a Brooklyn high school, Erasmus Hall, before World War II, when it was still a required text. I remembered only one detail from it: the epic passage about the American whaling ships running (the passage) like a great wave from the mountains of ice and frozen recesses of Hudson's Bay and Davis's Straits all the way down to Falkland Island and the frigid Antipodes, from the whalers' striking the harpoon on the coast of Africa to running the longitude in pursuit of the gigantic game along the coast of Brazil. I was an avid Melville reader then, so the passage stayed with me; the words were grand and made me feel American pride. I did not have the understanding to remember the passage's lovely peroration, with its reverence for the free, unconstrained development of the "happy form" of colonial society.

> [W]hen I know that the colonies in general owe little or nothing to any care of ours, and that they are not squeezed into this happy form by the constraints of a watchful and suspicious government, but that through a wise and salutary neglect, a generous nature has been suffered to take her own way to perfection. . . . I feel all the pride of power sink, and all the presumption in the wisdom of human contrivance melt, and die away within me. My rigour relents. I pardon something to the spirit of Liberty.

Do not, he urged the British, insist on your abstract rights of sovereignty. "The question with me is, not whether you have a right to render your people miserable, but whether it is not your interest to make them happy." But the British insisted on their sovereign rights.

With the American colonies it had been possible to imagine the empire as a body held together by the noble bond of liberty. That was not possible in India's case. Doubt of the imperial idea forced itself on Burke and grew into a violent indignation at the East India Company's plundering of the country and abuse of the Indian princes and population. He waged a fourteen-year campaign to expose the Company's crimes and impeach its governor general. His passion astonished the English, who thought him mad unless they thought him actuated by personal or party motives. Such hysterical carrying on over a remote place and people with unpleasant (to say the least) customs! But his reply to the honest question of a young friend wasn't in the least hysterical: "I have no party in this business, my dear Miss Palmer, but among a set of people who have none of your lilies and roses in their faces, but who are the images of the great Pattern as well as you or I. I know what I am doing; whether the white people like it or not." India, which he called his proudest effort, proved yet another defeat. His bill to reform the East India Company was killed in the House of Lords in 1783 and the governor general, Hastings, ultimately exonerated.

Burke grew old and tired. Embittered by what he felt was "his perpetual failure," he quoted Ovid: "Shame when an old man is a soldier." Perhaps he would retire. And then came 1789. Into battle he rushed again with his *Reflections on the Revolution in France.* He had stood in the past against monarchical power and the oppression of subject peoples. A man of notable humanity, in lesser matters as in great, he had stood for kinder treatments and gentler punishments. Now he had taken his stand on the other side, on the side of kings and old oppression—or so it appeared in 1790 to his shocked friend, the Whig leader Charles James Fox, to the Whig party, to the reformers, and to his correspondent and friend of sorts, the radical Tom Paine. He was a Whig; he belonged to the party of the English Revolution; how could he oppose the French one?

Burke's answer was, he had defended liberty against the monarchical threat, now he was defending it against the "democratist" one ("democratist" meaning the direct [street] democracy of the Paris sans-culottes). At the end of the *Reflections* he wrote that it was no intention of his "to belie the tenour of his life"; as in a vessel overloaded on one side, he had shifted the "small weight of his reasons" to the other side so as "to preserve the equipoise." But to his former allies he hadn't preserved the balance of the Whig vessel, he had jumped ship and deserted to the enemy.

Burke was a staunch upholder of Whiggism first and last, the founding principle of which was the rejection of absolutism. He would advocate a war against Jacobinism with furious insistence but never a Restoration. Yet his Whiggism *had* changed. He had come to fear for the survival of the England that he knew, for England's *ancien régime,* as Professor Clark calls it. The *Reflections,* as much about England as France, was a retort to a November 1789 sermon by a "political theologian and theological politician," Dr. Richard Price, a dissenting divine who interpreted the Glorious Revolution of 1688 in a radical democratic sense and hailed the French Revolution as a still more glorious triumph signalling the downfall of tyranny and priestcraft and a utopian future of benevolence and world citizenship. A year later Dr. Price proposed a toast: "The Parliament of *Britain*—May it become a NATIONAL ASSEMBLY." (If there is such a thing as a historical shudder, this produces it.) "Burke's aim until the 1780s," writes Clark, "was to win power within the old order of society by condemning its vices and championing its virtues." But then becoming alarmed at the union of religious and political heterodoxy, which was to be found even in a section of the peerage (even in his friend the Duke of Richmond), his aim changed "in the 1790s [to one of] defend[ing] the old order as such, virtues and vices together."

Events justified Burke against his critics about the direction in which the French Revolution would go. It ushered in no ideal state, no brave new world, nor even a constitutional monarchy; on the contrary, it brought about a euphoric-anarchic convulsion of street, assembly, and countryside. The first *government* it achieved was the Jacobin dictatorship of terror and war in 1793–94. Fox clung for years to the notion that 1789 was the French 1688, until he could no more. After which, it was reported, he said that Burke was right after all, he was often right, "only he was right too soon." An anticipation of "premature anti-communism"!

Burke was right after all, he was *politically* right. Liberty, however, which is first of all a political thing, came in time to be less regarded. As the nineteenth century turned into the twentieth, representative government, with its noisy contentions of political parties, fell into contempt, which it partly earned by scandal and corruption. The liberal democratic social order was condemned as a whole, from the left and from the right. To understand this, we need to go back to Rousseau, who was among the first to envisage and judge society as a whole. His influence, extraordinary in the eighteenth century, is by no means dead. One Rousseauvian influence is stronger than ever. Ernst Cassirer expressed succinctly what it is: "Rousseau created a new responsibility for evil; neither God nor man but human society." There was a personal motive involved in this new accounting for evil: Rousseau's desire to shift from himself the responsibility for his long succession of contemptible acts. They did not touch his inner being, his soul, he said in the *Confessions*; his virtue kept its purity. If he wasn't responsible for his own actions, who was? Society, Rousseau declared, meaning the rich and powerful. In finding society guilty, "poor Jean-Jacques," as he called himself—Tartuffe, as François Mauriac called him—attempted to get himself off the hook. In extending this principle to a general truth, he got us all off the hook.

To recognize that society bears a heavy responsibility for the evil in the world was indeed to discover a great truth, a sociological truth. But this scientific truth was seized on self-justifyingly to make the modern claim of universal innocence. As Joseph K. tells the priest in *The Trial*: "Wie kann denn ein Mensch überhaupt schuldig sein?" (How can a man—any man—be called guilty?) Rousseau argued that what made men bad were the institutions of inequality, by which society is structured in depth.

It seemed to follow that politics was a superficial agitation of the surface, while the real movement of things took place down below, in the social depths. The bright light of un-covered social truth, shining upwards, exposed the political lie. Britain's celebrated liberty, what was it but the rule of an oligarchy? What was the democratic freedom of America but the freedom of cotton-growers to enslave blacks, of capitalists to enslave workers? The Marx of the British Library and *Capital* also dismissed political action as ineffectual. What would bring capitalist society down were its internal con-tradictions—it would fall not by the action of parties (which is to say the concerted efforts of individuals) but of impersonal forces. But since it is only in the political that one finds liberty, the devaluation of politics was the devaluation of liberty. Movements—which is to say organized mobs—supplanted or challenged political parties in much of Europe and elsewhere, proclaiming one or another kind of social justice. Social equality isn't liberty. It can be obtained without liberty. Burke, as an undistracted political man, never lost sight of the interest of liberty, whether in America, India, Ireland, or revolutionary France.

In 1788 he had hoped to see France reform herself into a society enjoying constitutional liberties under a constitutional king. What he saw in 1789 was a France turned completely upside down, a democratic ideology proclaimed (not a democratic system established) and equality achieved in the street in the form of what Simon Schama calls "the liberation of disrespect." Liberty, whose agency was the Revolution's representative assemblies, was weak from the start, menaced by the sans-culotte mob. Artisans, shopkeepers, and rentiers for the most part (but no *misérables*, no wretched of the earth)—who but themselves, the Paris sans-culottes believed (and were assured), were the embodiment of the sovereign, Rousseauvian unitary people's will, which the different fac-tions competed in claiming to represent? The power of the sans-culottes, put forth in successives *journées*, drove but didn't direct the Revolution. Mob disorder was often tolerated in eighteenth-century France (and England). But the revolutionary National Assembly didn't tolerate it; it embraced popular violence. When a week after the storming of the Bastille two royal officials accused of trying to starve Paris were caught by an angry crowd, lynched, and their heads paraded through the streets, it drew from the very cultivated, the very distinguished deputy from Stendhal's Grenoble, Antoine Barnave, the comment, "Was this blood then so pure?" With such words—which the guillotine made the poor man eat in 1793—the terror was being recognized right off as an element of the Revolution and not an accident. The Paris mob's interest was in bread, price controls, and assistance to the needy, not in liberty whether economic or political, never mind what the deputies believed. Suspicious of middle-class representatives, they sat in at the Constitutional Assembly's sessions with Marat's *L'Ami du peuple* sticking out of their pockets, shouting and cursing. Sometimes they climbed down from the gallery and sat among the representatives. The deputies, Burke wrote,

> act like the comedians of a fair before a riotous audience . . .
> amidst the tumultuous cries of a mixed mob . . . who . . .
> direct, control, applaud, explode [hoot] them; and sometimes
> mix and take their seats amongst them.

Such an overthrow of absolutism inspiring no enthusiasm in Burke, his head was clear to see what a century and a half of democratic and radical opinion ignored or excused: that the Revolution would allow no room for disagreement, much less opposition. "The dictators in Paris," as he called them, "proceed in argument as if . . . those who reprobate their crude and violent schemes of liberty ought to be treated as advocates for servitude. . . . Have these gentlemen never heard . . . of anything between the despotism of the monarch and the despotism of the multitude?" Differing from reigning revolutionary opinion was to advocate counter-revolution; opposing it was counter-revolution itself. "In the groves of *their* academy, at the end of every vista, you see nothing but the gallows."

Burke recognized the ideological character of the French Revolution. "It is a revolution of doctrine and theoretic dogma," he wrote in *Thoughts on French Affairs* (1791), resembling "those made on religious grounds. . . . [T]he interest in opinions (merely as opinions, and without experimental reference to their effects) when once they take strong hold of the mind, become the most operative of all interests." This understanding of ideas as "operative" in the Revolution, after the long domination of the *marxisant* interpretation of them as disguised expressions of material (bourgeois) interests, was renewed and extended in recent times, especially by the late François Furet. Under French absolutism there had been no class with political authority and experience. To fill this void, Tocqueville wrote, "the most literate nation on earth" called on its Enlightened *philosophes* and men of letters—or as we say, intellectuals. About politics—about political facts, means, power, and action—these intellectuals knew nothing. What they knew about (which they thought was to know everything) was abstract rights, general principles, values, and goals. Thanks to them the eighteenth-century atmosphere vibrated with moral sentiment, love of humanity and equality, the cult of virtue, veneration of the Creator. With 1789 these ideas underwent a harsh precipitation into a revolutionary credo for which "nothing existed," Furet wrote, "but patriotism and treason, the people and the aristocratic plots," virtue and counter-revolution, the saved and the damned.

The liberal representatives of the Constituent Assembly courted the illiberal democracy of the sans-culottes in what Burke called an "auction of popularity." It was an uneasy alliance: the mob saved the Revolution in 1789 and it could unsave it—which it did in 1792. Down the pseudo-constitutional regime fell before the mob's invasion of the Tuileries on August 10. The slaughter at the Tuileries was outdone in September—when it was learned that the Prussians had taken Verdun—by the sadistic, drunken massacres of the Paris prison population. Those responsible for order, Danton and Roland, did nothing. The Girondins, after beating the drums for war and denouncing royal plots, now justified-deplored the massacres they had done so much to provoke.

Burke, in his 1794 "Preface" to a translation of an address by the Girondin leader Brissot, quoted from a letter the always moral Roland wrote to the assembly, as the slaughter continued at full swing. (The italicization of Roland's circumlocutions and lies is Burke's, with one exception.)

> Yesterday was a day upon the events of which it is perhaps necessary to leave a *veil*; I know that that people with their vengeance *mingled a sort of justice*; they did not take for victims *all who presented themselves to their fury*; they directed it *to them who for a long time had been spared by the sword of law*, and who they *believed*, from the peril of circumstances, should be sacrificed without delay. But I know that it is easy to *villains and traitors* to misrepresent this *effervescence*, and that it must be checked.

This is perfect newspeak: "victims who presented themselves" for slaughter (less mad in the idiomatic French); mass murder as "effervescence" when committed by the virtuous populace of Paris. "The whole compass of the language," Burke commented, "is tried to find synonyms and circumlocutions for massacre and murder." One hundred and fifty years later, J. H. Plumb, in his *England in the Eighteenth Century*, wrote:

> In Paris the Committee of Public Safety . . . was transforming the French economy. The flamboyant use of the guillotine has

distracted attention from the extraordinary efficiency of the Terror in mobilizing the industrial resources and manpower of France.

Flamboyant! It's a match for Roland's "effervescence." The two light-hearted words, centuries apart, have the same purpose: to defend the indefensible. They deprecate urbanely a horrified human response to the appalling barbarism of the Terror, excused by Roland as *a sort of justice* and credited by Plumb with the *extraordinary efficiency* with which the Jacobins, institutionalizing it, organized the war effort.

How did intelligent, cultivated people, then and later, come to excuse these abominations which ordinary simplicity sees for what they are? One answer, of course partial, seems to be the deep shift, anticipated by Rousseau, of moral feeling away from concern for liberty to concern for social justice.

The cause of liberty rallied men in the nineteenth century against the European dynasties. But even as Parliamentary democracy triumphed, it was attacked by a left intelligentsia tending towards socialism and a right intelligentsia refusing modern conditions. Liberal democracy in the first half of the twentieth century was always taken to task (for good and bad reasons) and taken for granted, at the same time. But then, at tremendous cost, one learned. I recollect reading recently what a historian of present-day slavery (which continues to exist in many parts of the world) said about the phrase "peculiar institution," once a periphrasis for black servitude in the American South: "Peculiar institution? Slavery isn't peculiar. What's peculiar is liberty."

BURKE HAS BEEN CALLED a liberal, a conservative, a reactionary. He was none of these. They are all terms from the political taxonomy of our world, not his. Whether you are for or against him, he touches you on your own political pulse— whereupon history tends to fly out the window. Consider the exchange between Conor Cruise O'Brien and Isaiah Berlin (appended to the former's biography of Burke, *The Great Melody*). O'Brien, arguing that Burke "was a liberal and pluralist [!] opponent" of the murderous utopian absolutism of the French Revolution, called on Berlin to retract his charge (in *The Crooked Timber of Humanity*) that Burke was a reactionary. Good-humoredly, Berlin complied at once: O'Brien was right; Berlin's knowledge of Burke was no more than the common stuff one picks up: "all honor" to Burke for "seeing through the fallacy and danger of utopian universalism." He had, however, some qualifications: Burke was "deeply illiberal [in his] respect for hierarchy, and for rule by a gentlemanly elite"; in his opposition to democracy; in his failure to recognize general human rights. Wasn't Burke "in some way" a defender "of some kind of *ancien régime*, though not perhaps to the degree to which my maverick colleague in All Souls, Jonathan [C. D.] Clark tries to make out? . . . Don't you think Burke might have been somewhat Pétainiste" if he had been a Frenchman of that later time? (What a question!) Berlin thus retracted his retraction. To be "somewhat Pétainiste" is to be as reactionary as you can get, is to be "somewhat" liable to the death sentence for betraying your country.

You throw your hands up in dismay to see how all historical sense has deserted both men.

Of course Burke was no reactionary. How would he wish to turn the clock back? The time it told—the hour of a hereditarian, aristocratic, constitutional Britain—was the very hour in which he lived and moved and had his being.

Of course Burke, as a Whig upholder of hierarchy and degree, was no liberal. Liberals hardly existed yet. What kind of liberal would believe your station in life was appointed by Providence?

Of course Burke, as a Whig reformer (except in the case of electoral reform), was no conservative. Conservatives also did not yet exist. "People will not look forward to posterity," he wrote in the *Reflections*, "who never look backward to their ancestors." His traditionalism looked *forward*.

Of course Burke was a defender of what the "maverick" Clark, as an historian, called England's *ancien régime*. But for Burke living under it, it wasn't *ancien*, it was *actuel*.

Then what more specifically than a Whig may one call Burke without insulting history? The maverick Clark provides, I think, a fitting word for a man (like Orwell) hard to pigeonhole: libertarian, a man of liberty.

When the chips were down in dire totalitarian times, it was patrician leaders who showed themselves the most stubborn defenders of liberty: Churchill, de Gaulle, Franklin Roosevelt. Such men were understood by Burke (as I quoted David Bromwich earlier as putting it) as "the steadiest resource of liberty." And the same may be said of the Irish commoner who spoke for them.

The Pillars of the
Temple of Liberty

by Diana Schaub

At what point shall we expect the approach of danger? By what means shall we fortify against it? Shall we expect some transatlantic military giant, to step the Ocean, and crush us at a blow? Never! All the armies of Europe, Asia and Africa combined, with all the treasure of the earth (our own excepted) in their military chest; with a Buonaparte for a commander, could not by force, take a drink from the Ohio, or make a track on the Blue Ridge, in a trial of a thousand years.

—Abraham Lincoln,
Address before the Springfield Young Men's Lyceum, 1838

ARE WE TO THINK that September 11 proved Lincoln wrong? Certainly, there are many Americans who now feel vulnerable. In losing their sense of security, they may also have lost their sense of American exceptionalism. While it might have been true that America was once geographically blessed, our moated fortress is no longer unbreachable. Nature's gift has been undone by our own technological ingenuity. It does not even require an intercontinental ballistic missile to "step the Ocean"—an airplane will do. A few foresighted observers had long (and unavailingly) warned that the advances of modernity might be turned against us by anti-modern crusaders who would take a sick delight in the irony of such death-dealing. It seems that in the future our protection will depend more on ourselves than on Providence, and will largely be a matter of defending ourselves against the vicious application of our own inventions, devices, appliances, and agents.

At the start of the Lyceum Address—the most profound meditation we have on the perpetuation of our political institutions—Lincoln says that each post-founding generation has two tasks: to transmit the possession of "this goodly land . . . unprofaned by the foot of an invader" and to transmit the "political edifice of liberty and equal rights . . . undecayed by the lapse of time, and untorn by usurpation." The attack on September 11 was a profanation. By the standards of world history, it was a minor one, but not so in the American collective consciousness. Yet the fact that we can express the sum total of our experience of foreign attack with such concision—December 7 and September 11—is a testament still to American exceptionalism. No enemy is marching along the Blue Ridge and, I daresay, none will be. Thus, it seems to me that Lincoln is still essentially correct. There is no American equivalent of the Fall of France, the Battle of Britain, the Siege of Stalingrad, or the Austrian Anschluss. What we have are two infamous days—days that stir us to such anger and overwhelming counterattack that they are not soon repeated. Moreover, it is worth remembering that the Islamic militants do not have in view a takeover of America; they left a footprint intended to insult and panic us, but have no plan (or at least no reasonable expectation) of placing a jackboot on our supine neck forever. Their tyrannical aspirations are directed closer to home where they are engaged in an intra-Islamic struggle. If they hoped to provoke our withdrawal from the Arabian Peninsula, they chose a singularly stupid tactic that may well prove suicidal not just for the bombers but for the movement as a whole. The enshrinement of suicide at the heart of an enterprise is likely to become a self-fulfilling prophecy.

Lincoln believed that the task of maintaining "the political edifice of liberty and equal rights" against the twin threats of "time" and "usurpation" was a much more daunting task than that of protecting the land from invaders. Here is what he says:

> At what point then is the approach of danger to be expected? I answer, if it ever reach us, it must spring up amongst us. It cannot come from abroad. If destruction be our lot, we must ourselves be its author and finisher.

In the immediate wake of September 11, there was a worry that we would harm ourselves (and grant the terrorists a victory) if we allowed the fear of further attack to alter our way of life. We were cautioned against curtailing either our civil liberties or our spending habits (hence, zero-percent financing on a new car to "Keep America Rolling"). This attitude of hardy disdain has much to recommend it. It was the first reaction of Londoners to the Blitz. In *Their Finest Hour*, Churchill says that "everybody went about his business and pleasure and dined and slept as he usually did. The theatres were full, and the darkened streets were crowded with casual traffic." Although the wisdom of taking sensible precautions soon became apparent, Churchill describes that initial refusal to admit disruption as "a healthy reaction," far superior to "the frightful squawk which the defeatist elements in Paris had put up on the occasion when they were first seriously raided."

Civil libertarians want to tough it out as well. What they fear more than loss of American lives is that certain forms of self-defense will grant a lasting and insidious victory to the enemy. They worry about self-inflicted damage to the system—a kind of home-front equivalent of "friendly fire." It is already obvious that the terrorists know how to manipulate our political system (especially the freedom to travel and the protections of the person against arbitrary search, seizure, and arrest), just as they know how to manipulate our technology. They would use liberty to undermine liberty. Hitler's exploitation of legality to bring about the collapse of the Weimar regime is the classic example of democracy's liability to subversion. Must we accept that this is a vulnerability inseparable from our form of government? In the name of liberty, must we allow liberty to be abused? Or can we defend liberty without sacrificing or sullying the end for which we are fighting by the means that unscrupulous enemies make necessary?

Given that Lincoln was himself willing to use strong measures against saboteurs, it does not seem that his fears of self-inflicted damage were the same as the ACLU's. It is good to remember what Lincoln said in defense of his suspension of the privilege of the writ of habeas corpus (in accord with Article 1, section 9 of the Constitution which explicitly allows for such suspension "when in Cases of Rebellion or Invasion the public Safety may require it"). Lincoln compared the measure, in his strikingly homely fashion, to an emetic. He did not anticipate any permanent damage from the use of emergency powers, since he didn't believe either individuals or nations develop a taste for foul medicines:

> Nor am I able to appreciate the danger . . . that the American people will, by means of military arrests during the rebellion, lose the right of public discussion, the liberty of speech and the press, the law of evidence, trial by jury, and Habeas corpus, throughout the indefinite peaceful future which I trust lies before them, any more than I am able to believe that a man could contract so strong an appetite for emetics during temporary illness, as to persist in feeding upon them through the remainder of his healthful life.

Lincoln may be right, but what gives one pause with respect to the creation of the Office of Homeland Security is that it does not seem to be conceived as a temporary wartime measure. It has all the trappings of a permanent establishment. If Americans are now to understand themselves as under a lasting and indefinite threat, with the home front indistinguishable from the front line, it really would mean a sea change. While a few of the preparedness measures (e.g., better training and coordination of emergency personnel) are probably smart things to do, I nonetheless suspect that we could (and should) abandon many of the costly and time-consuming security measures, which are both ineffective and insulting. Instead of treating every citizen like a potential terrorist, why not trust the eagle eyes of the flying public? The necessary virtue is courage—a virtue that does not flourish in overly bureaucratized, overly policed states.

Leaving aside questions about the intended scope and tenure of the Office of Homeland Security, I wonder about the wisdom of pressing into service the term "homeland." It is a word that comes into currency when national survival is at stake and will, I believe, under more normal circumstances, sound overheated. Indeed, even in times of national danger, it is not a term that leaps naturally to the American tongue, perhaps because in a nation of immigrants "homeland" could never have quite the resonance that it has for older, more homogeneous peoples. Even for second-, third-, and fourth-generation Americans, the homeland is the place one's ancestors left. Certainly, "fatherland" and "motherland" have a distinctly un-American ring to them. Filial piety may contribute to American patriotism, but it is not its foundation. Accordingly, American patriotic songs rhapsodize as much about the flag as about the land (witness especially "The Star-Spangled Banner" and "You're a Grand Old Flag"). When they do celebrate the land, it is in unique ways, as in the remarkable verse "This is my country! Land of my choice!" I doubt that a survey of anthems from around the world would produce any equivalent.

Other nations emphasize autochthony: "Thou art the gentle mother of the children of this soil, Beloved land,

Brazil" or "Think, beloved fatherland, that heaven gave you a soldier in each son" (Mexico) or "Indonesia, my native land, my place of birth, where I stand guard, over my motherland." America being such a vast, geographically diverse land produces other unusual effects. Lyrical tributes often catalogue the variety: "From the mountains, to the prairies, to the oceans white with foam" or "From California to the New York Islands, from the Redwood Forests to the Gulf Stream waters, this land is made for you and me." The United States could have no equivalent of "Edelweiss." Yes, "Edelweiss" was written by Rodgers and Hammerstein for *The Sound of Music*; nonetheless, it perfectly captures the rooted character of patriotism in a small, alpine nation. By contrast, American songs convey a bird's-eye view of the whole "from sea to shining sea." The diversity of the land is matched, of course, by the diversity of individuals who choose this land as their own. Woody Guthrie's line "this land is made for you and me" implies that America is broad enough (physically and metaphysically) to accommodate both "you" and "me." What transforms you and me into "us" is not a shared nativity, but our pledged allegiance to the flag "and to the republic for which it stands."

Since September 11, there has been a phenomenal resurgence of flag-waving. The symbolic stand-in for the republic stands proud and upright, but how about the republic itself. How—and for what—does the republic stand? Perhaps not as sturdily or as undivided as one would hope. This was Lincoln's worry in 1838 and must still be ours today to the extent that Americans are confused about, ignorant of, contending over, and (whether consciously or not) departing from the founding principles of the republic.

THERE HAVE BEEN painful recent reminders of our self-division. Witness the flap over the proposed memorial to the New York firefighters who lost their lives at the World Trade

Center. The commissioned statue was to be based on the widely circulated photo, first published in the Bergen County *Record*, of three firemen raising an American flag at Ground Zero—a photo strikingly reminiscent of the even more famous photo of six American servicemen raising the flag at Iwo Jima. The World War II photo was translated into bronze, becoming the U.S. Marine Corps Memorial. The Fire Department of New York wanted a similarly monumental rendering of the image and moment of its heroism. Before casting the scene into bronze, however, it made a decision to change the cast of characters. Instead of the three white firemen of the photo, there were to be one white, one black, and one Hispanic. The recasting, however, met with objections, and then the objections to the recasting met with objections, and soon enough everyone was offended. The most flattering light in which to put the incident would be to say that Americans of all complexions love their flag so much they fight over the honor of raising it (and the honor of dying for it). A less flattering light would reveal how many of our judgments are filtered and distorted by racially polarizing lenses.

I see no reason to doubt that most of those who object to the photo's alteration do so on principle. They want the statue to reflect the grim and glorious reality of that moment. Those were real men acting in real time. They don't want a gussied up, public relations version. Such "diversity" (which pretends to an inclusiveness and racial proportionality that does not in fact exist in the FDNY) might be fine for recruiting brochures, but the appeal of the photo was in the way it bodied forth inner qualities. It was the soulfulness of the picture that captured the nation's attention. If the flag-raisers had been all black or all female, I trust that the advocates of historical memory would be demanding the same fidelity to the moment and that the photo (despite its superficial unrepresentativeness) would still be regarded as a natural for commemoration. Yet, under the current ideological dispensation, one is not allowed simply to see character. The eye is arrested by the surface. It is color that must be seen. If the rainbow isn't there, it must be added.

Since it is the expression of dedication and heroism that counts, one might ask what difference a little "artistic license" makes. The argument of "artistic license," however, seems stretched since the reason for the change is not aesthetic but political. Those who corrected the photo say they wished to pay tribute to all the firefighters who died, some of whom were African American and Hispanic. Presumably the firefighters were also of varying religion, marital status, sexual orientation, height, handedness, and moral quality. Why is race the relevant category? And if racial designations are so important, must artistic and symbolic renditions be accurate, neither over- nor underrepresenting the 24 martyred firemen, out of 343, who were minorities?

Perhaps it would help if we remembered that the purpose of any memorial is to honor the dead, not necessarily to depict them. The photo was of living firemen captured in a spontaneous act of honoring their fallen brothers. It was one degree removed or abstracted from the actual event. By what reasoning must the honor guard mirror the racial composition of the honored dead? If the brotherhood is real, what matters the race of the honorer? It would be suggestive of segregation rather than integration if a black fireman had to be added in order to deliver honor to the fallen black firefighters, since the governing presumption would then be that one can honor only those of one's own hue. It would certainly give new meaning to the term "color guard."

Perhaps what generated most offense was the implication that there was something wrong with the event as it actually transpired. Being airbrushed (or firehosed) out of the picture cannot help but be perceived as a denigration of the individuals involved and, by extension, of white firemen in general (since what was wrong was their race). If the racial homogeneity of the original group constituted an insuperable objection, then the idea of using the photo should have been dropped to avoid the Orwellian insult.

The opponents of political correctness have found some unlikely allies among black commentators. Clarence Page, columnist for the *Chicago Tribune*, has argued that a multiracial memorial would serve only to "mask patterns of discrimination that fire departments have practiced for decades." Since this is a department that is 94 percent white, the monochrome of the photo was not accidental. For the Fire Department of New York to offer a retouched self-presentation, driven by bad conscience, in which minority representation swells from 6 percent to 66 percent is mendacious. Thus, the call for historical accuracy cuts in different directions. The picture that seemed so right—because so expressive of sacrifice and bravery—is now bedimmed and just as likely to be interpreted as evidence of ongoing institutional racism. There are those who would reinstate the white-guy originals not for their originality but for their whiteness. Thereby the memorial would become "exhibit A" in the court of racial opinion, where there is no protection against self-incrimination.

Although as a nation we are often greatly divided on racial matters, rarely is there a straight black/white divide. For that, I suppose, we should be thankful. Despite predictions of eventual "race war" from commentators the likes of Thomas Jefferson and Alexis de Tocqueville, America's racial battles have not, in the main, been racial in the sense of being fought out between the races. They have instead been contests between the holders of alternative understandings of justice and alternative visions of what conduces to racial accord. Like so much else in America, the disputes are fundamentally doctrinal. Happily enough—happy at least for those who believe in the freedom of the mind—race, sex, and class do not turn out to be reliable proxies for viewpoint.

Lincoln, of course, became a protagonist in the greatest of

these doctrinal disputes. Already in 1838, well before the rent in the Union became manifest, he warned of the danger of self-destruction: "As a nation of freemen, we must live through all time, or die by suicide." Freedom is invulnerable to all but self-inflicted wounds. It is for this reason that Lincoln agrees with the ancient authors who argued for the priority of domestic over foreign affairs. Again, even more against the modern bias, Lincoln did not regard economic matters as the essence of domestic affairs. If the "body politic" can be said to have a soul, then the alimentary is elemental, but subordinate. Subscribing to the "statecraft as soulcraft" school, Lincoln elevated virtue above security (whether economic or physical) and education above defense. Or, rather, he saw virtue and education as the only true means of defense against the twin threats of "time" and "usurpation." Similarly, when *The New Criterion* sponsors an inquiry into the "survival of culture," it expresses a concern not for survival but for culture, or not simply for survival but rather for the survival of a thing that transcends mere survival. As Aristotle noted of the political community, "while it comes into being for the sake of living, it exists for the sake of living well"— "well" being defined as living by law and justice, living nobly rather than richly.

For Lincoln, the perpetuation of our political institutions depends decisively on the rightness of our self-understanding. Indeed, in 1855, Lincoln said he was prepared to withdraw his allegiance should our divarication from orthodoxy go much further. In a letter to a slave-owning friend, he closed with these mordant lines:

Our progress in degeneracy appears to me to be pretty rapid. As a nation, we began by declaring that "*all men are created equal*." We now practically read it "all men are created equal, *except negroes*." When the Know-Nothings get control, it will read "all men are created equal, except negroes, *and foreigners*, *and catholics.*" When it comes to this I should prefer emigrating to some country where they make no pretence of loving liberty—to Russia, for instance, where despotism can be taken pure, and without the base alloy of hypocracy.

Unlike Jefferson, who wrote so sanguinely of "the progress of the human mind," Lincoln concluded that the mind, or at any rate the American mind, was more likely to retrogress and digress. Principles that had been clearly understood in the beginning (despite their frequent violation in practice) were being lost to sight, covered over, distorted, repudiated, and forgotten (perhaps because of their too-long-permitted violation).

IN THE LYCEUM ADDRESS, Lincoln diagnosed the decay brought about by "the lapse of time." His metaphor was architectural. He spoke of "the temple of liberty," originally supported by "pillars," now "crumbled away." Those pillars were "the *passions* of the people" or more precisely the sound form which the passions assumed as a result of the impress of "the interesting scenes of the revolution." During the fight for liberty, the people's worst passions were either suppressed (as were "jealousy, envy, and avarice") or redirected outward against the enemy (as was the case with "hate" and "revenge"). Once the fight was over, however, and more especially once the memory of the fight had faded, the base passions lost their structural and supportive form. Lincoln declares that "[p]assion has helped us; but can do so no more. It will in future be our enemy." Lincoln recommends the crafting of wholly new pillars, "hewn from the solid quarry of sober reason."

Although Lincoln's aim is the perpetuation of our political institutions, his method is not that of a historic preservationist. He does not strive to repair or reproduce the original pillars. Perpetuation can be achieved only by a fundamental improvement: the substitution of imperishable reason for perishable passion. Lincoln's depreciation of passion leads him to expect little from the study of history. There can be no lasting appeal to "the scenes of the revolution." The history books cannot inspire patriotism. What rendered those scenes once powerful was the *"living history"* of the men who figured in them,

> a history bearing the indubitable testimonies of its own authenticity, in the limbs mangled, in the scars of wounds received . . . —a history, too, that could be read and understood alike by all, the wise and the ignorant. . . . But *those* histories are gone. They *can* be read no more forever. They *were* a fortress of strength; but, what invading foemen could *never do*, the silent artillery of time *has done*.

In keeping with his choice of reason over passion, Lincoln emphasizes the texts that perdure (the Declaration, Constitution, and laws) rather than the vanishing "scenes of the revolution." He favors the word over the spectacle. His discipline is political philosophy, not history.

Lincoln's new pillars would demand much more of the people. While the passions of the people were sufficient to erect the political edifice, its maintenance will depend on "their judgment." Self-government begins with the self. A well-ordered state cannot be formed out of disordered individuals. Here again, Lincoln runs counter to the modern claim that private vice can conduce to public benefits if only the vices be ingeniously arrayed. From Machiavelli to Kant, we have been promised that moderation will be the automatic, systemic consequence of immoderate, competitive interaction—no need for the old-fashioned version of moderation which consisted in the habit of saying no to the desires.

Lincoln's paean to the rulership of reason in the individual soul calls for reason to be molded into three qualities: *"general intelligence, sound morality* and, in particular, *a reverence for the constitution and laws.*" The last of these, which allies reason with reverence, is the most intriguing. Whereas scenes and spectacles fade over time, words and texts can acquire greater force, taking on an almost scriptural status. It is as if religious feeling is transposed onto the plane of politics. While some might consider reverence a passion, Lincoln describes it as crafted from the material of "cold, calculating, unimpassioned reason." In this he seems to disagree with Madison who, as Father of the Constitution, was also very keen on reverence. Although Madison admits that "in a nation of philosophers . . . a reverence for the laws would be sufficiently inculcated by the voice of an enlightened reason," he suspects that ordinary nations will discover reverence to be a salutary public prejudice, dependent on factors other than the abstract rightness of obedience to law. Reverence is more a function of the stability (and hence antiquity) of the government. In Federalist 49, Madison recommends that this conservative prejudice be carefully encouraged, primarily by not involving the people too often in large and troublesome questions that would disturb their tranquility.

In Lincoln's day, public tranquility (the key ingredient of non-philosophic reverence) was already compromised "by the operation of this mobocratic spirit, which all must admit, is now abroad in the land." Under the circumstance of "increasing disregard for law," Lincoln could not trust time to settle the inflammation. He had to address the public on the most significant and sensitive issue and he had to do so through reason alone. His speeches are remarkable for the non-impassioned, almost mathematical spareness and rigor of their argumentation. Lord Charnwood, in his biography of Lincoln, says that "[h]e put himself in a position in which if his argument were not sound nothing could save his speech from failure as a speech." This willingness to trust to the compulsion of logic was a great act of faith in the capacities of the people. If self-government is a real possibility, then even a mob must have its "better angels." Perhaps Lincoln's democratic faith helps explain how these same speeches are often suffused with religious language and culminate in moments of deep but restrained reverence. Think of the final paragraphs of the Lyceum Address, the Cooper Union Address, and the First Inaugural, as well as virtually the whole of the Gettysburg Address and the Second Inaugural.

Lincoln's speeches are in themselves demonstrations of how "reverence for the constitution and laws" can proceed from reason alone. The efforts he made to reduce his thoughts to the cleanest, most crystalline formulations were in the service of a recovery of orthodox constitutionalism. It was Lincoln's conviction that the Constitution, properly understood and venerated, offered the only hope for a solution to the slavery crisis—a solution that would do justice to all, South as well as North, and achieve justice for all, black as well as white. If slavery could be once again placed where the Founders had placed it—namely "where the public mind shall rest in the belief that it was in the course of ultimate extinction"—then all might yet be well. To prove it, Lincoln undertook patient, textual explications of the principles informing the founding charters and equally patient elaborations of the public policy implications of those principles.

In one sense, Lincoln failed miserably. His attempt to engraft these new pillars seemed to shake the edifice itself. The election of the man most dedicated to reason provoked an unreasoning rebellion. The faded scenes of the revolution were replaced with fresh (but unwholesome) scenes of civil war, where hate and revenge turned inward.

Yet the conflict issued in something sublime: the Union was saved and refounded on the fundamental principle of emancipation. And all understood that this was Lincoln's achievement. Walt Whitman described the culmination of the war of secession in the martyrdom of Lincoln as "that seal of the emancipation of three million slaves—that parturition and delivery of our at last really free Republic, born again, henceforth to commence its career of genuine homogeneous Union, compact, consistent with itself." According to Whitman, the death of Lincoln provided

> a cement to the whole people, subtler, more underlying, than any thing in written constitution, or courts or armies— namely, the cement of a death identified thoroughly with that people, at its head, and for its sake. Strange, (is it not?) that battles, martyrs, agonies, blood, even assassination, should so condense—perhaps only really, lastingly condense—a Nationality.

Whitman emphatically sides with history and the commemorative muse of poetry. If Lincoln's analysis in the Lyceum Address is correct, however, then the scenes of the Civil War, including its murderous climax—what Whitman calls "its highest poetic, single, central, pictorial denouement"—will fade. So too all subsequent American scenes of moral grandeur. We live right now on the cusp of the loss of the "living history" of World War II—the history that bears "the indubitable testimonies of its own authenticity, in the limbs mangled, in the scars of wounds received." The recent tributes to "the greatest generation," fitting though they are, will not prevent the action of "the all-resistless hurricane" of time.

There is a direct connection between these perils of "time" and that other danger mentioned by Lincoln: "usurpation." Because the very passions that proved a pillar of liberty at the time of the nation's framing will, in later days, become instruments for demagogic manipulation and demolition, only new pillars "hewn from the solid quarry of sober reason" could succeed in upholding liberty. Reason prepares the people to resist usurpation by teaching them how to recognize it. Unlike invasion by an avowed enemy (which in all but the most debilitated nations would prompt self-defense), usurpation can occur imperceptibly, particularly when it is ideological rather than personal in character. Mistaken understandings insinuate themselves into the public mind and become habitual. To usurp means literally "to take possession of by use," and that is precisely how false philosophy comes to seize public opinion. (Of course, if false philosophy goes far enough, it can blind a nation to external threats as well and weaken self-preservative reflexes.) Resistance to usurpation begins with the ability to recognize what is pernicious, to understand which streams of thought are dangerously at odds with the principles of republican self-government.

Aware that reflection must supersede reflex, Lincoln dedicated his entire political career to educating Americans in the meaning of their original charters. It was an education conducted by means of electoral contests with the usurpers (or their progeny), from John C. Calhoun—the man who began what Lincoln termed "an insidious debauching of the public mind"—to Stephen A. Douglas, whose doctrine of "popular sovereignty" effected a reinterpretation of the Declaration that left it "without the *germ* or even the *suggestion* of the individual rights of man," thereby rendering it "mere rubbish" and "old wadding." Even Lincoln's prosecution of the war entailed teaching—namely, "teaching men that what they cannot take by an election, neither can they take it by a war." Bullets were far from the only weapons employed to defend the sanctity of the ballot. As much as the rebel army, it was the rebel argument about the legitimacy of secession that had to be defeated. Lincoln did so by revealing the articulation of the principle of free elections, the doctrine of the social compact, and the original truth of human equality, at each point contrasting it with the counter-trinity of secession, state rights, and slavery.

The inscription on the Lincoln Memorial reads: "In this

temple, as in the hearts of the people, for whom he saved the Union, the memory of Abraham Lincoln is enshrined forever." Despite those words, we must wonder whether there is anything imperishable in Lincoln's statesmanship, never forgetting that in Lincoln's own estimation, memory by itself is insufficient. This is true even in the First Inaugural, where he famously refers to "mystic chords of memory, stretching from every battlefield, and patriot grave, to every living heart and hearthstone, all over this broad land." Lincoln goes on to say, however, that the mystic chords of memory must be activated or sounded by something else within us, namely "the better angels of our nature," which I take to mean intellect and understanding—after all, the whole of the First Inaugural is a carefully argued logical appeal which waxes poetic only in its final lines. Once again, it is reason that stirs reverence; it is dialectics that "will yet swell the chorus of the Union." (The cosmos operates the same way: without mathematics there would be no music of the spheres.) The lesson I would draw is that the memory of Lincoln is vitalized only when we think the thoughts he thought. Accordingly, the Lincoln Memorial rightly includes, on flanking walls, the full texts of the Gettysburg Address and the Second Inaugural—texts that in turn direct the reader to other texts: the Declaration of Independence, the Constitution, and the Bible. As the Gettysburg Address tells us, it is fitting to grieve and pay our respects to the dead, but the only complete commemoration is for the living to dedicate themselves to the same "cause" and "unfinished task," so that the dead "shall not have died in vain."

SINCE IT IS A RARE THING to encounter politicians capable of serving as preceptors of the people, the task of citizen education falls heavily upon the schools. To the extent that they have even bothered with it, their approach has been historical—tending to err either in the direction of hagiography or in a debunking revisionism that essentially criminalizes the nation's founding. It has not worked. And I don't believe it can work. Students are much more receptive to a philosophic approach—one that puts reason before reverence (or irreverence). Such an approach, in fact, fits well with many of their predispositions and allergies. Being inclined toward cynicism, they are suspicious of pious story telling. At the same time, despite having been exposed to a lot of "feet-of-clay" historiography, they long to have America's past—and especially the idea of America—restored to respectability (so long as it can be done without a whitewash). While I have focused almost exclusively on Lincoln here, one would proceed very differently in a course, substituting dialectics for exhortation. Students would read works by Calhoun, Douglas, and the abolitionists (especially Frederick Douglass), in addition to Lincoln. Unlike so many other intellectual projects, this one grabs them because it is connected with their sense of self. They want to know how they ought to regard their nation. They want to know how to think about equality and liberty.

Despite the best efforts of the deconstructionists, young people often venerate the Constitution. When they encounter the debate between Jefferson and Madison on the desirability of regular change in the laws, they all immediately side with Jefferson (since "laws and institutions must go hand in hand with the progress of the human mind"), but when they realize that Jefferson wanted a Constitutional Convention every twenty years, these supposed partisans of the new are horrified. It is as Madison had hoped: undisturbed longevity has produced veneration. The problem, however, is that the veneration is often devoid of any knowledge, and so the content of their political ideas is frequently at odds with the documents they claim to respect. Respecting a document is not as straightforward as respecting a person. Without philosophic literacy, it is easy for public opinion to be shanghaied.

To give an example: when affirmative action was adopted more than a generation ago, it was widely understood to be a violation of the fundamental principle of color blindness. It was justified as a temporary expedient to reverse the effects of discrimination and exclusion. In other words, it was thought to be a necessary evil—desirable in the circumstances, but not desirable in and of itself. Privilege and preference, once established, however, are not readily relinquished. To make the policy permanent a new rationale was needed: hence the call for "diversity," which makes race-consciousness a positive good. "Diversity" dismisses the old standard of color-blindness, declaring it not only impossible, but also undesirable. This movement from affirmative action to diversity parallels the transformation in antebellum thought which began by recognizing slavery as a necessary evil and ended by hailing it as a positive good (the better to maintain race-based privileges). I don't mean to suggest that the injustice of quotas is on a par with the injustice of slavery, but I do mean to say that the doctrine of the equality of rights-bearing individuals would condemn both. It makes no difference which group— white or black, majority or minority—is arguing for (or being benefited by) the permanence of race-based preferences. If it were understood that the genealogy of the "diversity" argument owes more to Calhoun (who pioneered the shift from the constitutional protection of individual rights to group rights) than to the Declaration's assertion of natural human equality, then the generous lip-service paid to the notion might become less fashionable. Well-intentioned idiocy can be almost as detrimental as malice aforethought.

A better understanding of natural right would improve the quality of public reflection (and the resultant public policy) not just on race, but on a whole range of issues, from foreign policy to genetic engineering and cloning, not to mention our contemporary equivalent of "the crisis of the house divided": abortion. Although such an education can be readily accomplished through the study of the Founders and Lincoln, there are all sorts of other ways to do it as well, since it is not fundamentally an historical enterprise, but a philosophic one. However it's done, it must challenge the usurping ideas that have slipped in over time—which turn out to be closely related (though not identical) to those Lincoln confronted. I am not suggesting a civic catechism (which is likely to be about as efficacious as the religious version).

What Americans need is a searching exploration of the meaning of the founding charters, and that would include an examination of the most powerful dissenting views. Moreover, as Lincoln understood, the recovery of old insights would not mean a return to square one, but an ascent—a "new birth of freedom." The aim is not to get back to the past, but "back to the future." Fundamentalism and progress are conjoined. Orthodoxy can be the most creative stance. No one, particularly not democratic man, wants to feel like an epigone. The example of Lincoln shows us how our pride can be satisfied, not through departures and deconstruction, but through fidelity and humility. It is by means of a refreshed and deepened understanding of self-government—by means of the building of new pillars—that we might make the bold claim of having secured for ourselves "the blessings of liberty."

Adversary Jurisprudence
by Robert H. Bork

The prophecies of what the courts will do in fact, and nothing more pretentious, are what I mean by law.
—Oliver Wendell Holmes

Every law or rule of conduct must, whether its author perceives the fact or not, lay down or rest upon some general principle, and must therefore, if it succeeds in attaining its end, commend the principle to public attention and imitation and thus affect legislative opinion.
—A. V. Dicey

The nightmare of the American intellectual is that the control of public policy should fall into the hands of the American people. . . . [P]olicymaking by the justices of the Supreme Court, intellectuals all, in the name of the Constitution, is the only way in which this can be prevented.
—Lino Graglia

UNTIL RECENTLY, the name of Charles Pickering was hardly a household word. That changed the moment President Bush nominated the obscure federal trial judge for a seat on a court of appeals. Overnight, Judge Pickering became the latest casualty of the cultural wars. If there was no compelling reason that Pickering should have been elevated to an appeals court, there was certainly no good reason why he should not have been. Candidates no better qualified have in the past been routinely confirmed by the Senate. He was not.

Instead, in a scenario that has become depressingly familiar, he was vilified by the media and anti-Bush partisans. His candidacy was scuttled by a party-line vote in the Judiciary Committee, which denied him consideration by the full Senate, where he probably would have been confirmed.

What was surprising about the unfortunate Pickering's travails was the brutality of the campaign against him. We have, alas, become accustomed to such battles over Supreme Court nominees. Until now, however, such battles had not extended to nominations to the lower courts. The immediate explanation, of course, was that the Democratic Party and its allies—People for the American Way, NOW, NARAL, and other left-wing groups—immolated Pickering to warn George Bush that they had the votes in the Committee to defeat any Supreme Court nominees who bore the slightest resemblance to Justices Antonin Scalia and Clarence Thomas.

The political struggle for control of the courts has become open and savage precisely because it is a major battleground in our culture war, a struggle for dominance between opposed moral visions of our future. In that battle, Supreme Court Justices are the major prize, but appeals court nominees are also important because those courts are final for all but the tiny sliver of cases accepted by the Supreme Court for review.

The outcome of the struggle for control of the courts will determine the future of the rule of law and hence the prospects for the survival of traditional American culture. The culture war has been best described by James Davison Hunter, who first adapted the term to the American context. On one side are traditionalists who accord a presumption of legitimacy and worth to longstanding sources of cultural authority, sources whose strength is eroded or whose continued existence is brought into doubt by the clamor for liberation of the individual. On the other side are the emancipationists, who are highly critical of constituted authorities and institutions and wish to liberate the individual will from such restraints. That is a process that must have limits if a coherent culture is to survive. Our courts, however, continually test and frequently transgress those limits. The disagreement is not merely philosophical; it is intensely political and generates furious passions. It may be roughly summarized as a battle between the ethos of the student radicals of the Sixties and that of adherence to bourgeois virtues.

The emancipationist party is led by—in fact it almost entirely consists of—intellectuals, a group that, as Friedrich Hayek noted, "has long been characterized by disillusionment with [the West's] principles, disparagement of its achievements, and exclusive concern with the creation of 'better worlds.'" This destructive utopianism was not too serious as long as intellectuals were an ineffective minority, but they increased in size and influence after World War II, and in the Sixties their values came to predominate.

We are accustomed to manifestations of the liberationist impulse in the institutions controlled by intellectuals: the press (print and electronic), universities, Hollywood, main line churches, foundations, and other "elite" institutions that engage in shaping or trying to shape our attitudes. Most people, however, do not think of the judiciary—insofar as they think about the judiciary at all—in the same way. They should. Television and motion pictures powerfully influence the direction of our culture but they do not claim to speak with the authority of the Constitution, nor do they possess the judges' power to coerce. In truth, television and motion pictures would not have the unfortunate cultural impact they do if courts had not broken the restraints of enacted law. Behavior and language are now routine that not long ago would have met not only with social disapproval but also with legal sanctions. No doubt public attitudes were changing in any event, but they could not have moved so far and so fast if the courts had not weakened moral curbs and made legal restraint impossible.

As many thinkers have noted, the Enlightenment has had a dark as well as a cheerful legacy. If it bequeathed us greater freedom, it also brought with it an attenuated sense of tradition and weaker attachments to communal, familial, and religious values. Although these disruptions accelerated in the 1960s, their real beginning was the growing view that what one did with one's life was almost entirely a matter of personal choice, owing little to the wishes of family, religion, or community. Today, this disintegration of the culture, and hence of the society, goes by the apparently respectable name of libertarianism, a catchword rather than a philosophy, and one with very unhappy consequences.

To say that this is a general cultural movement that we do not know how to stop or reverse is not to absolve activist courts from their responsibility in causing the damage we see about us. The courts, and especially the Supreme Court, have led the way to cultural dissolution by breaking down the legal barriers that restrain radical individualism. And, in destroying those barriers, an enterprise wicked enough in itself, the Court has also fostered the immoral attitude that the individual will must be completely emancipated, no matter what the cost. The judiciary has in large measure become the enemy of traditional culture. This enterprise of the law deserves the title of adversary jurisprudence.

The political manifestation of the culture war was the 1972 takeover of the Democratic Party by the McGovernites. To put the matter crudely, but by no means inaccurately, since that time the Democratic Party has come to represent the values of the Sixties, while the Republican Party, insofar as it has a pulse, tends to a traditionalist stance on social issues. If it seems odd to refer to politicians as intellectuals, it must be remembered that the term does not signify any particular skill at intellectual work. Ted Turner, Cornel West, and Barbra Streisand qualify; you get the idea. The intelligentsia are influential beyond their numbers because they control the institutions that shape attitudes, ration information, and offer prestige and comfortable lives to the young they recruit. *The New York Times*, Harvard Law School, the Ford Foundation, and NBC's nightly news are a few of many examples.

The performance of the Supreme Court over the past half century follows the agenda of the intelligentsia. The Court majority's spirit is activist and emancipationist: it liberates the individual will in constitutional issues of speech, religion, abortion, sexuality, welfare, public education, and much else. This is what liberalism has become in our time. Judicial activism, a term of abuse flung about freely without much thought, properly refers to the practice of some judges of enunciating principles and reaching conclusions that cannot plausibly be derived from the Constitution they purport to be interpreting. Activism consists in the assumption by the judiciary of powers not entrusted to it by the document that alone justifies its authority. The results are twofold: the erosion of democracy and the movement of the culture in a left-liberal direction. If the text, history, and structure of the Constitution no longer guide and confine the judge, he has nowhere to look but to his own ideas of justice, and these are likely to be formed by the assumptions of the intellectualized elites he has known for most of his life and whose approval he very much wants. When the judge's views are claimed, however implausibly, to be based on the Constitution, the legislators and the public are helpless. For better or for worse, on crucial issues, an activist Court, not the Constitution, leads and shapes the culture.

At the apex of all our courts, federal and state, sits the Supreme Court of the United States. Its rulings are not merely final but are highly visible and influential statements of the principles our most fundamental document is said, not always credibly, to enshrine for our governance and contemplation. Though these principles are the same as those on the intellectual class agenda, it must be said that there is more diversity of opinion on the Court than there is in the faculty lounges of the law schools. That fact makes the liberal Left anxious and determined to control every new appointment. So far they have been successful. No matter how many Justices are appointed by Republican presidents, the works of the Warren Court and the victories of the ACLU are not reversed.

The small sampling of cases that can be discussed here nevertheless constitutes a cornucopia of judicial activism: no court could arrive at such results by reasoning from the text, history, or structure of the Constitution. Here, as elsewhere in our national life, attitude trumps reason.

THE FIRST AMENDMENT to the United States Constitution is a major focal point of the culture war.

Consider freedom of speech. The First Amendment to the Constitution, dealing with speech and religion, is central to America's understanding of itself and its freedoms. The first words of the Amendment are: "Congress shall make no law respecting an establishment of religion, or prohibiting the free exercise thereof; or abridging the freedom of speech, or of the press."

The Court has since extended these prohibitions from Congress to all federal, state, and local governments. But that is of secondary importance to the explosive expansion it has given the words "speech" and "establishment." It is indicative both of the Court's radically altered importance in cultural matters and of the late rise of the intellectual class that neither the Speech Clause nor the Establishment Clause, adopted in 1791, occasioned Supreme Court review of official acts until well into the twentieth century.

American law concerning freedom of speech, and perhaps much wider areas of constitutional law, has been deformed by the almost irrebuttable presumption of unswerving rationality and freedom of individual choice embodied in Justice Oliver Wendell Holmes's foolish and dangerous metaphor of the marketplace of ideas. That notion made its debut in 1919 in the much-lauded dissent by Holmes, joined by Louis Brandeis, in *Abrams* v. *United States*. The Court majority upheld the convictions under the Espionage Act of Russian immigrants, self-proclaimed "revolutionists" who distributed circulars in New York City advocating a general strike and urging that workers stop producing ammunition to be used against the revolutionaries in Russia. The theory of the prosecution was that the strike, though not so intended, would harm the war effort against Germany. Holmes would have set aside the convictions on statutory grounds, which would have been entirely proper, but he went on to introduce into the First Amendment an unfortunate assumption:

> [W]hen men have realized that time has upset many fighting faiths, they may come to believe even more than they believe the very foundations of their own conduct that the ultimate good desired is better reached by free trade in ideas—that the test of truth is the power of thought to get itself accepted in the competition of the market.

Holmes certainly knew that horrible ideas are often accepted in the market. The market for ideas has few of the self-correcting features of the market for goods and services. When he wrote, Holmes of course knew nothing of Soviet Communism or German Nazism, but his own experience in the Civil War demonstrated that when ideas differ sharply enough, the truth of one or the other is not settled in the competition of the market but in the slaughter of the battlefield. Nevertheless, the compelling quality of his prose and the attractiveness to intellectuals of the supposed ultimate supremacy of good ideas has served, down to our own day, to make his absurd notion dominant in First Amendment jurisprudence and, more remotely, in other fields of constitutional law.

The metaphor of the marketplace not only assumes the

goodwill and rationality of most men who have to choose among the ideas offered, but also, by the nature of a market, the choices, desires, and gratifications of the individual are of first importance. Given that assumption, it is an easy step to the thought that no idea should be kept from the market. Individualism is placed above the welfare of the community, a theme that runs throughout constitutional law.

But Holmes, joined again by Brandeis, elevated that thought to incoherence. *Gitlow* v. *New York* (1925) upheld a conviction under a criminal anarchy statute for publishing a call for the violent overthrow of the government. "If in the long run [Holmes wrote in dissent] the beliefs expressed in proletarian dictatorship are destined to be accepted by the dominant forces of the community, the only meaning of free speech is that they should be given their chance and have their way." This in a case where the defendant urged violent action by a minority to institute a dictatorship that would put a stop to free speech? What happened to the marketplace of ideas? Why, on Holmes's reasoning, were the dominant forces of the community that enacted the criminal anarchy law not allowed to have their way? That they should, on his reasoning, must be the only meaning of free speech. There is an alarming frivolity in these dissents. "If in the long run the belief, let us say, in genocide is destined to be accepted by the dominant forces of the community, the only meaning of free speech is that it should be given its chance and have its way. Do we believe that?" Alexander Bickel asked. "Do we accept it?" Funny little mustached men wearing raincoats stand on street corners preaching obviously crackpot notions that may one day become the policy of a nation, "where nothing is unspeakable, nothing is undoable."

The themes of the Holmes-Brandeis dissents were ready at hand for adoption by the intellectualized post–World War II Court. After some wavering, the essence of those dissents became the law in *Brandenberg* v. *Ohio* (1969). The Court there reversed the conviction under the Ohio Criminal Syndicalism statute of a Ku Klux Klan leader who made a speech threatening to blacks and Jews, ruling that "the constitutional guarantees of free speech and free press do not permit a State to forbid or proscribe advocacy of the use of force or of law violation except where such advocacy is directed to inciting or producing imminent lawless action and is likely to produce such action." To wait until violence is imminent, of course, is likely to wait too long to prevent it.

What benefits can such speech have in a country committed to representative democracy? The ideas involved, if such expostulations can be called ideas, could be offered in Holmes's marketplace uncoupled from calls to violence. A nation that fears only violence but is otherwise indifferent to fundamental republican principles, as the *Abrams* and *Gitlow* dissents and *Brandenberg* would have it, is unlikely to show persistent determination in defending its culture.

Individualistic relativism appears even more clearly in cases dealing with vulgarity, pornography, and obscenity. The prime example is *Cohen v. California* (1971) which overturned a conviction for disorderly conduct of a man who entered a courthouse wearing a jacket bearing the words "F . . . the Draft" (without the ellipsis). The majority opinion by Justice Harlan asked "How is one to distinguish this from any other offensive word?" and answered that no distinction could be made since "one man's vulgarity is another's lyric." The Court would never dream of saying that one man's armed robbery is another's redistribution of wealth in pursuit of social justice. (Although, come to think of it, the Warren Court's solicitude for criminals may have come close to that.)

Cohen was just the beginning. The following year the Court decided *Rosenfeld v. New Jersey*, *Lewis v. New Orleans*, and *Brown v. Oklahoma*. Rosenfeld addressed a school board meeting of about 150 people, including about 40 children, and on four occasions used the adjective "motherf . . . ing" to describe the teachers, the school board, the town, and the United States. Lewis shouted the same epithet at police officers who were arresting her son. Brown used the same language in a meeting in a university chapel. None of the convictions—for disorderly conduct, breach of the peace, and use of obscene language in a public place—was allowed to stand. The relativism of these decisions seems to reflect a loss of will to maintain conventional standards. The Court refused to allow punishment for the same obscene and assaultive speech that was tolerated by supine university faculties and administrators in the late 1960s and early 1970s. When the faculties collapsed, the universities were corrupted; when the Supreme Court gave way, the national culture was defiled. Now, of course, such language is routine on television and in motion pictures.

Pervasive vulgarity was guaranteed by *Miller* v. *California* (1973) which laid down the conditions under which a state could regulate obscenity. That test is a maze whose center cannot be reached. The most damaging condition is that the work, taken as a whole, must lack serious literary, artistic, political, or scientific value. How can a jury find that *anything* lacks serious artistic value when museums, our cultural authorities on what is art, exhibit Robert Mapplethorpe's photograph of one man urinating in the mouth of another, a picture of the Virgin Mary spattered with dung, and jars of excrement as works of art? There will, in any event, always be a gaggle of professors eager to testify that the most blatant pornography is actually a profound parable about the horrors of capitalism or the oppressiveness of bourgeois culture.

The themes the Court had been developing reached a crescendo of sorts in *United States* v. *Playboy Entertainment Group, Inc.* (2000). The decision held unconstitutional a congressional statute that required cable television channels "primarily dedicated to sexually-oriented programming" to limit their transmission to hours when children are unlikely to be viewing. The Court majority found the law a restriction on the content of speech that was not justified because there appeared to be less restrictive methods of protecting children.

The Justices, equating sex and speech, said, "Basic speech principles are at stake in this case." That is a peculiar view of fundamentals since Playboy advertised, as Justice Scalia pointed out in dissent, that its channel depicted such things as "female masturbation/external," "girl/girl sex," and "oral sex/cunnilingus." Most of the speech in such entertainment probably consisted of simulated moans of ecstasy which the females are required to utter in order to excite viewers.

The legislation and the Court both focused on the danger that children would be exposed to erotic sounds or pictures. The Court's discussion centered upon the pleasures of adults. No weight was given to the interest of society in preserving some vestige of a moral tone. "Where the designed benefit of a content-based speech restriction is to shield the sensibilities of listeners, the general rule is that the right of expression prevails, even where no less restrictive alternative exists. We are expected to protect our own sensibilities 'simply by averting [our] eyes.'" Many of the people around us will not avert their eyes, and that fact will certainly produce a moral and aesthetic environment which it is impossible to ignore. We are forced to live in an increasingly ugly society.

Indeed, the Court majority refuted its own avert-your-eyes solution when it said: "It is through speech that our convictions and beliefs are influenced, expressed, and tested. It is through speech that we bring those beliefs to bear on Government and society. It is through speech that our personalities are formed and expressed." Try substituting "consuming pornography" or "watching female masturbation/external" for the word "speech" in that passage and see how persuasive it remains.

Apparently aware that this line of cases has been criticized, the majority opinion essays a rebuttal:

When a student first encounters our free speech jurisprudence, he or she might think it is influenced by the philosophy that one idea is as good as any other, and that in art and literature objective standards of style, taste, decorum, beauty, and esthetics are deemed by the Constitution to be inappropriate, indeed unattainable. Quite the opposite is true. The Constitution no more enforces a relativistic philosophy or moral nihilism than it does any other point of view. The Constitution exists precisely so that opinions and judgments, including esthetic and moral judgments about art and literature, can be formed, tested, and expressed. What the Constitution says is that these judgments are for the individual to make, not for the Government to decree, even with the mandate or approval of a majority.

In a word, what the Constitution says, as interpreted by today's Court, is that one idea *is* as good as another so far as the law is concerned; only the omnipotent individual may judge. A majority may not enact its belief, apparently self-evidently wrong-headed, that the production and consumption of obscenity and pornography work social harms. That is a relativistic philosophy or moral nihilism, if anything is. And it is not the Constitution's philosophy; it is the Court's.

It is not too much to say that the suffocating vulgarity of popular culture is in large measure the work of the Court. The Court did not create vulgarity, but it defeated attempts of communities to contain and minimize vulgarity. Base instincts are always present in humans, but better instincts attempt, through law as well as moral disapproval, to suppress pornography, obscenity, and vulgarity. When the law is declared unfit to survive, not only are base instincts freed, they are also validated.

The triumph of the individual over the community advanced in a new direction in *Texas* v. *Johnson* (1989), a five-to-four decision invalidating federal law and the laws of forty-eight states prohibiting the physical desecration or defilement of the American flag. While chanting insults to the United States, Johnson burned the flag in public to show contempt for this country. He was not prosecuted for his words but only for the burning. Equating an expressive *act* with speech, itself an extremely dubious proposition, Justice Brennan said the government could not prohibit the expression of an idea on the grounds of offensiveness. Unifying symbols are essential to an increasingly divided community, but the strain of individualism in its precedents left the Court majority unable to accept that fact.

THE PERVERSION of the First Amendment took the opposite tack when legislative majorities cut at the heart of the Speech Clause by diminishing and biasing political speech.

Buckley v. *Valeo* (1976) upheld portions of the Federal Election Campaign Act that severely limited individual contributions to political campaigns on the theory that large contributions may lead to the corruption of politics or may create a public impression of corruption. Had limits so severe then been in effect they would have made impossible Eugene McCarthy's primary challenge that led Lyndon Johnson not to run for re-election. Yet freedom of political speech is conceded to lie at the core of the Speech Clause.

Any hope that *Buckley* was an aberration that the appointment of new justices would cure was dashed by *Nixon* v. *Shrink Missouri Government PAC* (2000). Missouri law set limits on campaign contributions for state elections that were considerably more severe than the limits set by the federal law. The Court once more held that corruption or the possible appearance of corruption was an adequate ground to regulate contributions. Justice Stevens concurred, insisting on "one simple point. Money is property; it is not speech." A soapbox is also property, not speech, but the speech of an orator in Hyde Park would be much less effective without it. Television equipment, paid for by contributions, is also property, but speech could not reach a mass audience without it. Justice Breyer's concurrence, while conceding that money enables speech, argued that limiting the size of the largest contributions serves "to democratize the influence that money itself may bring to bear upon the electoral process." Real democratization would justify restrictions upon media commentary that is obviously one-sided in support of liberal candidates and policies. Had the speech been pornographic it would have gained greater protection. Those, including the President, who are counting on the Supreme Court to rescue the political process from the excesses of the new campaign finance law may be unpleasantly surprised.

The Court's deformation of the Speech Clause is outdone by its treatment of religion. Tocqueville saw that religion should be "considered as the first of [the Americans'] political institutions; for if it does not give them the taste for freedom, it singularly facilitates their use of it" because it "prevents them from conceiving everything and forbids them to dare everything." That was then. Now the restraints for which Tocqueville praised religion are seen as intolerable limitations on the individual will. The power of religion to prevent and forbid is greatly attenuated and no little part of that decline is due to the Supreme Court's endorsement of intellectual class secularism. This decline, in turn, bears directly upon the Court's interpretation of the freedom of speech, since in that area there is no longer much that cannot be conceived and dared.

The Establishment Clause has spawned a welter of cases, but it is necessary to examine only a few to see the themes that run through them. *Engel* v. *Vitale* (1962) was the first case dealing with a nondenominational prayer initiated by New York school officials. Officially sanctioned prayer had long been a feature of public schooling, but now the Court, perceiving a forbidden establishment of religion, started down a path leading to the official equality of religion and irreligion. In truth, irreligion seems the preferred constitutional value. A year later, *Abington*

School District v. *Schempp* (1963) invalidated a Pennsylvania law requiring that the school day begin with a reading of verses from the Bible and student recitation of the Lord's Prayer. Although any student could be excused upon the written request of his parent, the Court said "the breach of [constitutional] neutrality that is today a trickling stream may all too soon become a raging torrent." That was extravagant hyperbole. In all of American constitutional history, the trickling stream has never achieved the status of even a sluggish creek.

The Court said the state must maintain neutrality by "neither aiding nor opposing religion." The long-standing policy, dating back to George Washington's presidency and the first Congress, that the state should favor religion in general was ignored. Faith and atheism may seem now to stand on equal footing, but only faith is barred from official recognition. That may be appealing to many moderns, but it certainly was not the view of those who wrote, the Congress that proposed, and the states that ratified the First Amendment.

So drastic has the antagonism to religion become that *Wallace* v. *Jaffree* (1985) struck down an Alabama statute permitting one minute of silent prayer or meditation in public schools. No one would know whether a student was praying, meditating, or daydreaming. The difficulty, according to Justice Stevens, was that by adding the option of silent prayer, the state characterized prayer as a favored practice.

The Court's treatment of religion became even more draconian in *Lee* v. *Weisman* (1992) which held unconstitutional a rabbi's recitation of a nonsectarian prayer at a middle-school graduation ceremony. Justice Souter disparaged evidence that after adoption of the First Amendment the founding generation encouraged public support for religion, saying that such acts "prove only that public officials, no matter when they serve, can turn a blind eye to constitutional principle." That is an extraordinary dismissal of the evidence that the same Congress that proposed the no-establishment principle also hired chaplains for both Houses and the armed forces, and successfully called upon presidents to declare national days of thanksgiving to God. History is in fact quite clear that the founding generation thought the state could and should encourage religion. The prayer was harmful to plaintiff Deborah Weisman, the Court said, because public or peer pressure might cause her to stand or at least maintain a respectful silence during its reading. She could constitutionally be required to stand or remain silent during the reading of any other material—the Communist Manifesto, say, or Darwinian theory—so long as it had no hint of religious content. But then such philosophical trickles, which have upon occasion become raging torrents, are not religious, at least not in the conventional sense.

One of the most extreme examples of anti-religious animus was presented by *Board of Education of Kiryas Joel Village School District* v. *Grumet* (1994). The Satmar Hasidim, who practiced a strict form of Judaism, established a village that excluded all but Satmars. Their children were educated in private religious schools. Federal law entitled handicapped children "the deaf, mentally retarded, and those suffering from various physical, mental, or emotional disorders" to special education services, but a Supreme Court ruling forced them to attend public schools outside the village. Their parents withdrew the children because of "the panic, fear and trauma [the children] suffered in leaving their own community and being with people whose ways were so different." The State of New York responded by constituting the village a separate school district to enable it to provide for itself the special services needed.

The Supreme Court, however, in an opinion by Justice Souter, found this to be a forbidden establishment of religion. Justice Stevens, joined by Blackmun and Kennedy, concurred, offering the advice that "the State could have taken steps to alleviate the children's fear by teaching their schoolmates to be tolerant and respectful of Satmar customs." Teaching grade schoolers to be tolerant and respectful of handicapped, strangely dressed classmates who spoke Yiddish and practiced what the classmates would see as a weird religion would be a Sisyphean task at best. The Justices must have forgotten how cruel children can be to those they regard as even mildly eccentric.

"The isolation of these children," the concurrence went on to say, "while it may protect them from 'panic, fear and trauma,' also unquestionably increased the likelihood that they would remain within the fold, faithful adherents of their parents' religious faith." Why families' freedom to raise their children as they think best should be suspect and what relevance the observation had to the Establishment Clause went unexplained. The concurrence spoke for social atomization.

Justice Scalia, in a dissent joined by Chief Justice Rehnquist and Justice Thomas, wrote that the Grand Rebbe, who brought the Satmars from Europe to escape religious persecution, would be "astounded" to learn that the sect was so powerful as to have become an "establishment" of New York State, and the Founding Fathers would be "astonished" that the Establishment Clause was used to prohibit a characteristically American accommodation of the religious practices of a tiny minority sect. "I, however," Scalia continued, "am not surprised. Once this Court has abandoned text and history as guides, nothing prevents it from calling religious toleration the establishment of religion." (Actually, once text and history are jettisoned, nothing prevents the Court from doing anything it chooses with any part of the Constitution.) Souter inadvertently conceded the point by rebuking Scalia for "his inability to accept the fact that this Court has long held that the First Amendment reaches more than classic, eighteenth-century establishments." Unfortunately for that riposte, the Establishment Clause is a product of the eighteenth century.

The same radical individualism determined the result in *Santa Fe Independent School District* v. *Doe* (2000). The school district authorized two student elections, one to decide whether invocations, messages, or statements should be delivered at home football games and a second to select a student to deliver them. The Court held the school district's policy a forbidden establishment of religion. Dislike of majority rule surfaced in Justice Stevens's opinion for the majority: "[T]his student election does nothing to protect minority views but rather places the students who hold such views at the mercy of the majority. School sponsorship of a religious message is impermissible because it sends the ancillary message to members of the audience who are nonadherents 'that they are outsiders, not full members of the political community, and an accompanying message to adherents that they are insiders, favored members of the political community.'" Religious speech must have extraordinary political power. All of us have heard actual *political* speech with which we heartily disagreed without feeling any the less members of the political community. But where religion is concerned, even imaginary discomfort to a hypothetical individual overrides the reasonable desires of the community.

This year the Court narrowly upheld the constitutionality of a voucher program that provides tuition aid for certain students in Cleveland public schools. The aid is given to parents who may use it for tutorial assistance or for any accredited schools, public or private, religious or secular. A large majority of the students participating attended religious schools, most of them Catholic. The Court majority held that the program was neutral with respect to religion because aid was given to parents who in turn direct the aid to religious or secular schools as a result of their independent choice. The outcome of the case was welcome but it may be that it had less to do with reining in an Establishment Clause jurisprudence run wild than it did with sympathy for poor black families whose children are trapped in public schools so bad that it condemns them to lives of ignorance, poverty, and for some, crime.

The weakness of the case as a guide to future decisions about the relationship of religion and government is suggested by the fact that the majority opinion by Chief Justice Rehnquist was an exercise in fencing within the confines of rules that themselves have no foundation in anything the Framers of the First Amendment intended. Had Rehnquist made a frontal assault on the legitimacy of those rules, as in past dissents he has, he could not have mustered a majority of the Court. The preposterous nature of those rules was illustrated when the Court of Appeals for the Ninth Circuit recently held in *Newdow* v. *United States Congress* that the words "under God," added to the Pledge of Allegiance by a 1954 federal statute, were unconstitutional. The plaintiff's case was that his eight-year-old daughter was injured, though she was not required to recite the Pledge or to say the added words, because she had to watch and listen as the teacher led her classmates in the recitation. The case is one more illustration of our judiciary's willingness to take seriously the most inane grievances about religion. The dissenting judge pointed out that the words found offensive have no tendency to establish a religion "except in the fevered eye of persons who most fervently would like to drive" all traces of religion from public life. It is impossible, he remarked, to accept both the theory of the majority and the singing of "God Bless America," "America the Beautiful," the third stanza of the "Star Spangled Banner," and the fourth of "My Country 'Tis of Thee" in many public settings.

The Establishment Clause, as interpreted by the Supreme Court, is a mess. Nothing makes that more obvious than that the majority's result in *Newdow* can easily be defended in terms of Supreme Court precedents. That those precedents are utterly without support in the First Amendment has now been made clearer than ever by Philip Hamburger's new book, *Separation of Church and State.* Our courts are forcing upon us a constitutional myth which reached its apogee with the

Ninth Circuit's statement, solidly grounded in Supreme Court cases, though not in history, that the Establishment Clause prohibits not only the endorsement of a particular religion at the expense of others (quite true) "but also of religion at the expense of atheism" (wholly false).

THERE IS ALSO the issue of feminism. *United States v. Virginia* (1996) held 7–1 that Virginia Military Institute, which is supported by the state, could not, under the Equal Protection Clause of the Fourteenth Amendment, remain an all-male school. The school was founded in 1839. The Fourteenth Amendment, designed to protect the newly freed slaves, was not ratified until 1868. Nobody at the time suggested that the Amendment banned single-sex education. In fact, it was not until 1971, over a hundred years later, that the Court first applied the Amendment to an irrational distinction between men and women. The ratifiers would have been aghast that a military school could not be all male.

VMI featured strict discipline, hard physical performance, and an absolute lack of privacy, something, in fact, very like Marine boot camp. The admission of women required modifications, as they have in every military college. VMI's distinctive character, it was pointed out, would be lost. The Court attached no weight to this prospect. The Court insisted on the abstract equality of men and women in all things, undeterred by the historical meaning of the Equal Protection Clause, the value of well over a century of unquestioned excellence and tradition, and most certainly not by the heretical thought that there might be some areas of life suited to masculinity that feminism should not be permitted to destroy. Masculinity is a highly suspect idea in today's elite culture and it cannot, therefore, be expected to find lodgement in the Supreme Court's version of constitutional law.

There is no limit to what the Court can do with the Equal Protection Clause. As Justice Scalia said in dissent, the "current equal-protection jurisprudence . . . regards this Court as free to evaluate everything under the sun." That is exactly right. Every law makes a distinction between lawful and unlawful behavior. Every law, therefore, produces inequality because some conduct is allowed while other conduct is forbidden. The Court's equal protection jurisprudence thus allows scrutiny of all law to see if it meets the Justices' views of appropriate policy.

It might appear that the Court's theme of equality is contrary to the theme of emancipated individualism, but that is a misunderstanding. Equality denies the right of the majority to impose standards that require some individuals to desist from activities they enjoy. When the clause is applied to erase such distinctions, the individual is liberated, even if we think he ought not to be. Emancipation of the will is then quite selective. One is reminded of the folks who deny the existence of any objective truth or moral standard even while fiercely imposing their truths on others. They are not in fact nihilists, since they clearly believe in something, even if it is only the protection of their own prerogatives. Equality can be a means of breaking down traditional authority so that a new morality may be imposed. Though equal rights authoritarians demand nonjudgmentalism, they are very judgmental about traditionalists who oppose them. The emancipation of the individual will turns out to be about power.

The intelligentsia are not through with VMI. The college has a tradition of a "brief, nonsectarian, inclusive blessing" before the evening meal. The ACLU persuaded a district court to prohibit even that. VMI's superintendent said, no doubt pensively, "Hearing a brief prayer before supper is no more the establishment of religion than the singing of 'God Bless America.'" True, but he shouldn't have given the ACLU any ideas for an additional lawsuit.

The Court's intervention has also been disruptive in the matter of sexuality. Much of the Court's activism is concerned with sexuality as the abortion cases *Roe* v. *Wade* (1973), *Planned Parenthood* v. *Casey* (1992), and *Stenberg* v. *Carhart* (2000) make clear. The chosen instrument in these cases was the Due Process Clause of the Fourteenth Amendment, which requires that no one be deprived of life, liberty, or property without due process of law. The language obviously requires only fair procedures in the application of substantive law. But in *Dred Scott* v. *Sanford*, an 1857 decision, Chief Justice Roger Taney transformed the identical Due Process Clause of the Fifth Amendment to require that statutes have substantive meanings which judges approve. He and a majority of the Court did not approve of a federal statute which, quite arguably, would have freed a slave taken by his owner to territory where slavery was forbidden. Taney wrote that depriving a man of his property, regardless of procedural regularity, could hardly be called due process. "Substantive due process," an oxymoron, was born.

Regardless of the shame in which it was conceived, and its internal contradiction, substantive due process has proved too valuable for judicial activism to be given up. In 1965, *Griswold* v. *Connecticut* gave birth to the Court-invented and undefined "right of privacy" which in turn spawned *Roe* v. *Wade*, a case that, without even a pretense of legal reasoning, announced a right to abortion. In an opinion of just over fifty-one pages, Justice Harry Blackmun surveyed such subjects as the view of abortion taken in the Persian Empire, the English common law, and by the American Medical Association, before announcing without further ado that the right of privacy was "broad enough" to cover a right to abortion. In *Planned Parenthood* v. *Casey*, the concurring opinion of three Justices, which created a majority to sustain a somewhat modified right to abortion, fashioned a right to "personal dignity and autonomy": "At the heart of liberty"—runs the by-now famous "mystery passage"—"is the right to define one's own concept of existence, of meaning, of the universe, and of the mystery of human life." Though the liberty to be protected is left entirely unclear by this fogbound rhetoric, the mood is certainly one of radical individualism. The three-justice opinion simply refuses to explain what it is talking about, just as *Roe* v. *Wade* did almost twenty years earlier.

Worse was to come. In *Stenberg* v. *Carhart*, the Court struck down a Nebraska statute banning partial birth abortions, a procedure in which a live baby is almost entirely removed from the mother, its skull pierced and its brain vacuumed out, before the carcass is taken from the birth canal. The procedure is morally indistinguishable from infanticide, but the Court majority held that an exception for cases in which the mother's life was otherwise endangered was not sufficient; there must be an exception to preserve the mother's health. Though it is never true that the mother's health would be adversely affected unless a partial birth abortion were performed, the ruling means that such abortions cannot be banned at all. There will always be an abortionist willing to certify that the procedure is essential to health.

In view of the territory the Court has claimed, it is worth examining the title deed composed in the *Griswold* decision. At issue was an ancient and unenforced statute prohibiting the use of contraceptives. Justice William O. Douglas reasoned that various provisions of the Bill of Rights protected aspects of privacy. That being so, the emanations from such rights formed a penumbra from which a larger, unmentioned right of privacy could be deduced. That reasoning assumes that the framers and ratifiers of the Bill of Rights had a sense that there was a more encompassing right which they were unable to articulate and so had to settle for a list of specific guarantees. In this view, the Court must finish the drafting by discerning a meaning the founders could not. The word "hubris" comes to mind. Bogus as it was, Douglas's sleight of hand seemed harmless, but it became the rhetorical cover for the far more serious decisions that followed. It is on that bastardized version of constitutional reasoning that the entire edifice of so-called "reproductive rights" rests.

The radical individualism of the abortion cases has off-shoots. In *Eisenstadt* v. *Baird* (1972), the Court moved beyond the rationale of *Griswold*, which purported to rest upon the marriage relationship, to decide that the same rationale must apply to the distribution of contraceptives to unmarried people. Justice William Brennan announced that "If the right of privacy means anything, it is the right of the *individual*, married or single, to be free from unwarranted governmental intrusion into matters so fundamentally affecting a person as the decision whether to bear or beget a child." It would be quibbling to point out that the right of privacy does not, in fact, mean anything, except what a majority of the Court wants it to mean on any given day. There was, of course, no explanation why the law in question was an "unwarranted" intrusion. The point to notice is that, once more, in-dividualism triumphed over majority morality.

THE COURT'S concern with sexuality has taken it into the subject of homosexual behavior. Justice Harry Blackmun's dissenting opinion in *Bowers* v. *Hardwick* (1986) is perhaps the leading example of judicial insistence upon an individualism so unconfined as to be useless for any practical purpose other than rhetorical bludgeoning. The majority upheld the con-stitutionality of making homosexual sodomy a criminal of-fense. Blackmun's dissent dismissed the relevance of prior cases that seemed to confine the claimed "right of privacy" to the protection of the family: "We protect those rights not be-cause they contribute, in some direct and material way, to the general public welfare, but because they form so central a part of an individual's life." This casual dismissal of the family, heretofore considered the most important unit of society, was in keeping with the modern attitudes of the intellectual class. On Blackmun's reasoning, since the individual is all, no-fault divorce must be a constitutional right. But he immediately went on to make matters worse: "[T]he concept of privacy embodies 'the moral fact that a person belongs to himself and not others nor to society as a whole.'" In short, the individual owes nothing to family, neighborhood, friends, nation, or anything outside his own skin, if that would interfere with his own pleasures. The four justices who signed the dissent cannot really have meant that, of course, but the fact that it could be written at all shows how far committed to individualism some of the justices have become.

Romer v. *Evans* (1996) took the next step and overruled *Bowers* without mentioning that case. By referendum the citizens of Colorado amended the state constitution to prevent localities from adding sexual orientation to the list of characteristics—race, sex, etc.—that were protected from private discrimination. The Court struck down the amendment on the theory that it treated homosexuals differently from other protected groups and thus violated the Equal Protection Clause. The rationale can best be described as incoherent. In order to gain legal immunity from private discrimination, homosexuals would have to seek it at the state level while the other groups would not. The fact is, of course, that all statewide or national laws require some groups to go beyond local government in order to change those laws. The Bill of Rights itself states principles that cannot be changed except by constitutional amendment. The most that can be made of *Romer* is that homosexuality is now a subject of special judicial solicitude. Individuals must be free to engage in homosexual behavior regardless of the community's moral standards.

A number of observers predict that within a few years the Court will announce that the principle of equality requires a constitutional right to same-sex marriage. If Jane is free to marry John, why doesn't equal protection require that Fred be equally able to marry John? Two state courts, of course, have already taken that step, to the intense displeasure of their citizens.

Since the Court is a central prize in the culture war, the fight to control it is political, engaging the White House and the Senate. There is, however, an equally important arena consisting of academic lawyers and pressure groups. These are heavily on the side of the emancipationists or liberals. Their tactic is frequently to insist, contrary to obvious reality, that the Supreme Court is dominated by conservatives.

Harvard's Laurence Tribe, for example, calls the current Justices "the most activist in our history." He said that "the astonishing weakness and vulnerability of the majority opinion in *Bush* v. *Gore*, and of the majority opinions in a number of other democracy-denying decisions in whose mold it was cast, are functions in part of the uniquely narrow spectrum of views . . . covered by the membership of the current Court." It must come as a revelation to the Justices themselves to learn that Stevens and Souter advance almost the same views as Scalia and Thomas. Tribe describes the Court's makeup as "four justices distinctly on the right, two moderate conservatives, a conservative moderate, two moderates, and no liberals." Cass Sunstein of Chicago states that today's Court has no liberals, which can only be true if he defines liberals as extreme radicals. Yale's Bruce Ackerman urges the Senate not to confirm anyone nominated by George Bush.

It is only on the misunderstanding that the proper function of judges is to advance an ideological agenda that Abner Mikva, once a judge on the court on which I sat and later counsel to President Clinton, can urge the Senate not to confirm any Bush nominees to the Court because that might disturb the "delicate balance on the court on fundamental issues." That "delicate balance" means a Court that is predominantly liberal. In his next sentence, Mikva clarifies the balance he praises by noting, with obvious approval, that the Warren Court, which was heavily liberal, made fundamental changes by substantial majorities. Balance is desirable only when a Republican president might tip the Court in a neutral direction. When liberals say "balance" they mean a Court that will rewrite the Constitution to make it ever more liberal.

It is hard not to think such remarks disingenuous. The Court as a whole lists heavily to the cultural left. A "narrow spectrum of views" hardly describes a Court that though it splits on important cultural issues, almost invariably comes down on the liberal side and whose members regularly denounce one another in heated terms. Tribe himself rebuts his narrow-spectrum description by saying that "the recurring 5–4 majority on the Court on these matters has become a genuine threat to our system of government." How close votes threaten our system of government is unspecified. That Tribe is committed to the judicial activism he decries is demonstrated by his four (at last count) attempts to find an acceptable rationale for *Roe* v. *Wade*. The problem is not that he fails—success is impossible—but that he will not stop trying. Abortion must be a constitutional right even if no one can explain why.

The interest groups of the Left proceed by systematic lying about judicial nominees who adopt the traditional approach of interpreting the Constitution according to its actual meaning. In opposing Judge Pickering, Ralph Neas of the hard-left People for the American Way said, "Achieving ideological domination of the federal judiciary is the top goal of right-wing activists inside and outside the Bush administration." The left wing has discovered an effective tactic of labeling any conventional jurist an ideologue with a right-wing agenda and hence "outside the mainstream."

In this enterprise, the left wing is abetted by its academic branch. There is far more diversity of opinion on the Court than is to be found on law school faculties. In the last three decades, as the students of the Sixties became professors, law scholarship has become increasingly left wing and intellectually disordered. Faculties are less and less engaged in scholarship that might conceivably be of use to practitioners and judges or to the reform of legal doctrine. As Harry Edwards, formerly chief judge of the Court of Appeals for the District of Columbia Circuit, put it, "there is a growing disjunction between legal education and the legal profession," which is reflected in the gradual replacement of older, traditional scholars by younger faculty whose work is often so theoretical as to be of little use outside the coterie of like-minded professors who engage in impractical discourse. The division, Edwards says, "is permeated by rancor, contempt and ill will." The newer scholarship is politically motivated: "Many, although not all, of the legal theorists would like to bring about a radical transformation of society. In many cases, their work amounts to an attack on classical liberalism, which they would like to see replaced with a philosophical or political theory that will lead to a much more egalitarian society."

Arthur Austin, a professor of jurisprudence at Case Western Reserve University, reports, "Reading hundreds of articles in researching a book on legal scholarship confirms that politically correct writing appears with increasing frequency." In the university community, he writes, political correctness "is associated with language modification, oppression studies, race and gender victimization, rejection of the white male canon," which it sees as a culture of "objectivity and rationality." This began with the critical legal studies movement which attempted to deconstruct the intellectual foundations of existing law and traditional legal scholarship, without, however, indicating what might be substituted. A liberal professor states that "critical legal studies is a political location for a group of people on the Left who share the project of supporting and extending the domain of the Left in the legal academy." Austin says that the advocates of political correctness now come from "Critical Race theorists, composed of Blacks and females, feminists, plus the remnants of the Critical Legal Studies movement." Austin continues: "One of the more esteemed techniques is the use of personal experiences to convey the emotion and agony of persevering in an alien environment of patriarchy, hierarchy, and objectification." Thus some work of "scholars" consists of storytelling. Their narratives are published in law reviews and have been sufficient for the award of tenure. This intellectual collapse is now praised as "postmodern jurisprudence," a term that itself ought to be an embarrassment to the legal academics involved.

There have emerged almost innumerable competing theories of how the Constitution should be "interpreted." None of these has proved satisfactory to the competing theorists so that now we have reached a state of advanced nihilism in which articles and books are written on the impossibility of all normative theories of constitutional law or the "misguided quest for constitutional foundations." Were these counsels of despair accurate, the only honest conclusion would be that since they cannot make sense of what they are doing, judges should abandon judicial review altogether. That conclusion is never drawn, however. Constitutional law is about power, and professors will never relinquish their bit of that power.

IF THE LEGAL academy is hopeless, one might suppose that at least some Justices would by now have undertaken a justification for their habitual departures from any conceivable meaning of the Constitution they claim as their authority. But search as one may, the opinions of the Court are utterly devoid of any such attempt. The most the Court has ever offered is the statement that it has never felt its power confined by the original understanding of the document. That much is certainly true, but it is hardly a justification. Persistent invasions of territory belonging to the people and their elected representatives cannot establish an easement across territory that the Constitution assigns to the democratic process.

It is not obvious what, if anything, can be done to bring the American judiciary back to legitimacy in a polity whose basic character is supposed to be democratic. It was once argued that a wayward Court would be corrected by professional criticism. The bar, however, is largely uninterested and academic constitutional commentary is largely intellectually corrupt.

Perhaps there is no remedy for judicial activism, perhaps a preference for immediate victories and short-term gratification of desires is characteristic of the spirit of our times. The public does seem ready to jettison long-term safeguards and the benefits of process for the short-term satisfaction of desires. That is always and everywhere the human temptation. But it is precisely that temptation that a constitution and its judicial spokesmen are supposed to protect us against. Constitutions speak for permanent values and judges are supposed to give those values voice. Instead, representatives of our judiciary are all too often, and increasingly, exemplars of disrespect for the rule of law. That situation is inconsistent with the survival of the culture that has for so long sustained American freedom and well-being. The example of lawless courts teaches a lesson of disrespect for process to all other actors in that system, the lesson that winning outside the rules is legitimate, and that political victory is the only virtue.

Born in Europe, central to the American founding, and fundamental to Western civilization, the ideal of the rule of law no longer commands much more than verbal allegiance. If prophecies of what the Court will do in fact is the meaning of law, then, in cultural matters the law may be predicted by the known personal inclinations of the Justices, nothing more pretentious. That is not the rule of law; it is the rule of judges. It would have been unthinkable until recently that so many areas of our national life would be controlled by judges. What is today unthinkable may well become not only thinkable but also actual in the next half century.

The liberal mindset refuses to recognize that real institutions can never approximate their ideal institutions. The pursuit of the ideal necessarily proceeds by and teaches an abstract, universalistic style of reasoning and legal argument. It leads to an incessant harping on rights that impoverishes political, cultural, and legal discourse. Universalistic rhetoric teaches disrespect for the actual institutions of the nation. Those institutions slow change, allow compromise, tame absolutisms, and thus embody inconsistencies that are, on balance, wholesome. They work, in short, to do things, albeit democratically and therefore messily, that abstract generalizations about the just society bring into contempt.

A Court that in one context after another lays down general principles of emancipation commends that principle to public attention and imitation and thus affects legislative opinion. Many people assume that what is legal is also moral, and they are all too likely to believe that what has been declared unconstitutional is immoral. Resistance to judicial imperialism in the name of the Constitution itself comes to be seen as immoral.

Writing last year in *The Wall Street Journal*, Charles Murray reflected on Arnold Toynbee's thesis about the decline of civilizations. One reliable sign of decline, Toynbee suggested, was when elites began to imitate those at the bottom of society. In robust societies, those at the bottom tend to imitate "their betters"—a phrase whose departure from common usage betokens the degradation Toynbee prophesied. One does not have to look far to see the vulgarization of the elites in contemporary American society. There is no more elite institution in America than the Supreme Court of the United States. The sampling of cases discussed here suggests that the Court is ahead of the general public in approving, and to a degree enforcing, the vulgarization or proletarianization of our culture.

Yet it is precisely that for which the Court is most admired by the intelligentsia and in our law schools. The names of

Warren, Douglas, and Brennan are enshrined in the liberal pantheon. Justices who performed their duties more faithfully are often less well-known or even almost entirely forgotten. The career of Chief Justice Morrison Waite is a case in point. Probably not one in twenty law professors and not one in a hundred lawyers even recognizes his name. Yet Professor Felix Frankfurter, in praising Waite, identified the characteristic judicial sin: "When dealing with such large conceptions as the rights and duties of property, judges lacking some governing directions are easily lost in the fog of abstraction." That may be even more true today as the Court multiplies vaguely defined rights.

Frankfurter said that Waite has become

> a dim figure in constitutional history because his opinions are not delectable reading. . . . But the limited appeal of his opinions is due in part to something else—to the fulfillment of one of the greatest duties of a judge, the duty not to enlarge his authority. . . . The distinction between those who are makers of policy and those concerned solely with questions [of the Constitution's allocations] of ultimate power probably marks the deepest cleavage among the men who have sat on the Supreme Bench. . . . The conception of significant achievement on the Supreme Court has been too much identified with largeness of utterance, and too little governed by inquiry into the extent to which judges have fulfilled their professed role in the American constitutional system.

Unless it takes its law from the original understanding of the Constitution's principles, the Court will continue to be an adversary to democratic government and to the morality of our traditional culture.

The Fortunes of Permanence
by Roger Kimball

Do not be proud of the fact that your grandmother was shocked at some-thing which you are accustomed to seeing or hearing without being shocked. . . . It may be that your grandmother was an extremely lively and vital animal, and that you are a paralytic.
—G. K. Chesterton, *As I Was Saying*

How but in custom and in ceremony
Are innocence and beauty born?
Ceremony's a name for the rich horn,
And custom the spreading laurel tree.
—W. B. Yeats, "A Prayer for My Daughter"

"Seven and a half hours of mild, unexhausting labour, and then the soma *ration and games and unrestricted copulation and the feelies. What more can they ask for?"*
—Mustapha Mond in Huxley's *Brave New World*

I REMEMBER the first time I noticed the legend "cultural instructions" on the brochure that accompanied some seedlings. "How quaint," I thought, as I pursued the advisory: this much water and that much sun, certain tips about fer-tilizer, soil, and drainage. Planting one sort of flower nearby keeps the bugs away but proximity to another sort makes bad things happen. Young shoots might need stakes, and watch out for beetles, weeds, and unseasonable frosts. . . .

The more I pondered it, the less quaint, the more profound, those cultural instructions seemed. I suppose I had once known that the word "culture" comes from the capacious Latin verb "*colo*," which means everything from "live, dwell, inhabit," to "observe a religious rite" (whence our word "cult"), "care, tend, nurture," and "promote the growth or advancement of." I never thought much about it.

I should have. There is a lot of wisdom in etymology. The noun "*cultura*" (which derives from *colo*) means first of all "the tilling or cultivation of land" and "the care or cultivation of plants." But it, too, has ambitious tentacles: "the observance of a religious rite," "well groomed" (of hair), "smart" (of someone's appearance), "chic, polished, sophisticated" (of a literary or intellectual style).

It was Cicero, in a famous passage of the *Tusculan Disputations*, who gave currency to the metaphor of culture as a specifically intellectual pursuit. "Just as a field, however good the ground, cannot be productive without cultivation, so the soul cannot be productive without education." Philosophy, he said, is a sort of "*cultura animi*," a cultivation of the mind or spirit: "it pulls out vices by the roots," "makes souls fit for the reception of seed," and sows in order to bring forth "the richest fruit." But even the best care, he warned, does not inevitably bring good results: the influence of education, of *cultura animi*, "cannot be the same for all: its effect is great when it has secured a hold upon a character suited to it." The results of cultivation depend not only on the quality of the care but the inherent nature of the thing being cultivated. How much of what Cicero said do we still understand?

In current parlance, "culture" (in addition to its use as a biological term) has both a descriptive and an evaluative meaning. In its anthropological sense, "culture" is neutral. It describes the habits and customs of a particular population: what its members do, not what they should do. Its task is to inventory, to docket, not judge.

But we also speak of "high culture," meaning not just social practices but a world of artistic, intellectual, and moral endeavor in which the notion of hierarchy, of a rank-ordering of accomplishment, is integral. (More etymology: "hierarchy" derives from words meaning "sacred order." Egalitarians are opposed to hierarchies in principle; what does that tell us about egalitarianism?) Culture in the evaluative sense does not merely admit, it requires judgment as a kind of coefficient or auxiliary: comparison, discrimination, evaluation are its lifeblood. "We never really get near a book," Henry James remarked in an essay on American letters, "save on the question of its being good or bad, of its really treating, that is, or not treating, its subject." It was for the sake of culture in this sense that Matthew Arnold extolled criticism as "the disinterested endeavour to learn and propagate the best that is known and thought in the world."

It is of course culture in the Arnoldian sense that we have primarily in view when we speak of "the survival of culture." And it is the fate of culture in this sense that I will be chiefly concerned with in this essay. But it would be foolish to draw too firm a distinction between the realms of culture. There is much confluence and interchange between them. Ultimately, they exist symbiotically, nurturing, supplementing, contending with each other. The manners, habits, rituals, institutions, and patterns of behavior that define culture for the anthropologist provide the sediment, the ground out of which culture in the Arnoldian sense takes root—or fails to take root. Failure or degradation in one area instigates failure or degradation in the other. (Some people regard the astonishing collapse of manners and civility in our society as a superficial event. They are wrong. The fate of decorum expresses the fate of a culture's dignity, its attitude toward its animating values.)

THE PROBLEM with metaphors is not that they are false but that they do not tell the whole truth. The organic image of culture we have inherited from Cicero is illuminating. Among other things, it reminds us that we do not exist as self-sufficient atoms but have our place in a continuum that stretches before and after us in time. Like other metaphors, however, it can be elevated into an absurdity if it is pushed too far. Oswald Spengler's sprawling, two-volume lament, *The Decline of the West*, is a good illustration of what happens when genius is captivated by a metaphor. Spengler's book, published in the immediate aftermath of World War I, epitomized the end-of-everything mood of the times and was hailed as the brilliant key to understanding—well, just about everything. And Spengler really is brilliant. For example, his remarks about how the triumph of scepticism breeds a "second religiousness" in which "men dispense with proof, desire only to believe and not to dissect," have great pertinence to an age, like ours, that is awash in new-age spiritual counterfeits. Nevertheless, Spengler's deterministic allegiance to the analogy between civilizations and organisms ultimately infuses his discussion with an air of unreality. One is reminded, reading Spengler, of T. S. Eliot's definition of a heretic: "a person who seizes upon a truth and pushes it to the point at which it becomes a falsehood."

That said, for anyone who is concerned about the survival of culture, there are some important lessons in the armory of cultural instructions accompanying a humble tomato plant. Perhaps the chief lesson has to do with time and continuity, the evolving permanence that *cultura animi* no less than agricultural cultivation requires if it is to be successful. All those tips, habits, prohibitions, and necessities that have been accumulated from time out of mind and passed down, generation after generation: How much in our society militates against such antidotes to anarchy and decay!

Culture survives and develops under the aegis of permanence. And yet instantaneity—the enemy of permanence—is one of the chief imperatives of our time. It renders anything lasting, anything inherited, suspicious by definition. As Kenneth Minogue observed earlier in this volume, "The idea is that one not only lives for the present, but also *ought* to live thus." We want what is faster, newer, less encumbered by the past. If we also cultivate a nostalgia for a simpler, slower time, that just shows the extent to which we are separated from what, in our efforts to decorate our lives, we long for. Nostalgia (Greek for "homesickness") is a version of sentimentality —a predilection, that is to say, to distort rather than acknowledge reality.

The political philosopher Hannah Arendt dilated on one essential aspect of the problem when she argued against taking an instrumental, "self-help" approach to culture. "What is at stake here," Arendt observed in "The Crisis in Culture,"

> is the objective status of the cultural world, which, insofar as it contains tangible things—books and paintings, statues, buildings, and music—comprehends, and gives testimony to, the entire recorded past of countries, nations, and ultimately mankind. As such, the only nonsocial and authentic criterion for judging these specifically cultural things is their relative permanence and even eventual immortality. Only what will last through the centuries can ultimately claim to be a cultural object. The point of the matter is that, as soon as the immortal works of the past became the object of social and individual refinement and the status accorded to it, they lost their most important and elemental quality, which is to grasp and move the reader or the spectator over the centuries.

The "objective status" of the cultural world to which Arendt appeals is precisely the aspect of culture we find hardest to accommodate. If there is a "nonsocial and authentic criterion" for judging cultural achievements, then what happens to the ideology of equivalence that has become such a powerful force in Western societies? Are we not committed to the proposition that *all* values are social? Isn't this part of what social constructionists like Richard Rorty mean when they say language goes "all the way down"? That there is no self, no value, no achievement, no criteria independent of the twitterings of fashion, which in turn are ultimately the twitterings of social power?

The attack on permanence comes in many guises. When trendy literary critics declare that "there is no such thing as intrinsic meaning," they are denying permanent values that transcend the prerogatives of their lucubrations. When a deconstructionist tells us that truth is relative to language, or to power, or to certain social arrangements, he seeks to trump the unanswerable claims of permanent realities with the vacillations of his ingenuity. When the multiculturalist celebrates the fundamental equality of all cultures—excepting, of course, the culture of the West, which he reflexively disparages—he substitutes ephemeral political passions for the recognition of objective cultural achievement. "A pair of boots," a nineteenth-century Russian slogan tells us, "is worth more than Shakespeare." We have here a process of leveling that turns out to be a revolution in values. The implication, as the French philosopher Alain Finkielkraut observed, is that

> the footballer and the choreographer, the painter and the couturier, the writer and the ad-man, the musician and the rock-and-roller, are all the same: creators. We must scrap the prejudice which restricts that title to certain people and regards others as sub-cultural.

But what seems at first to be an effort to establish cultural parity turns out to be a campaign for cultural reversal. When Sir Elton John is put on the same level as Bach, the effect is not cultural equality but cultural insurrection. (If it seems farfetched to compare Elton John and Bach, recall the literary critic Richard Poirier's remark, in *Partisan Review* in 1967, that "sometimes [the Beatles] are like Monteverdi and sometimes their songs are even better than Schumann's.") It might also be worth asking what had to happen in English society for there to be such a thing as "Sir Elton John." What does *that* tell us about the survival of culture? But some subjects are too painful. Let us draw a veil. . . .

"The history of philosophy," Jean-François Revel observed in *The Flight from Truth* (1991), "can be divided into two different periods. During the first, philosophers sought the truth; during the second, they fought against it." That fight has escaped from the parlors of professional sceptics and has increasingly become the moral coin of the realm. As Anthony Daniels observed in his essay for this volume, it is now routine for academics and intellectuals to use "all the instruments of an exaggerated scepticism . . . not to find truth but to destroy traditions, customs, institutions, and confidence in the worth of civilization itself." The most basic suppositions and distinctions suddenly crumble, like the acidic pages of a poorly made book, eaten away from within. "*A rebours*" becomes the rallying cry of the anti-cultural cultural elite. Culture degenerates from being a *cultura animi* to a *corruptio animi*.

ALDOUS HUXLEY's *Brave New World* may be a second-rate novel—its characters wooden, its narrative overly didactic—but it has turned out to have been first-rate prognostication. Published in 1932, it touches everywhere on twenty-first-century anxieties. Perhaps the aspect of Huxley's dystopian—what to call it: fable? prophecy? admonition?—that is most frequently adduced is its vision of a society that has perfected what we have come to call genetic engineering. Among other things, it is a world in which reproduction has been entirely handed over to the experts. The word "parents" no longer describes a loving moral commitment but only an attenuated biological datum. Babies are not born but designed according to exacting specifications and "decanted" at sanitary depots like The Central London Hatchery and Conditioning Centre with which the book opens.

As with all efforts to picture future technology, Huxley's description of the equipment and procedures employed at the hatchery seems almost charmingly antiquated, like a space ship imagined by Jules Verne. But Huxley's portrait of the human toll of human ingenuity is very up-to-date. Indeed, we have not—not quite, not yet—caught up with the situation he describes. We do not—not quite, not yet—inhabit a world where "mother" and "monogamy" are blasphemous terms from which people have been conditioned to recoil in visceral revulsion. Maybe it will never come to that. (Though monogamy, of course, has long been high on the social and sexual revolutionary's list of hated institutions.) Still, it is a nice question whether developments in reproductive technology will not soon make other aspects of Huxley's fantasy a reality. Thinkers as different as Michel Foucault and Francis Fukuyama have pondered the advent of a "posthuman" future, eagerly or with dismay, as the case may be. Scientists busily manipulating DNA may give substance to their speculations. It is often suggested that what is most disturbing about *Brave New World* is its portrait of eugenics in action: its vision of humanity deliberately divided into genetically ordered castes, a few super-smart Alpha-pluses down through a multitude of drone-like Epsilons who do the heavy lifting. Such deliberately instituted inequality offends our democratic sensibilities.

What is sometimes overlooked or downplayed is the possibility that the most disturbing aspect of the future Huxley pictured has less to do with eugenics than genetics. That is to say, perhaps what is centrally repellent about Huxley's hatcheries is not that they codify inequality—nature already does that effectively—but that they exist at all. Are they not a textbook example of Promethean hubris in action? It is worth stepping back to ponder that possibility.

In the seventeenth century, Descartes predicted that his

scientific method would make man "the master and possessor of nature": are we not fast closing in on the technology that proves him right? And this raises another question. Is there a point at which scientific development can no longer be described, humanly, as progress? We know the benisons of technology. Consider only electricity, the automobile, modern medicine. They have transformed the world and underscored the old observation that art, that *techne*, is man's nature. Nevertheless, the question remains whether, after two hundred years of breathtaking progress, we are about to become more closely acquainted with the depredations of technology. It would take a brave man, or a rash one, to venture a confident prediction either way. For example, if, as in *Brave New World*, we manage to bypass the "inconvenience" of human pregnancy altogether, should we do it? If—or rather when— that is possible, will it also be desirable? Well, why not? Why should a woman go through the discomfort and danger of pregnancy if a fetus could be safely incubated, or cloned, elsewhere? Wouldn't motherhood by proxy be a good thing—the ultimate labor-saving device? Most readers will hesitate about saying yes. What does that tell us? Some readers will have no hesitation about saying yes; what does *that* tell us?[1]

As Huxley saw, a world in which reproduction was "rationalized" and emancipated from love was also a world in which culture in the Arnoldian sense was not only otiose but dangerous. This is also a sub-theme of that other great dystopian novel, George Orwell's *1984*, which ends with the work of "various writers, such as Shakespeare, Milton, Swift, Byron, Dickens," being vandalized by being translated into,

---

1 A recent article in *The Wall Street Journal* reported on the new popularity of using continuous birth-control pills or other methods to suppress women's menstrual cycles. The article quoted one obstetrician-gynecologist who, noting that most women in primitive societies had many more pregnancies than women today, argued that stopping monthly periods "gets women to a more natural state." Really?

Newspeak. When that laborious propaganda effort is finally complete, the "original writings, with all else that survived of the literature of the past, would be destroyed." The point is that culture has roots. It limns the future through its implications with the past. Moving the reader or spectator over the centuries, in Arendt's phrase, the monuments of culture transcend the local imperatives of the present. They escape the obsolescence that fashion demands, the predictability that planning requires. They speak of love and hatred, honor and shame, beauty and courage and cowardice—permanent realities of the human situation insofar as it remains human.

The denizens of Huxley's brave new world are designed and educated—perhaps his word, "conditioned," is more accurate—to be rootless, without culture. When a relic of the old order of civilization—a savage who had been born, not decanted—is brought from a reservation into the brave new world, he is surprised to discover that the literary past is forbidden to most of the population.

> "But why is it prohibited?" asked the Savage. In the excitement of meeting a man who had read Shakespeare he had momentarily forgotten everything else.
>
> The Controller shrugged his shoulders. "Because it's old; that's the chief reason. We haven't any use for old things here."
>
> "Even when they're beautiful?"
>
> "Particularly when they're beautiful. Beauty's attractive, and we don't want people to be attracted by old things. We want them to like the new ones."

Huxley's brave new world is above all a superficial world. People are encouraged to like what is new, to live in the moment, because that makes them less complicated and more pliable. Emotional commitments are even more strictly rationed than Shakespeare. (The same, again, is true of *1984*.) In the place of emotional commitments, sensations—thrilling, mind-numbing sensations—are available on demand through drugs and motion pictures that neurologically stimulate viewers to experience certain emotions and feelings. The fact that they are artificially produced is not a drawback but their very point. Which is to say that the brave new world is a virtual world: experience is increasingly vivid but decreasingly real. The question of meaning is deliberately short-circuited. "You've got to choose," the Resident World Controller for Western Europe patiently explains to the Savage,

> "between happiness and what people used to call high art. We've sacrificed the high art. We have the feelies and the scent organ instead."
> "But they don't mean anything."
> "They mean themselves; they mean a lot of agreeable sensations to the audience."

If this seems like a prescription for arrested development, that, too, is part of the point: "It is their duty to be infantile," the Controller explains, "even against their inclination." Promiscuity is encouraged because it is a prophylactic against emotional depth. The question of meaning is never pursued beyond the instrumental question of what produces the most pleasure. Socrates told us that the unexamined life is not worth living. Huxley (yet again like Orwell) pictures a world in which the unexamined life is the only one available.

Huxley's imagination failed him in one area. He understood that in a world in which reproduction was emancipated from the body, sexual congress would degenerate into a purely recreational activity, an amusement not inherently different from one's *soma* ration or the tactile movies. He pictured a world of casual, indeed mandatory, promiscuity. But he thought it would develop along completely conventional lines. He ought to have known that the quest for "agreeable sensations" would issue in a pansexual carnival. In this area, anyway, we seem to have proceeded a good deal further than the characters who inhabit Huxley's dystopia.

In part, the attack on permanence is an attack on the idea that anything possesses inherent value. Absolute fungibility— the substitution of anything for anything—is the ideal. In one sense, this is a product of what the philosopher Michael Oakeshott criticized as "rationalism." "To the Rationalist," Oakeshott wrote in the late 1940s, "nothing is of value merely because it exists (and certainly not because it has existed for many generations), familiarity has no worth and nothing is to be left standing for want of scrutiny." The realm of sexuality is one area where the effects of such rationalism are dramatically evident. It was not so long ago that the description from Genesis—"male and female created he them"—was taken as a basic existential fact. True, the obstinacy of sexual difference has always been a thorn in the side of utopian rationalism. But it is only in recent decades that the engines of judicial meddlesomeness, on the one hand, and surgical know-how, on the other, have effectively assaulted that once permanent-seeming reality.

For an illustration of how sexual politics has been enlisted in the attack on permanence, consider the recently acquired habit of using the term "gender" when we mean "sex." This may seem an innocent, nearly a euphemistic, innovation. But it is not innocent. It issues not from any residual sense of modesty about sexual matters but from a hubristic effort to reduce sex to gender. The term "gender" has its home in grammar: it names a certain linguistic convention. Sex describes a basic biological division. As the columnist George Will noted recently, the substitution of "gender" for "sex" is so widespread because it suggests that sexual differences are themselves a matter of convention—"socially constructed" and therefore susceptible to social deconstruction: susceptible to being "erased by sufficiently determined social engineers." A powerful legal tool in the campaign to substitute gender for sex is Title IX, which celebrated its thirtieth anniversary in May 2002. Written to prohibit discrimination on the basis of sex, it has, in the hands of what Will calls "Title IX fanatics," become a legal bludgeon that is wielded to deny the reality of sexual differences. It has already been used to gut the athletic programs of hundreds of schools and colleges across the country; the next target, Will suggests, will be the curriculum: if a college has an engineering department, it must also have proportional representation of the sexes—sorry, the genders—in that department. Anything less would be an insult to the ideal of equality.

A more florid example of sexual fungibility at work is the explosion of interest in—indeed, the incipient normalization of—"gender reassignment surgery" and other adventures in sexual plasticity. A glance at the personal ads of any "alternative" newspaper—to say nothing of internet sex sites—will reveal a burgeoning sexual demi-monde where the "transsexual," "pansexual," and "virtually sexual" heartily compete with more traditional promiscuities.

Nor are such phenomena confined to such "help wanted" venues. Headline from a California newspaper in summer 2001: "San Francisco is about to embark on another first in the nation: providing health care benefits for city workers undergoing sex-change procedures." "Oh, well," you say: "It's California, what do you expect?" Here's another headline: "Britain's free health care service should provide sex-change operations for transsexuals because they suffer from a legitimate illness, a court has ruled." Not to be left behind, *The New York Times* Sunday magazine recently ran a long and sympathetic cover story about a "transgendered" thirteen-year-old who, though born as a girl, has lived for the last several years as a boy.

Real-life transsexuals are what we might call the objective correlative of an increasingly prominent strand in our culture's fantasy life. Consider, to take just one example, the British artists Dinos and Jake Chapman. Their signature works are pubescent female mannequins studded with erect penises, vaginas, and anuses, fused together in various postures of sexual congress. The thing to notice is not how outrageous but how common such items are. The Chapman brothers are not a back-alley, plain-brown-wrapper phenomenon. Their works are exhibited in major, once staid, galleries like the Royal Academy in London and the Brooklyn Museum in New York. They are "transgressive," all right. But the point is that the transgressions they announce have been to a large extent domesticated and welcomed into the mainstream. It would be bootless to multiply examples—readers will doubtless have lists of their own. Hardly anyone is shocked anymore, but that is a testament not to public enlightenment but to widespread moral anaesthesia. (The question of aesthetics, of distinctively artistic achievement, does not even enter the calculation: what does that tell us?)

What we are seeing in sexual life is the fulfillment, in some segments of society, of the radical emancipatory vision enunciated in the 1960s by such gurus as Herbert Marcuse and Norman O. Brown. In *Eros and Civilization* Marcuse looked forward to the establishment of a "non-repressive reality principle" in which "the body in its entirety would become . . . an instrument of pleasure." The sexual liberation Marcuse hailed was not a fecund liberation. As in *Brave New World*, children do not enter into the equation. The issue is pleasure, not progeny. Marcuse speaks glowingly of "a resurgence of pregenital polymorphous sexuality" that "protests against the repressive order of procreative sexuality." A look at the alarmingly low birth rates of most affluent nations today suggests that the protest has been effective. When Tocqueville warned about the peculiar form of despotism that threatened democracy, he noted that instead of tyrannizing men, as past despotisms had done, it tended to infantilize them, keeping "them fixed irrevocably in childhood." What Tocqueville warned about, Marcuse celebrated, extolling the benefits of returning to a state of "primary narcissism" in which one will find "the redemption of pleasure, the halt of time, the absorption of death; silence, sleep, night, paradise—the Nirvana principle not as death but as life." What Marcuse encouraged, in other words, is solipsism, not as a philosophical principle but as a moral indulgence, a way of life.

It is often said that we are entering the "information age." There is doubtless some truth in that. But what does it mean? The shocking bulletins appear with clocklike regularity: students seem to know less and less history, less and less mathematics, less and less literature, less and less geography. In May 2002, Diane Ravitch bemoaned the "truly abysmal scores" high-school seniors made in an American history examination: only one in ten did well enough to be considered proficient in the subject. The week before, some other report had bad news about other students and some other subject. A look in the papers today will reveal yet another depressing finding about the failure of education.

Welcome to the information age. Data, data everywhere, but no one knows a thing. In the West, at least, practically everybody has instant access to huge databases and news-retrieval services, to say nothing of television and other media. With a few clicks of the mouse we can bring up every line of Shakespeare that contains the word "darkling" or the complete texts of Aeschylus in Greek or in translation. Information about contract law in ancient Rome or yesterday's developments in microchip technology in Japan is at our fingertips. If we are traveling to Paris, we can book our airline ticket and hotel reservation online, check the local weather, and find out the best place to have dinner near the Place des Vosges. We can correspond and exchange documents with friends on the other side of the globe in the twinkling of an eye. Our command of information is staggering.

And yet with that command comes a great temptation. Partly, it is the temptation to confuse an excellent means of communication with communications that are excellent. We confuse, that is to say, process with product. What Eric Ormsby observed about contemporary librarians in his essay for this volume goes for the rest of us: our fascination with means has led us "to ignore and neglect the ends."

That is not the only confusion. There is also a tendency to confuse propinquity with possession. The fact that some text is available online or on CD-ROM does not mean that one has read and absorbed its contents. When I was in graduate school, there were always students who tended to suppose that by making a Xerox copy of some document they had also read, or half-read, or at least looked into it. Today that same tendency is exacerbated by high-speed internet access. We can download a veritable library of material to our computer in a few minutes; that does not mean we have mastered its riches. Information is not synonymous with knowledge, let alone wisdom.

This is not a new insight. At the end of the *Phaedrus*, Plato has Socrates tell the story of the god Theuth, who, legend has it, invented the art of writing. When Theuth presented his new invention to the king of Egypt, he promised the king that it would make his people "wiser and improve their memories." But the king disagreed, claiming that the habit of writing, far from improving memories, would "implant forgetfulness" by encouraging people to rely on external marks rather than "the living speech graven in the soul."

WELL, NONE OF US would wish to do without writing—or computers, come to that. Nor, I think, would Plato have wanted us to. (Though he would probably have been severe about television. That bane of intelligence could have been ordered up specially to illustrate Plato's idea that most people inhabit a kind of existential "cave" in which they mistake flickering images for realities.) Plato's indirect comments— through the mouth of Socrates recounting an old story he picked up somewhere—have less to do with writing (an art, after all, in which Plato excelled) than with the priority of im- mediate experience: the "living speech graven in the soul."

Plato may have been an idealist. But here as elsewhere he appears as an apostle of vital, first-hand experience: a realist in the deepest sense of the term.

The problem with computers is not the worlds they give us instant access to but the world they encourage us to neglect. Everyone knows about the studies showing the bad effects on children and teenagers of too much time in cyberspace (or, indeed, in front of the television set). It cuts them off from their family and friends, fosters asocial behavior, disrupts their ability to concentrate, and makes it harder for them to distinguish between fantasy and reality. I suspect, however, that the real problem is not so much the sorry cases that make headlines but a more generally disseminated attitude toward the world.

When I entered the phrase "virtual reality," the Google search engine (at last count, 2,073,418,204 pages indexed) returned 1,260,000 hits in .12 seconds. There are many, many organizations like the Virtual Reality Society, "an international society dedicated to the discussion and advancement of virtual reality and synthetic environments." Computer simulations, video games, special effects: in some areas of life, virtual reality seems to be crowding out the other variety. It gives a whole new significance to Villiers de L'Isle-Adam's world-weary mot: *Vivre? Les serviteurs feront cela pour nous.*

The issue is not, or not only, the digital revolution—the sudden explosion of computers and e-mail and the internet. It is rather the effect of such developments on our moral and imaginative life, and even our cognitive life. Why bother to get Shakespeare by heart when you can look it up in a nonce on the internet? One reason, of course, is that a passage memorized is a passage internalized: it becomes part of the mental sustenance of the soul. It's the difference between a living limb and a crutch.

It used to be said that in dreams begin responsibilities. What responsibilities does a virtual world inspire? Virtual responsibilities, perhaps: responsibilities undertaken on spec, as it were. A virtual world is a world that can be created, manipulated, and dissolved at will. It is a world whose reverberations are subject to endless revision. The Delete key is always available. Whatever is done can be undone. Whatever is undone can be redone.

Of course, as the meditations of Huxley in the 1930s and Marcuse in the 1960s suggest, computers and the internet do not create the temptations of virtual reality; they merely exacerbate those temptations. They magnify a perennial human possibility. Human beings do not need cyberspace to book a vacation from reality. The problem is not computers or indeed any particular technology but rather our disposition toward the common world that culture defines. When we ask about the survival of culture and the fortunes of permanence, we are asking about the fate of that common world. In many respects it is a political question—or, more precisely, a question regarding the limits of politics. When Susan Sontag, in the mid-1960s, championed the "new sensibility" she saw erupting across American society, she rightly observed that its representatives "have broken, whether they know it or not, with the Matthew Arnold notion of culture, finding it historically and humanly obsolescent."

What exactly is the "Matthew Arnold notion of culture" that Sontag and her cadre of hip intellectuals rejected as outmoded and irrelevant? For one thing, as we have seen, it is culture understood as a repository of mankind's noblest spiritual and intellectual aspirations: "the best," as Arnold put it, "that has been thought and said in the world." The "Matthew Arnold notion of culture" is thus a hierarchical idea of culture—a vision of culture as a "sacred order" whose majesty depends on its relevance to our deepest cares and concerns.

A second feature of the "Matthew Arnold notion of culture" is its independence—what Arnold summed up in the term "disinterestedness." Criticism achieves disinterestedness, Arnold said, by keeping aloof from what is called "the practical view of things"; by resolutely following the law of its own nature, which is to be a free play of the mind on all subjects which it touches. By steadily refusing to lend itself to any of those ulterior, political, practical considerations about ideas . . .

Understood in one way, Arnold's ideal of disinterestedness— with its emphasis on "a free play of the mind on all subjects"—might seem to be a prescription for moral quietism or frivolous aestheticism. What rescues it from that fundamental unseriousness is Arnold's unwavering commitment to truth and honesty. The business of criticism, he said, is to know and propagate the best, to "create a current of true and fresh ideas," and "to do this with inflexible honesty." It tells us a great deal about the state of culture that Arnold's demanding ideal of disinterestedness is not merely neglected but actively repudiated by many influential academics and intellectuals today.

A third feature of the "Matthew Arnold notion of culture" is its immediacy, its emphasis not on virtual but on first-hand experience. "Here," Arnold noted, "the great safeguard is never to let oneself become abstract, always to retain an intimate and lively consciousness of the truth of what one is saying, and, the moment this fails us, to be sure that something is wrong." The "Matthew Arnold notion of culture," then, comes armed with a sixth sense against the seductions of the spurious, the attractions of the ersatz.

Ultimately, what Sontag had against Arnold's view of culture was its earnestness, its seriousness. When she celebrated the Camp sensibility, she did so largely because in Camp she found a nimble ally in her effort "to dethrone the serious." Her praise of pop culture, pornography, and the pullulating ephemera of the counterculture must be understood as part of her battle against seriousness as traditionally defined. We have here that curious compact of moral levity and grim self-absorption that has characterized so many partisans of "advanced" opinion from Oscar Wilde on down to our own time. Redacted by the political passions of the 1960s, that strange compact resulted in the vertiginous relativisms that have overpopulated the academy, the art world, and other bastions of elite culture throughout Western society.

Part of what makes those relativisms vertiginous is their inconsistency. What we see in contemporary culture is relativism with a vengeance. It is a *directed*, activist relativism, forgiving and nonjudgmental about anything hostile to the perpetuation of traditional Western culture, full of self-righteous retribution when it comes to individuals and institutions friendly to the West. It incubates what Mark Steyn described above as "the slyer virus": "the vague sense that the West's success must somehow be responsible for the rest's failure." It is in effect a sort of secularized Jansenism: we are always in the wrong, not in the eyes of God but in the eyes of the exotic Other as imagined by us.

IT HAS LONG been obvious that "multiculturalism" is an ornate synonym for "anti-Americanism." It is anti-Americanism on a peculiar moralistic jag. Its effect has been to pervert institutions hitherto entrusted with the preservation and transmission of our spiritual, political, and intellectual heritage. The institutions persist, but their purpose is stymied. Wherever we look—at our schools and colleges, at our churches, museums, courts, and legislatures—we see well under way a process of abdication: a process whereby institutions created to protect certain values have been "deconstructed" and turned against the very things they were meant to preserve.

Consider what has happened to the judiciary. In any society that enjoys the rule of law, courts are a custodian of permanence. The task of judges is to uphold the laws that have been passed down to them, not make new ones. But as Robert Bork has shown—and as we see all around us—the

American judiciary has to an extraordinary extent become the "enemy of traditional culture." On issues from free speech and religion to sexuality, feminism, education, and race, the courts have acted less as defenders of the law than as an avant-garde establishing new beachheads to promulgate the gospel of left-liberal enlightenment. The recent attempt by the Ninth Circuit Court of Appeals in California to declare the Pledge of Allegiance unconstitutional because it includes the phrase "under God" is one of the more risible efforts in this campaign. The overall effect has been to inure society to rule by diktat, a situation in this country that is as novel as it is ominous. "It would," Judge Bork observes, "have been unthinkable until recently that so many areas of our national life would be controlled by judges." One again recalls Tocqueville's warning about democratic despotism. Only now it is not the sovereign but the judiciary that

> extends its arms over society as a whole; it covers its surface with a network of small, complicated, painstaking, uniform rules through which the most original minds and the most vigorous souls cannot clear a way to surpass the crowd; it does not break wills, but it softens them, bends them, and directs them; it rarely forces one to act, but it constantly opposes itself to one's acting; it does not destroy, it prevents things from being born; it does not tyrannize, it hinders, compromises, enervates, extinguishes, dazes, and finally reduces each nation to being nothing more than a herd of timid and industrious animals of which the government is the shepherd.

The attack on permanence is a failure of principle that results in moral paralysis. Chesterton once defined madness as "using mental activity so as to reach mental helplessness." That is an apt description of a process we see at work in many segments of our social and intellectual life. It is not so much a version of Hamlet's disease—being sicklied o'er with the pale cast of thought—as an example of what happens when conscience is no longer animated by principle and belief.

Item: Friday, May 17, 2002: "Hamas founder says suicide attacks will continue." Really? And what about us: what do we have to say about that abomination? Mostly, we wring our hands and mumble about restarting the "peace process." In a recent column, Linda Chavez reported on an episode of National Public Radio's "All Things Considered" in which a group of second- and third-generation Palestinian Americans living in Northern Virginia were interviewed. If you had been thinking of taking a holiday there, you may wish to reconsider, or at least be sure that your life insurance premiums are paid up. As Ms. Chavez noted, the sentiments expressed could have come from Hamas. "It doesn't matter who dies," said one young boy who idolizes the suicide bombers, "just as long as they're Israeli." His mother blames Israel: "They've made him violent and hate them." His father swells with paternal pride: "If his time has come, he will die, regardless of where he is. But at least he will die for a cause. I will live the rest of my life being proud of him." What about the rule of law? Forget it. American democratic values? Don't make me laugh. What we have here, Ms. Chavez observes, is "a reflection of our new multicultural America, where young people are taught that one's allegiance to one's ethnic group takes precedence over allegiance to the United States or adherence to democratic values." Thus it is, as David Pryce-Jones observes in his essay, that "contempt for democratic institutions was translated into contempt for the moral values that had underpinned those institutions."

When immigrants become American citizens, they take an oath of allegiance. Among other things, they must "absolutely and entirely renounce and abjure all allegiance and fidelity to any foreign prince, potentate, state, or sovereignty of whom or which [they] have heretofore been a subject or citizen." But such promises are only so many words to a population cut adrift from the permanent values enshrined in America's political principles. The fault lies with the elites who no longer respect and stand up for those principles. "No taxation without representation" is a splendid demand. But so is "no immigration without assimilation." Where is the simple imperative that one live up to one's oaths or face the consequences? If one becomes an American citizen, then one must become an American citizen, with the rights *and duties* pertaining thereto. If that proves too onerous, perhaps citizenship should be revoked and a one-way ticket to elsewhere provided. Such drastic measures would not be a sign of excessive rigor but an example of beneficence in action. It is kindness to stymie the forces of anarchy. By supporting the permanent values that undergird society, such enforcement would be a vote for civilization against chaos.

Since September 11, questions about the survival of culture have naturally taken on a new urgency. The focus suddenly shifted away from the airier purlieus of cultural endeavor to survival in the most visceral sense. The murderous fanatics who destroyed the World Trade Center, smashed into the Pentagon, and killed thousands of innocent civilians took the issue of multiculturalism out of the fetid atmosphere of the graduate seminar and into the streets. Or, rather, they dramatized the fact that multiculturalism was never a merely academic matter. In a sense, the actions of those terrorists were less an attack on the United States than part of what Binyamin Netanyahu called "a war to reverse the triumph of the West." We are very far from being in a position to assess the full significance of September 11 for the simple reason that the detonations that began that day continue to reverberate and destroy. A battle of wills, a contest of values, was initiated or at least openly acknowledged on September 11. It is much too early to predict the course of that conflict.

September 11 precipitated a crisis the end of which we cannot see. Part of the task that faces us now is to acknowledge the depth of barbarism that challenges the survival of culture. And part of that acknowledgment lies in reaffirming the core values that are under attack. Ultimately, victory in the conflict that besieges us will be determined not by smart weapons but by smart heads. That is to say, the conflict is not so much— not only—a military conflict as a conflict of worldviews. It is convenient to command the carrier battle groups and cruise missiles; it is essential to possess the will to use them and the faith that our cause, the cause of culture, is the best hope for mankind. Mark Steyn put it well: "If we are as ashamed as we insist we are—of ourselves, our culture and our history—then inevitably we will invite our own destruction." The horrifying slaughter of September 11 tempts us to draw a line around that day and treat it and its immediate consequences as an exceptional case. There is a deep sense, however, in which the terrorist attacks underscore not the fragility of normality but the normality of fragility. This is a point that C. S. Lewis made with great eloquence in a sermon he preached at Oxford in 1939. "I think it important," he said,

> to try to see the present calamity in a true perspective. The war creates no absolutely new situation: it simply aggravates the permanent human situation so that we can no longer ignore it. Human life has always been lived on the edge of a precipice. Human culture has always had to exist under the shadow of something infinitely more important than itself. If men had postponed the search for knowledge and beauty until they were secure, the search would never have begun.
>
> We are mistaken when we compare war with "normal life." Life has never been normal. Even those periods which we think most tranquil, like the nineteenth century, turn out, on closer inspection, to be full of crises, alarms, difficulties, emergencies. Plausible reasons have never been lacking for putting off all merely cultural activities until some imminent danger has been averted or some crying injustice put right. But hu-

manity long ago chose to neglect those plausible reasons. They wanted knowledge and beauty now, and would not wait for the suitable moment that never comes. Periclean Athens leaves us not only the Parthenon but, significantly, the Funeral Oration. The insects have chosen a different line: they have sought first the material welfare and security of the hive, and presumably they have their reward.

Men are different. They propound mathematical theorems in beleaguered cities, conduct metaphysical arguments in condemned cells, make jokes on scaffolds, discuss the latest new poem while advancing to the walls of Quebec, and comb their hair at Thermopylae. This is not panache: it is our nature.

Lewis's meditation is by turns cheering and sobering. On the one hand, it testifies to the heartiness of culture, which is the heartiness of the human spirit. Sonnets in Siberia, mathematical formulae in the besieged fortress. There is no time when cultural instructions are not pertinent. On the other hand, Lewis's meditation reminds us that culture, and the humanity that defines it, is constantly under threat. No achievement may be taken for granted; yesterday's gain may be tomorrow's loss; permanent values require permanent vigilance and permanent renewal.

What lessons may we draw from these Janus-faced conclusions? One is that it is always later than you think. Another is that it is never too late to start anew. Our French friends have lately taken to disparaging the "*simplisme*" of America's foreign policy. In their subtlety they ignore the fact that most important truths are—I use the adverb advisedly—terribly simple. Our complexity is much more likely to lead us astray than any simplicity we may follow.

In *Notes Towards the Definition of Culture*, T. S. Eliot observed that "If any definite conclusions emerge from this study, one of them surely is this, that culture is the one thing that we cannot deliberately aim at. It is the product of a variety of more or less harmonious activities, each pursued for its own sake." "For its own sake." That is one simple idea that is everywhere imperiled today. When we plant a garden, it is bootless to strive directly for camellias. They are the natural product of our care, nurture, and time. We can manage that when it comes to agriculture. When we turn our hands to *cultura animi*, we seem to be considerably less successful. The historian John Lukacs has just published a gloomy book called *At the End of an Age*. He argues that "we in the West are living near the end of an entire age," that the Modern Age, which began with the Renaissance, is jerking, crumbling irretrievably to its end. I believe Lukacs is precipitate. After all, prophecies of the end have been with us since the beginning. It seems especially odd that an historian of Lukacs's delicacy and insight would indulge in what amounts to a reprise of Spengler's thesis about the "decline of the West." How many times must historical "inevitabilities" be confounded before they lose their hold on our imaginations?

Where Lukacs is on to something, however, is in his meditations on the ideology of progress. Science does not deserve the scare quotes with which Lukacs adorns it, far from it. But it is true that much that we have taken for progress looks with the passage of time more and more dubious. Our stupendous power has accustomed us to say "yes" to every innovation, in manners and morals as well as the laboratory. We have yet to learn—even now, even at this late date—that promises of liberation often turn out to conceal new enchantments and novel forms of bondage. Our prejudice against prejudice tempts us to neglect the deep wisdom of tradition and time-sanctioned answers to the human predicament. The survival of culture is never a sure thing. No more is its defeat. Our acknowledgment of those twin facts, to the extent that we manage it, is one important sign of our strength.

Contributors

ROBERT H. BORK is a senior fellow at the American Enterprise Institute and a professor at Ave Maria School of Law. He has served as a circuit court judge, lawyer, educator, Solicitor General, and acting Attorney General of the United States.

ANTHONY DANIELS is a doctor and writer whose most recent books are *Utopias Elsewhere* and *Monrovia Mon Amour*. He has practiced on three continents. He now works in a hospital in a British slum and in a nearby prison.

MARTIN GREENBERG's translation of Goethe's *Faust* is available from Yale University Press. A winner of the translation prize from the Academy of American Poets, Mr. Greenberg has also translated Heinrich von Kleist's stories (*Marquise of O and other stories*) and plays (*Five Plays*). He is a former editor of *Commentary*.

ROGER KIMBALL is the managing editor of *The New Criterion* and the author, most recently, of *Lives of the Mind: The Use and Abuse of Intelligence From Hegel to Wodehouse* (Ivan R. Dee) and *The Long March: How the Cultural Revolution of the 1960s Changed America* (Encounter Books).

KENNETH MINOGUE is Emeritus Professor of Political Science at the London School of Economics. He is the author of numerous books, ranging from *The Liberal Mind* (1962, 1967) to *Politics: A Very Short Introduction* (1995, 2000).

ERIC ORMSBY is a professor of Islamic studies at McGill University. He was Director of Libraries at McGill University from 1986 to 1996 and previously Library Director at Catholic University of America. His most recent book is *Facsimiles of Time: Essays on Poetry and Translation* (The Porcupine's Quill).

DAVID PRYCE-JONES has published nine novels and nine books of nonfiction, including *The War that Never Was*, about the end of the Soviet Empire, and *The Closed Circle: An Interpretation of the Arabs*, recently reissued in a new edition by Ivan R. Dee. He is a senior editor of *National Review*.

DIANA SCHAUB is associate professor and chair of the political science department at Loyola College in Maryland. A frequent contributor to *The National Interest* and *The American Enterprise*, she has written on a wide range of issues in political philosophy and American political thought. Her latest book is entitled *Erotic Liberalism: Women and Revolution in Montesquieu's "Persian Letters"* (Rowman & Littlefield).

MARK STEYN is the senior North American correspondent for Britain's Telegraph Group. In the United States, Mr. Steyn is theater critic of *The New Criterion* and a columnist for the *Chicago Sun-Times*. His most recent book is *Broadway Babies Say Goodnight*.

KEITH WINDSCHUTTLE is the author most recently of *The Killing of History: How Literary Critics and Social Theorists Are Murdering Our Past* (1997). He is the publisher of Macleay Press, Sydney.

Index